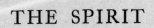

THE SPIRIT

MACMILLAN AND CO., Limited
LONDON · BOMBAY · CALCUTTA · MADRAS
MELBOURNE

THE MACMILLAN COMPANY
NEW YORK · BOSTON · CHICAGO
DALLAS · SAN FRANCISCO

THE MACMILLAN CO. OF CANADA, Ltd.
TORONTO

THE SPIRIT

GOD AND HIS RELATION TO MAN
CONSIDERED FROM THE STANDPOINT
OF PHILOSOPHY, PSYCHOLOGY AND ART

A. SETH PRINGLE-PATTISON   C. A. ANDERSON SCOTT
LILY DOUGALL   CYRIL W. EMMET
J. ARTHUR HADFIELD   A. CLUTTON-BROCK

AND

B. H. STREETER (EDITOR)

" In Him we live and move and have our being "

MACMILLAN AND CO., LIMITED
ST. MARTIN'S STREET, LONDON
1920

CONTENTS

INTRODUCTION

I. IMMANENCE AND TRANSCENDENCE

X. CHRIST THE CONSTRUCTIVE REVOLUTIONARY

"My wish is that I may perceive God, whom I find everywhere in the external world, in like manner within and inside me."

KEPLER.

"I cannot but think that the reformation in our day, which I expect to be more deep and searching than that of the sixteenth century, will turn upon the Spirit's presence and life, as that did upon the Justification by the Son."

F. D. MAURICE.

"The traditional doctrine of the Holy Spirit, neglected by the early theologians of the Church, even when the creeds were still in the formative period of their existence, has remained until this day in the background of inquiry, both for the theologians and for the philosophers. A favourite target for hostile, although often inarticulate, criticism on the part of the opponents of tradition, and a frequent object of reverential, but confessedly problematic and often very vague, exposition on the part of the defenders of the faith,—the article of the creed regarding the Holy Spirit is, I believe, the one matter about which most who discuss the problem of Christianity have least to say in the way of definite theory. Yet, if I am right, this is, in many respects, the really distinctive and therefore the capital article of the Christian creed, so far as that creed suggests a theory of the divine nature. This article, then, should be understood, if the spirit of Christianity, in its most human and vital of features, is to be understood at all. And this article should be philosophically expounded and defended, if any distinctively Christian article of the creed is to find a foundation in a rationally defensible metaphysical theory of the universe."

Professor ROYCE of Harvard.

INTRODUCTION

IF the advance of knowledge has long ago made
bankrupt the crude supernaturalism of traditional
Christianity, it seems well on the way towards discredit-
ing no less completely the crude materialism of Victorian
science. Supported by the prestige of men justly famed
for epoch-making discoveries, the philosophical system
known as Scientific Materialism could for a long while,
in the popular view, hold its own against a stream of
continual protest from the side of Metaphysics, Ethics,
and Aesthetics. But now that these protests are being
reinforced by the latest investigations in Biology,
Physiology, and especially Psychology, the case is altered.

The idea that mechanism is an adequate explanation
of life and that consciousness is a bye-product of the
dance of atoms, is one intrinsically so incredible that
it could secure general acceptance only if supported by
a consensus of the leaders of thought. Accordingly of
recent years the mind of the age has been moving
towards a more vitalistic conception of the nature of
the Power behind phenomena—a conception of which,
perhaps, the happiest expression is Boutroux's vague
but impressive formula "THE BEYOND THAT IS
WITHIN." There are few, however, who pause to
consider how far this is identical, how far diverse, from
that conception of the SPIRIT as the active indwelling
of the transcendent Divine in whom "we live and
move and have our being" which dazzled the minds
of a St. Paul or a St. John.

Essentially the two conceptions are the same—but

with one important difference. The early Christian is
more vivid, more vital, more definite. But this definiteness is precisely the element in it which modern thought
regards as unwarranted—and up to a point the objection
is well founded. The definiteness which traditional
Theology has given to the concept of the Spirit is a
definiteness of the wrong kind. On the one hand, the
Holy Ghost of the classical theology is a scholastic
abstraction. On the other, if we turn from that to
popular Christianity of the evangelical type, we find
indeed a conception of the Spirit which, through its
connection with a moving religious experience, is
indeed the reverse of abstract, but which is still definite
with a definiteness of the wrong kind. For only
certain types of experience are given spiritual significance, and no attempt is made to relate this experience
to a thought-out philosophy of the universe. It is not
therefore surprising that it should sometimes lead to
narrowness of outlook and a tendency to value religious
emotion for its own sake.

In religious discussions the question is often raised
whether " definiteness of the wrong kind " may not
after all be better than a " general vagueness." The
question is purely academic. Practical men do not
waste time in debating which of two evils is the worse,
unless and until it has become clear that another and
a more satisfactory alternative is not forthcoming.
When definiteness of the right kind is in sight it is
folly to rest content until it is attained. And it can
be attained. The relation of religion and the creative
thought of the day is quite different now from what
it was fifty, or even fifteen, years ago. On the one
side, the spirit of scientific inquiry has—it must be
confessed, only after a hard struggle—firmly established
itself in Christian Theology ; on the other, the leaders
of the world's thought have discovered that no
philosophy can hold water which has not sympathetic-
ally studied, and in its system found a place for, the

historical and psychological phenomena in which
religion has found expression. After centuries of
bickering, Religion and Science at last have shaken
hands—and if only they would go a step farther and
become fast friends, they could, by pooling their
resources, regenerate the world.

The Scholastic Theology, considered in relation to
its own age and the social and intellectual developments of its own time, is one of the greatest monuments
of human genius. But the survival of what is really,
though often unconsciously, the Scholastic standpoint
has forced upon the Church a timid and defensive
attitude towards all new discovery. Worse still, it
has erected an artificial barrier which has fenced off
modern thinkers from the greatest spiritual tradition
in the world's history. It is not sufficiently realised
that the divorce between the Church and the living
thought of the day has impoverished Philosophy as
much as it has enfeebled the Church.

The promise of a way out of the present *impasse*
would seem to lie in a re-examination of the conception
of the Spirit—considered as God in action—in the light
alike of the religious experience and theological reflection of the Christian Church throughout the ages, and
of present-day movements in Philosophy, Psychology,
and Art. In the way, however, of such an enterprise is
one outstanding difficulty. Nobody can reasonably
hope to produce work of any degree of originality in
any subject unless he has devoted to it the concentrated
study of many years ; and no one person can have
done this to all the subjects vitally connected with the
present quest. Accordingly the method of investigation
pursued has been the same as that used in the preparation of the books *Foundations*, *Concerning Prayer*, and
Immortality.[1] A series of conference-retreats, which the
majority of contributors were able to attend, supple-
mented by individual discussion for mutual criticism and

[1] The method is described at greater length in *Immortality*, pp. x-xiii.

information, has made it possible gradually to focus on a single point the results of a first-hand study, not only of Philosophy, Psychology, and the theory of Art, but of the relevant branches of modern scientific Theology.

It should perhaps be added that the Holy Spirit formed the subject of discussion at a joint retreat of the Anglican and Free Church Fellowships at Easter 1917, at which several of the contributors to this volume were present, and some read papers.   And this book owes not a little to that discussion, and still more to the insight into the meaning and possibilities of spiritual fellowship gained at this and at similar gatherings.

The Essays form a continuous series the order of which is self-explanatory—with one exception.   The Essay on "Spirit and Matter" by Mr. Clutton-Brock opens with an argument for the existence of spirit directed against the materialistic affirmation that matter is the only reality.   Logically this argument should have come very early in the book.   But the Essay in which it occurs and the Essay by the same author which precedes it present, if taken together, a constructive discussion of Spirit from the standpoint of Aesthetics which seems most appropriately placed in the later position.

To sum up, this volume is an attempt to put forward a conception of the Spirit of God which is definite but not scholastic, and which is capable of affording an intellectual basis both for a coherent Philosophy of the universe and for a Religion passionate and ethical, mystical and practical.   Of the success of the attempt it is not for the authors to judge ; but even to fail in a great task is to make the way easier for those who follow.

B. H. S.

CUTTS END, CUMNOR,
September 9, 1919.

I

IMMANENCE AND TRANSCENDENCE

BY

A. SETH PRINGLE-PATTISON, LL.D., D.C.L.

FELLOW OF THE BRITISH ACADEMY
PROFESSOR OF LOGIC AND METAPHYSICS IN THE UNIVERSITY OF EDINBURGH
AUTHOR OF " THE IDEA OF GOD IN THE LIGHT OF RECENT PHILOSOPHY," ETC.

SYNOPSIS

THE question of immanence or transcendence is a fundamental issue in religious philosophy, and the central doctrines of Christian theology are in the main directed towards a satisfactory solution.

A purely immanental view of the divine is equivalent to a pantheism which equates God and nature, to the extent of holding that God is present equally in everything. Such a view leaves no room for moral distinctions, or indeed for any distinction of higher and lower ; everything just as it exists is equally divine and therefore equally perfect. On the other hand, the conception of God as a purely transcendent and extra-mundane Being fails to realise His activity as indwelling Spirit. In the history of religious thought such a theory is known as Deism. It is exemplified in the rigid monotheism of the Hebrew religion and still more in Mohammedanism. In the Psalms the pity of God is compared to that of a father for his children, but there is a gulf between the sonship of man as thus conceived and as it is conceived, for example, in the Gospel of St. John.

Looked at philosophically, and apart from the obsolete terminology in which it is expressed, the Christian doctrine of the Incarnation, developed by the speculative theologians of the Eastern Church on the basis of the older doctrine of the Logos, may be regarded as an attempt on a grand scale to harmonise the ideas of immanence and transcendence. The inmost nature of God as self-giving Love is taken to be revealed in the human life and death of Jesus : "he that hath seen me hath seen the Father." And in the complementary conception of the indwelling and ever-active Spirit (originally identified with the eternal Logos), it is implied that the presence of the divine is not limited to any one age or individual. But popular Christianity, by reinstating the deistic conception of a purely transcendent and impassible Creator, and by stressing the divinity of the Christ in such a way as to make Him no longer truly man, loses hold of the vital significance of its own central doctrines. A God thus deistically conceived comes to be treated merely as a great First Cause, and the idea completes its natural evolution in modern thought as the Unknown and the Unknowable.

It is important, therefore, for religious thought to rid itself of a transcendency which seeks to magnify God's greatness by separating

2

Him from the world and making Him self-sufficient and complete without it. The process of the finite world is not extrinsic to the being of God ; on the contrary, it may be said that only in the process of creation and redemption do we touch the essential secret of the divine life. The word creation is apt perhaps to suggest primarily the calling into being of the material system of things. But, philosophically regarded, the material world is an abstraction when sundered from the conscious lives in which it culminates ; it is but God's medium for the shaping of souls. The whole meaning of creation lies in the origination of conscious spirits to whom God can reveal Himself and from whom He can obtain an appropriate response. Creation in this sense is demanded by the nature of God; and it implies a real agency and responsibility on the part of the beings created. Freedom, and to that extent contingency, is thus a condition of the existence of a finite world at all in any real sense. But the Spirit of God moving the hearts of men is the guiding and formative agency in the process, bearing with His creatures the whole stress and pain of the world and drawing them to Himself with the infinite patience of love. Such is the conception of the divine immanence suggested in Christian thought. Obviously such immanence does not imply the sheer identification of the being and life of God with the process of human history or with the last term (so far reached) of any finite attainment. This identification, made by some absolutist philosophers, stultifies itself, for it fails to explain even the progress so far achieved. The immanent God is always the infinitely transcendent, and it is the presence of the Infinite in our finite lives that alone explains the essential nature of man.

I

IMMANENCE AND TRANSCENDENCE

THE question of immanence and transcendence touches the fundamentals of religious philosophy ; and Christian theology in particular, in its main doctrines, is little else than a persistent attempt to reconcile these two views of the divine nature and action. Let us first try to clarify our ideas by considering the two views in their mutual opposition and exclusiveness. We can best do this by reference to philosophical types of the two extremes. A purely immanental view of the divine is equivalent to a sheer Pantheism in which no distinction whatever is drawn between God and nature. Spinoza's equation of *Deus sive Natura* is often taken as the typical example of such a position, but there are elements in Spinoza's thought, particularly his doctrine of "degrees of perfection," which carry us beyond it and point to a more satisfactory theory. Pure immanence or pure Pantheism is perhaps better exemplified in those phases of Eastern thought in which this doctrine of degrees seems entirely absent. "The learned"—so runs a typical saying— "behold God alike in the reverend Brahmin, in the ox and the elephant, in the dog and in him who eateth the flesh of dogs." In the popular religious cults in which this attitude is expressed, the immanental unity of the divine is little more than the idea of a teeming nature, and passes easily into a gross polytheism, whose deities represent and consecrate every

natural force and tendency. Such a view may be
called the Lower Pantheism in order to distinguish it
from the Higher Pantheism (in Tennyson's phrase),
the doctrine of the divine immanence which, as I
hold, must be the heart of any true philosophy.
There is much, however, to be said for a suggestion
of Dean Inge's that the name Pantheists "should be
reserved for those who hold that God is present
equally in every part of His creation." [1] Pope's often-
quoted phrases in the *Essay on Man*, though they
may be due to alliteration and antithesis rather than
to a full appreciation of their philosophical meaning,
are an exact expression of Pantheism in this sense :

> As full, as perfect, in a hair as heart . . .
> To Him no high, no low, no great, no small,
> He fills, He bounds, connects, and equals all !

In such a view there is no place either for aspiration
or condemnation. Morality and the most specific
experiences of religion become alike unmeaning. There
is neither good nor bad, neither better nor worse ;
for everything, just as it exists, is equally divine,
and therefore equally perfect. Existence and perfection become identical terms.

If a purely immanental doctrine is equivalent to
Pantheism in the sense just indicated, a doctrine of
pure transcendence might, I would suggest, be fitly
styled Deism, the term Theism being reserved for
such theories as attempt to mediate between the two
extremes and to combine the truths on which they
one-sidedly insist, in a way which does not override,
but on the contrary serves to explain, our moral and
religious experience. No doubt, etymologically, the
two terms, Deism and Theism, mean exactly the same
thing, and usage varies. Theism is used by some
writers to designate a position distinguished from, and
to some extent opposed to, the Christian doctrine of

[1] *Personal Idealism and Mysticism*, p. 43.

God. It will be found, however, that when Theism is so employed, the doctrine in view is one which treats God merely as a transcendent or extra-mundane Creator without recognition of His activity as indwelling Spirit. Now the term Deism acquired just this specific connotation in the beginning of the eighteenth century, when the English Deists, as they are styled, supported what they called "the religion of nature" as distinguished from the special tenets of Christianity as a "revealed" religion. It was an age not remarkable either for speculative insight or for depth of religious feeling ; and although the Deists were duly answered by orthodox Churchmen, the disputants on both sides accepted the same external view of the relation of God to the world. The Churchmen were just as far from being "Theists" in the modern sense of the term as their opponents were. The additional dogmas which they professed to accept were accepted not from the analysis of religious experience but on the authority of an external revelation; and the doctrines were powerless therefore to transform the defective deistic notion of God with which they started. Deism, in short, rather than Christianity, was the common creed of the age. It seems a pity, therefore, with the two terms at our disposal, to use them indiscriminately in the same sense ; they might be usefully specialised in the way I have suggested.

On the large scale of history the pure transcendency of the divine is exemplified in Judaism, out of which Christianity developed, and still more clearly by Mohammedanism, which is a conscious reaction against the central Christian doctrine of the Incarnation.

The monotheism of the Hebrews has been called the religion of Sublimity as contrasted with the religion of Beauty, the nature-religion of the Greeks. Nothing, indeed, can surpass in sublimity some of the utterances in the Psalms and the Prophets, or in the Book of Job. But to the Hebrew writers the sublimities of nature

are not in strictness a revelation of God ; they are
used rather to enhance the measureless and irresistible power of God by their nothingness before Him.[1]
" It is he that sitteth upon the circle of the earth,
and the inhabitants thereof are as grasshoppers. . . .
Behold, the nations are as a drop in the bucket, and are
counted as the small dust of the balance : behold, he
taketh up the isles as a very little thing (Isaiah xl.).
" He looketh on the earth and it trembleth : he
toucheth the hills and they smoke" (Ps. civ. 32).
" The voice of the Lord breaketh the cedars ; yea,
the Lord breaketh the cedars of Lebanon (Ps. xxix.).
" The earth saw and trembled. The hills melted
like wax at the presence of the Lord" (Ps. xcvii.).
Omnipotence which creates and destroys with a word,
enthroned above the heavens, immeasurably remote
from the thoughts and ways of men, an absolute
Will with something of the arbitrariness and irre-
sponsibility of an Eastern despot—such are perhaps
the foundational elements of the Jewish conception.
" By the word of the Lord were the heavens made.
. . . He spake and it was done" (Ps. xxxv.). " He
commanded and they were created " (Ps. cxlviii.). " I
form the light and create darkness ; I make peace and
create evil ; I, the Lord, do all these things. . . . Woe
unto him that striveth with his Maker ! Let the
potsherd strive with the potsherds of the earth. Shall
the clay say to him that fashioneth it, What makest
thou ? " (Isaiah xlv.).

The history of Jewish religion is the record of the
process by which the original conception of a vengeful
tribal deity, in very truth a Lord of Hosts, a God of
battles, was purified into this lofty monotheism without
weakening the national faith in Jehovah as the guide
and protector of His people. " The God of Heaven,"
" the God of the whole earth," is still in a special sense
" the God of Israel," the redeemer of His chosen people ;

[1] Cf. Caird's *Evolution of Religion*, i. 385.

and the realisation of this relationship prevents the sheer transcendency of the divine from producing its full effects. At the same time, the higher conception of God implies a rising above mere nationalism : the bond between Jehovah and His chosen people is thought of as founded in righteousness and obedience. As this is deepened and spiritualised in the prophetic teaching, the national relationship becomes also an individual relationship between the worshipper and his God, which gives us in the Psalms and the Prophets some of the most intimate expressions of devotional feeling. The distance is partially annulled : "The Lord is nigh unto them that are of a broken heart" (Ps. xxxiv.). "For thus saith the high and lofty One that inhabiteth eternity, whose name is Holy : I dwell in the high and holy place, with him also that is of a humble and contrite spirit" (Isaiah lvii. 15). "Like as a father pitieth his children, so the Lord pitieth them that fear him." But the very thought of the fatherly pity is linked with that of the infinite contrast between the divine and the human : it is the reflection on human frailty and transience that calls it forth. "For he knoweth our frame ; he remembereth that we are dust. As for man, his days are as grass : as a flower of the field, so he flourisheth. For the wind passeth over it, and it is gone ; and the place thereof shall know it no more" (Ps. ciii.). Pity may be akin to love, but it is not quite the same thing, and this fatherhood is still far removed from that implied in the sonship of which St. John speaks : "To them gave he power to become the sons of God."

"The Lord looketh from heaven. . . . From the place of his habitation he looketh upon all the inhabitants of the earth" (Ps. xxxiii. 13-14). "And the Word was made flesh and dwelt among us" (John i. 14). These two sayings measure the distance that divides the Psalms from the Fourth Gospel, and that is the difference between the Jewish and the Christian doctrine of God and man. As it has been well said, "the transition through which the meaning of the expression 'Word of God' passes in the interval between the Old Testament and the Gospel of St. John contains in it a whole history of the development of religion." [1]

It is no part of my purpose here to trace that transition in detail, even if I were competent to do so. It is sufficient to refer to the Hebrew conception of the Wisdom of God as developed in the Apocryphal books, and the fusion of this in Philo of Alexandria with the old Greek idea of the Logos or indwelling reason of the world. As philosophical speculation in that age, exaggerating the Platonic and Aristotelian tradition, stressed more and more the transcendence — the inaccessibility, the incomprehensibility—of the divine, the need became clamant for some principle to bridge the chasm, some mediator between God and man. Thus we get Philo's doctrine of "the second God," the Logos, the uttered Reason, the first-born Son, the Platonic world of Ideas conceived as a creative force through which God formed the world, conceived also in religious language as the high-priest who through his intercession creates and preserves relations between God and man. The Logos as the indwelling deity is knowable, while God Himself, as exalted beyond all predicates, remains unknowable. The identification of this eternal revelation of God in the cosmos with the historical revelation of the character of God and His purposes with men in the man Christ Jesus was the work of the speculative Christian theologians of the second and third centuries, and was fixed as the doctrine of the Church by Athanasius in the fourth. That doctrine, as elaborated in the heat of controversy and stated in the creed which goes by his name, is apt to appear as the climax of irrationality, a tissue of incredibilities, and the doctrine of Arius comparatively intelligible and credible. But Arianism is really a

[1] Caird, *op. cit.* i. 386.

reversion to the idea of a purely transcendent, an inaccessible and incommunicable God ; and the Arian Christ, a demigod called into existence to create the world, is a purely mythological being, neither God nor man, but standing midway between the two. As it has been said, " the supernatural being whom Arius sets forth as mediator between God and man does not unite but separates them, for he serves to reveal the infinite impassable gulf that lies between them. . . . Union with Deity according to such a theology is impossible." [1] On the other hand, whatever fault we may find with the philosophical terminology in which the Athanasian position is expressed, the position is broadly based by Athanasius himself on a philosophical doctrine of immanence inherited by the Alexandrians from Stoic philosophy, an immanence not restricted to a single historical individual. Because God is immanent in the world as a whole, and specifically in all mankind, Athanasius argues at times, there is nothing contrary to reason, nothing unworthy of the divine, in the idea that He should manifest Himself pre-eminently in one man.[2]

The controversy, to the modern mind so tedious and futile, which subsequently distracted theologians concerning the union of the two natures in Christ —as if they were two substances which refused to mingle, or two consciousnesses miraculously maintained in water-tight compartments within a single human organism—depended on the tacit denial of the spiritual unity asserted in the Incarnation. If I understand the doctrine of the Church aright, it teaches that just in so far as Jesus is perfect man, He is also, and thereby, the perfect revelation of the

[1] Allen, *The Continuity of Christian Thought*, p. 87.

[2] " If the Word of God is in the universe . . . if it beseems Him to unite Himself with the universe and to be made known in the whole, it must beseem Him also to appear in a human body and that by Him it should be illumined and work. . . . It cannot be absurd if, ordering as He does the whole and giving life to all things and having willed to make Himself known through men, He has used as an instrument a human body to manifest the truth and knowledge of the Father. For humanity, too, is an actual part of the whole " (cf. *De Incarnatione Verbi*, chaps. 41 and 42).

Father, the express image of His person. Spiritual things must be spiritually discerned. Clothed in an obsolete and misleading terminology, they degenerate into materialistic miracles and become a stumbling-block to faith instead of a help to living piety. Profound religious feeling will not go astray, but popular Christianity is probably in the main a kind of Arianism, if not a Tritheism. It is, to my mind, a great misfortune that " the spirit of God," the *influence* of God in the human soul, or, as it is alternatively called in the New Testament, " Christ," " the spirit of Jesus," the mystic presence of the Lord in the hearts of His followers, a spirit of comfort and consolation in their loss, revealing the mind of the Master whom on earth they had often so ill understood, and so guiding them and the Church after them into all truth—it is, I say, a misfortune that expressions like these, and the spiritual fact for which they stand, should have been materialised so as to suggest the existence of a third personality or agency distinct from both the Father and the Son. For what better word could be found to express just the fact of divine immanence on which the possibility of communion with God is based, the illuminative presence of God operative in every soul which He has created? The conception of the Spirit is, in fact, the final and complete account of the one God as the Father of spirits, their Creator, Inspirer, and Redeemer.

But popular Christianity is unable to assimilate this sublime mysticism, and falls back upon a deistic conception of the transcendent and impassible Creator, the unbending Judge of His sinful creatures; and so we arrive at forensic theories of the Atonement and similar doctrines which are neither ethical nor religious. For such a mode of thought the doctrine of the Incarnation itself loses its significance as an expression of the essential nature of God eternally giving and revealing Himself. It becomes, if one may say so, almost an after-thought resorted to as a remedy for the miscarriage of the divine

plan.   And this is because, for a deistic theory, the
whole process of the world—its creation and its redemption alike—is non-essential to the life of God.
But the course of modern thought shows conclusively
that the existence of such an extraneous self-involved
Deity is difficult to maintain, and that the notion of
such a Being rapidly loses all content, and consequently
ceases to possess any vital significance.   He had been
supposed to give evidence of His existence by interfering
with the course of nature from time to time ; but with
the growth of a scientific and critical temper of mind
the evidence of such interferences becomes more and
more suspect and the interferences themselves less and
less credible.   Hence the notion becomes attenuated
to the idea of a Great First Cause, and, as nothing
about the universe seems to be explained simply by
postulating a divine mechanic to set it agoing, the
Deism with which the eighteenth century opened passed,
towards its close, into the explicit Atheism of the
French Encyclopaedists or the shadowy belief on which
Hume makes theist and atheist shake hands at the
conclusion of his *Dialogues concerning Natural Religion*, seeing that the proposition on which they agree
"affords," as he says, "no inference that can affect
human life, or can be the source of any action or
forbearance."   In more recent times, no doubt with
more of reverence but by the same inevitable logic, we
see the notion reduced to that of the unknown God, or,
in more sweeping phrase, the Unknown and Unknowable.   This characteristic product of later nineteenth-
century thought reappears in Mr. Wells's new theology
as the Veiled Being, and Mr. Wells also is unable to
discover any religious value in such a conception.   He
proposes accordingly to transfer the name of God and
the effective qualities of deity to the mythological
being whom he styles the Invisible King—a being
purely mythological, as Mr. Wells presents him, but
one in whom it is easy enough for others than Mr.

Wells to recognise, in a mutilated form, some of the characteristic features of the Christ whom the author of the Epistle to the Hebrews spoke of long ago as the " Captain " of our salvation.

It is highly important, therefore, for religious thinking—and for philosophic thinking also—to rid itself of a transcendency which seeks to magnify God's greatness by separating Him from the world, placing Him at a distance from it, and making Him self-sufficient and complete without it. Transcendence in the only important sense is reached on other lines, as I hope to show ; but against this kind of transcendence it must be contended that God is not a *causa remota*, who created a universe once upon a time. He is its ever-present sustaining ground. The universe of the finite and everything in it exists from one moment to another only because He perpetually creates it. As the mediaeval thinkers taught, to sustain in existence is equivalent to continuous creation. Moreover, any account of creation in terms of mere *will* is fundamentally misleading. Yet this, I think, is beyond doubt the popular idea. The idea of creation as an act of will and the idea of creation as taking place once upon a time are, indeed, connected in the closest way. According to this conception, God existed in all His perfection and blessedness *before* the creation of the world : He *chose* to create a world, but He might equally have forborne to create, and his abstention would have made no difference to His already self-sufficient being. The world, in other words, is in no way organic to the divine life. It is something that happened, but it is an accident—in the old logical sense, that it cannot be deduced from the essential *nature* of God. It remains, as one may say, extrinsic to the courses of His being. Against such a view Spinoza insisted, I think rightly, that God is the cause of all things *per se*, not *per accidens*; that is to say, it belongs to His very nature to be Creator, or, in more modern and perhaps more religious language, God is essentially the self-revealing, the self-giving, and (shall we say ?) the self-sacrificing God. In the process of this revelation and self-giving consists His own very being and His eternal joy. "Verily," said the Hebrew prophet, "thou art a God that hidest thyself"; "clouds and darkness," says the Psalmist, "are round about him." But the true God is no *deus absconditus*, hidden, withdrawn from our sight, but a Creator that eternally utters Himself in and to His creatures.

The common objection to Spinoza's way of putting it—especially when he illustrates his thesis, as he is so fond of doing, from the necessity with which the properties of a triangle follow from the definition of the figure—is that God seems, if one may say so, to have no personal choice in the matter. If creation is a necessary act, then it is a process which seems to achieve itself independently of His will ; and, instead of a personal life, we are left, it is said, with a system of abstract necessity, which is little better than the all-embracing mechanism of the materialists. But such a conception of necessity as an external compulsion imposed upon the divine action, a kind of abstract fate which he passively carries into execution, is less than just to Spinoza's intention, though it may be fostered by his illustrations and may find support in certain features of his own system. For the necessity of which he speaks is the necessity of *the divine nature itself*, and, according to his doctrine, God alone enjoys perfect freedom because, as the sole self-subsistent Being, there is nothing external to Him which could affect His action. To perfect knowledge and perfect goodness there can be no *choice*, in our sense of the word, as a dubiety between alternatives and a making up of our minds for one or the other. He must act in every case out of the fulness of His own nature ; His action is simply the realisation of His nature. And that this is the ideal of action—this and not the so-called freedom

of choice, characteristic of the finite will—we acknowledge, when we envisage, as the goal of our own religious
endeavour, the "service" which is "perfect freedom,"
that state of moral being in which our actions shall
respond with a like spontaneity to "the mind of God,"
as we have learned to know it. They become the
expression, in other words, of a nature attuned to the
divine.

We find more thoughtful theologians recognising accordingly that the divine will must in every case be an
expression of the divine nature, and many of them, following out this line of thought, have accepted the idea of
creation as an eternal act, which means that God never
existed without a world in which He was manifested.
But although many would go thus far, I have found others
(and perhaps even some of those who would accept the
general idea of an eternal creation) protesting against
any form of words which seems, as they say, to "bind
up" God and the world in a relation of reciprocal implication ; for that is, they say, to make God "dependent"
upon man in a sense which contradicts the notion of
Him as the self-subsistent and infinitely perfect Being,
and is also at variance, it has been objected, with the
feeling of utter dependence on our part which has been
defined as the essence of religion, and which is at any
rate an abiding element in religious experience.   But
surely this is to strain at a word, as before in the case of
necessity, and to import into the idea of "dependence"
a meaning which could only attach to it if the finite
creatures were beings existing in their own right, and
capable, as it were, of entering into a concordat with the
Infinite, whereby finite and infinite should agree to
support one another in existence.   It may be freely
conceded that to represent God as dependent on anything ontologically extraneous to Himself contradicts
our whole conception of Him ; but surely nothing of
the kind is suggested in the view I have maintained.
Whatever ethical independence is conferred upon the

finite creature, he is sustained in existence at all only by the *concursus dei*, as the old theologians taught, and from the same infinite source he draws his rational and moral sustenance. Both for the fact of his existence and the content of his life he is thus utterly dependent, and the most heartfelt expressions of religious feeling are full of the acknowledgement of this dependence. Obviously it is not in this sense that God can be said to depend on the creature, and the word " dependent " is none of mine. But I say that in the nature of the case we can have no knowledge of God except in relation to the world of His creatures, and that in attempting to conceive His solitary and self-sufficient existence out of that relation, we make an abstraction for which we have no warrant; and if we think we are thereby framing a more elevated notion of Him we deceive ourselves; on the contrary, we are robbing Him of the perfections which we recognise to be most divine. Need I do more than mention the Christian conception of redemptive Love? That is surely no " accident " of the divine experience, but the very process in which God's life consists. If we believe this, it is unmeaning to say that " God's nature is complete without creation."

But it is important to be clear as to what we mean by creation. In the popular use of the term I think we are apt to have in our mind primarily the fabric of the material universe, and hence the process seems comparable to that of turning out a manufactured article; and the product, summoned somehow into existence, appears to stand there henceforth independent of God, as it is similarly independent of, and, as we say, external to, finite spirits like ourselves who are, on this view, the result of a subsequent and distinct act of creation. But, if we think philosophically, we must not think of creation as a serial process in which a material system of things was first brought into existence, to which conscious beings were afterwards added as its denizens. Such a way of thinking bestows an artificial independence upon the material cosmos and lands us in a number of difficulties, as, for instance, what meaning we can attach to the existence of unconscious material things entirely out of relation to the experience of conscious beings. If we think in terms of process (of time), we must at any rate remember that no process can be truly described unless it is viewed in its completeness, that is to say, in the light of its final result, that to which it all leads up. And the process of the material universe is towards life and consciousness. As Browning says :

> All tended to mankind
> And, man produced, all has its end thus far :
> But in completed man begins anew
> A tendency to God.[1]

Viewed thus, the whole meaning of creation is seen to be the origination of conscious spirits ; for to them alone God can reveal Himself, and from them only can He obtain a response. Everything else, the whole material fabric, is but God's medium, as it were, for the shaping of souls, and we need not involve ourselves in difficulties by thinking of it as something created independently and standing, so to speak, on its own basis. There is, in strictness, no creation—no finite universe at all—till spirits are created. And if, when we think of creation, we think primarily of the origination of conscious spirits, we shall not be tempted to relapse into what has been called the cabinetmaker theory of creation. For spirits are not things that are "made." The bold metaphor of the Creed, "begotten not made," would indeed seem better to suggest the relation of every potential son of God to the Being whose image he bears and of whose nature he is invited to partake.

But when we speak thus of creation as an eternal act, we mean simply that the basal constitution of the universe (using that term now in the largest sense) is eternally complete. If the ultimate definition of God is Love, then the divine life is *essentially* a process of

---

[1] *Paracelsus, ad fin.*

c

self-communication, a life in and through others, and
it is a contradiction to imagine Him existing without
objects of that love.[1]   The statement is not meant to
imply that we can eliminate considerations of time (of
process, of effort, of co-operation) when we think of
the dealings of God with any concrete individual or any
particular race.   Certainly it does not mean that what
we call the history of the world has no meaning for
God, inasmuch as the end is for Him one with the
beginning, and the whole predetermined in every detail.
That would be to belie the very meaning of creation as
we have used the term ; for it would mean that God
was the sole agent in everything that happened, we
being, in literal truth, God's puppets.   Such a view
acts like a paralysis upon the moral life.   Creation,
as demanded by the nature of God, implies, on the
contrary, a real independence, a real agency and responsibility, on the part of the beings created.   As a
matter of fact, such beings are not turned out like
ready-made articles ; they are rather given an opportunity of making themselves.   Freedom, and to that
extent contingence, is therefore a condition of there
being a finite world in any real sense at all.   The
Spirit of God moving in the hearts of men is the
guiding and formative agency in the process, operating
not as a natural force that overbears opposition, but as
an inward illumination, drawing them with the infinite
patience of love.   If we believe in the omnipotence of
love, the victorious issue may be secure—secure, that
is to say, in the long run and in general outline—but
nowise determined as to the details of its realisation in
individual lives or communities, and perhaps not even
certain of gathering all the sheep into the fold, so strange
is the power of self-determination vested in the finite
will.   If God is not thus active in the time-process,
bearing with His creatures the whole stress and pain of

---

[1] The doctrine of the eternal generation of the Son may be taken as symbolising
this ideal necessity.

it, the immanence of the Creative Spirit becomes an unmeaning phrase. However difficult it may be for us to realise the relation of the temporal to the eternal, no solution can be true which simply abolishes the one or the other. The time-process must be rooted in an eternal reality, but the eternal is not the timeless. It must be conceived as somehow comprehending the temporal as an element—and a necessary element—in its own being.

It should be almost needless to add that all this emphasis on the essentially creative nature of God, and the immanence, therefore, of God in His universe, must not be taken to mean the equation of the divine with the process of finite experience. Such a sheer identification of the two seems to be implied in the statements of many absolutist philosophies. Take Hegel's system, for example. Hegel traces in his *Philosophy of Law* and in his *Philosophy of History* the human record in these different spheres, and in each case the record of gradual advance is represented as the process by which the Absolute attains full self-consciousness—attains it, one is almost ashamed to add, in the social and political structure of Europe, and of Germany in particular—at the opening of the nineteenth century. And, similarly, as we unroll the history of philosophy we are supposed to have before us the successive stages by which God arrived at a knowledge of Himself, complete knowledge being attained in the Hegelian philosophy with which Hegel's record naturally terminates. The convinced Hegelians of the first generation debated in sober earnest what the further history of the world could consist in, seeing that by attaining to self-knowledge in the philosophy of the Master the world-spirit had already reached its goal. Such sublime self-satisfaction is perhaps only possible to certain types of the German mind, and it hardly needed Lotze's ridicule to expose the inherent absurdity of the "dialectical idyll" according to which the

" creative cause of the universe issued from its darkness into the light of manifestation only by the narrow path of earthly nature, and after having formed man and human life again retreated into infinity, as if with all its ends accomplished." [1] But in a less extreme form of expression the same tendency has invaded a good deal of modern philosophy. Because we may truly say that God is manifested in the mind of man and in the process of human history, philosophers pass on to treat the achievement of humanity, taken collectively, as the sole and sufficient self-realisation of the divine. But this extraordinary deification of the *status quo*—of man as he is—has only to be stated, it seems to me, in order to condemn itself. It means, of course, the denial of any divine selfhood, any actuality of God for Himself. There is no knowledge, that is to say, in the universe, no understanding of the scheme of things anywhere, more comprehensive than that which works itself out in laborious patchwork in this and the other human brain ; no goodness, no justice, no tenderness, save that which springs in the human heart. But such a theory does not even explain the *status quo* in which it rests ; for to accept any present as final is to misread the whole nature of development. If the indwelling God is just man as he is, there would be no consciousness of higher and lower, no ideal set before us, and no progress at all therefore possible. The principle which explains human progress is the presence of God, and, as grounded in God, that progress must be " on and always on," for no finite achievement can body forth the infinite perfection. Humility deepens with each step in advance. " Not as though I had already attained," says the Apostle, " either were already perfect, but I follow after . . . forgetting those things which are behind, and reaching forth unto those things which are before." On no other view is the process of human experience explicable.

---

[1] *Microcosmus*, i. 458 (English translation).

We speak naturally in this context of God and *man*. But we have only to lift our gaze to the midnight sky to remember that we have no right to restrict the revelation of God to the comparatively recent inhabitants of this humble planet.

> Worlds on worlds are rolling ever
> From creation to decay.

And in these worlds, or in worlds unseen by the bodily eye, multitudes of self-conscious spirits may exist, children of the same Father and admitted to the same fellowship. " Other sheep I have which are not of this fold." The words spoken by the Johannine Christ in a narrower reference may well be given this wider application. Man, therefore, in this context is merely representative of the finite spirit wherever found, and among those other spirits many may, in every form of spiritual excellence, vastly surpass mankind as we know it. But whatever range beyond range of experience and achievement may thus open before us, nothing is altered in principle as regards the relation of the finite spirit to the infinite Source of its aspirations. He that has gone farthest will be the foremost to declare that he has not already attained, and that it is not in his own strength that he has won his way thus far.

To return, in conclusion, to the opposite views of the divine nature and action which we set out to consider, the eternal contrast between the actual and the ideal seems to me to furnish the natural key to the problem of immanence and transcendence. Transcendence does not mean remoteness or aloofness. The distinction it points to is that between the perfect and the imperfect ; and by perfection we do not understand the possession of innumerable unknown attributes, but the perfect realisation of those very values which we recognise as the glory and crown of our human nature. This idea of perfection disclosing its features gradually, as men become able to apprehend the vision, is the immanent God, the inspiring Spirit to whom all progress is due. But the immanent God is thus always the infinitely transcendent. The two aspects imply one another. A purely immanental theory, as we saw in the earlier part of this paper, means the denial of the divine altogether as in any way distinguishable from the human, and involves, therefore, the unqualified acceptance of everything just as it is. A theory of pure transcendence, on the other hand, tends to leave us with a " mighty Darkness filling the seat of power," for only so far as God is present in our experience can we know anything about Him at all. It is the immanence of the transcendent, the presence of the infinite in our finite lives, that alone explains the essential nature of man— the "divine discontent" which is the root of all progress, the strange sense of doubleness in our being, the incessant conflict of the lower and the higher self, so graphically described by St. Paul as a law in his members warring against the law of his mind. And the more clearly we identify the call of the higher with our true self the more unfeignedly do we recognise the illumination of the divine Spirit. *Deus illuminatio mea*—" In Thy light shall we see light."

II

GOD IN ACTION

BY

LILY DOUGALL

AUTHOR OF "PRO CHRISTO ET ECCLESIA," ETC.

ANALYSIS

The Holy Spirit for the early Christians was the joyful indwelling force of love and life which they felt to be God.

Later the Spirit, as one Person of the Trinity, was regarded as God in action in the world of men.

I. The Spirit acts always in accord with nature, not by overriding natural ways and laws.

II. On this view consider how apparently miraculous or supernatural religious experience may be understood in the light of psychological law.

Such experience considered under four heads : Inward illumination ; Inspired utterance ; Unusual power of resisting temptation or of influencing other minds ; The reception of specific benefits in answer to prayer.

Such experiences may be shown to be in accord with psychological law.

The fact of free will does not result in man acting otherwise than in co-operation with natural law : nature, we conceive, is in the same way God's instrument by which He accomplishes the desire expressed in every true prayer.

Religious experience is evidence of God's action in the world, because in it the religious instinct gets satisfaction, not because the method of its getting satisfaction is magical or miraculous.

III. We must not regard all that happens as the work of the Spirit : He works always for good and opposes evil.

IV. The universal good for which the Spirit works is man's perfect correspondence with environment, i.e. the Kingdom of Heaven. The universal brotherhood implied in this does not come with the mere process of the ages ; it depends on the free choice and sacrificial work of men.

The difficulty in recognising the Spirit's work in the process of development arises from the constant sacrifice of the individual while the Kingdom lingers.

But the fact that, through human development of that self-sacrifice traceable in the whole biological system, the value of the individual is increasingly recognised, indicates that the Spirit is urging on this value and will justify it.

The adventure of world-creating in conscious communion with the Spirit brings about a better future, while it affords the individual who pursues it the fruition of all his permanent desires.

Jesus Christ discovered and proclaimed the power of the Spirit to enhance and harmonise all life and so to bring in the Kingdom of Heaven.

II

GOD IN ACTION

What thought and feeling rises unbidden in us when we hear some one speak of the Holy Ghost or the Holy Spirit?

In some it is a sort of wondering, half-respectful derision, such as we all feel when we come upon belief in creeds that we hold to be outworn. In others it is the simple boredom always experienced by the inferior mind when confronted with what is great in poetry or music or painting. In others, again, who do not doubt that the term signifies a great reality, the thought of holiness rouses only a sense of repulsion. For them the adjective " holy " is synonymous with " forbidding " — a perfection which imperfection, however well-intentioned, may not touch without being " thrust through with a dart."

Yet to spirit in all living creatures belong such life, hope, health, enterprise, curiosity, joy, kindness, love, as they may know. Stones or corpses do not know these affections ; therefore it is to the spirit in the universe that life and love belong. The associations of the word " spirit," therefore, ought not to be dulness or fear. It will be said that to spirit belong also animosities, pride, scorn, cruelty. True ; and these also have been, and are still, attributed to such invisible power or powers as many worship. Hence the notion of " holiness " as " taboo "—a notion compact of the unapproachable, the irrational, the terrible. The early Christians, whatever their mistakes, sins, and ignorances, did this interesting thing—they took the word "holy"

25

—which, originally having its roots in taboo, had been elevated by the Old Testament prophets to mean goodness, awful and exclusive,—they took this word and appropriated it to the Divine Spirit which made for fellowship.[1] It was a new use of the word. So used it served to distinguish the indwelling force they felt to be God from those demonic forces which they, in common with their world, believed to inspire men with animosities and diseases. They were hilarious, these early Christians. In their records we come constantly upon words that evince good spirits. Their delight in a new-found spiritual Friend triumphed over all their misfortunes. They upset the world with their joy and liveliness. They had the same sense of fellowship and enterprise as have the men of a regiment, and they went joyfully to meet persecution as men certain of victory go joyfully to battle. They felt themselves possessed by some external force of love and life which filled them with beautiful hopes and empowered them to carry out their desires.

After that, in the growth of the creed, we get the conception of the Trinity ; but all that we are here concerned with is that the " Holy Spirit " is the name given by Christians to *God in action in the world of men*.

It is essential to any developed religion to believe that God is a Spirit and that He acts in the world of men. To attain a right conception, therefore, of the nature of the Spirit, and of His action, is the most fundamental need of religious thought.

In this connection the chief questions which are exercising the minds of present-day thinkers are the following :—

I. Does the Spirit act in accordance with nature, or by overriding natural ways or laws?

II. If the Spirit works through nature, how may we explain apparently miraculous or supernatural religious experience ?

[1] Cf. Essay IV. p. 137.]

III. Are all things that happen the work of the Spirit ? or does He work for good and oppose evil ?

IV. If for good only, what is the nature of that good ? and if by natural processes, how may man attain to natural co-operation with Him ?

Spirit and the Reign of Law

Science is discarding the mechanistic and determinist conception of natural consequence. The term "law," used for the habits of whatever acts in a dependable and explicable manner, is ambiguous, but the phrase "laws of nature" is so engrafted in our speech that it is pedantic to avoid it.

The modern biologist, although believing that life is governed by law, describes something like choice and adventure at every stage of development, from the amoeba upwards. The psychologist, who long ago discovered that the reign of law prevails in the sphere of mind, is still able to treat each self as a centre of spontaneity. Science no longer compels us to regard nature as an iron-bound system, but at the same time insists that nature is entirely dependable. We may perhaps think now of the system of our universe as to be relied on as the actions of a good man of established character are to be entirely relied on because we know no motion of his mind will be eccentric. It is in this sense that we use the term "the reign of law," in considering its relation to the action of God.

I. Those who have been accustomed to teach the religious world have long brought forward, as proofs of God's existence and evidence of His character, certain events held to be more than natural. We who love God have been taught to fear that the world may ignore Him if He does not sometimes override nature. Yet if we can truly trust God, we shall perceive that there is nothing to fear, whatever the upshot of any truth-seeking. Whatever is true is God's way of revealing Himself ; we may fearlessly seek the fullest knowledge of that way, even though that involve the sacrifice of some favourite tradition.

A child taught to believe in the existence of the ocean because he has heard the roar and murmur of its surges when he puts the curling shell to his ear, may naturally suppose that the ocean itself is only a beautiful myth when the acoustic reason of the surging, throbbing sound of the shell against his ear is first explained to him. But the ocean is a fact too large and insistent to be ignored. And, what is more, the relation between the child's delicate sense of hearing and the echoing of the shell is the same relation as that between his ear and waves of sound made by the surf upon the shore, or the dance of the waves that clap their hands to the winds in mid-ocean. In so far as such sounds are music to him, in so far as such music raises in his consciousness images of beauty and thoughts of infinite spaces and wild delights, both the ocean and the shell bear the same relation to his own power of poetic interpretation. The only reason why he might temporarily doubt the existence of the ocean lies in the beautiful but erroneous nursery tradition that the sea sounds through the orifice of the shell.

It is a fundamental question whether in certain times and conditions we can think—as tradition teaches —of God's action as something so apart from and different from the ordinary working of nature as to be incalculable, and the evidence of something of which we have no other evidence, or whether we may believe that God works in the world only by the qualities and powers of the creatures and things in the world.

It is well that we should realise how small is the area that has ever been claimed by religion for God's miraculous action. Even in ancient times, when no intellectual difficulty was felt in admitting the direct visible action of invisible powers, we find that such action was only assumed with regard to events that appeared extraordinary and not otherwise explicable. And from the earliest times the progress of culture and education tended to restrict the area of divine interposition as it extended the area of human knowledge into the working of nature. This tendency to restrict the area of miracle has ebbed and flowed with the enlightenment, and the more or less emotional temper, of the age. We are all aware how greatly it has shrunk in our own age before the advance of modern science. Let us ask ourselves how far an orthodox Christian of to-day and a modern atheist would differ as to the evidence for the supernatural.

First, let us observe that the word " supernatural " is used by the orthodox to describe a larger area of experience than what is strictly miraculous : all that is miraculous is supernatural, but all that is supernatural is not called miraculous. God's supernatural grace, it is said, may be realised only as subjective, producing for the unbeliever no evidence of the operation of anything extraneous to nature. But a miracle is conceived as taking place irrespective of human expectation or mood, and is regarded as evidence, valid for any candid observer, of God's supernatural action. The area of the miraculous, always restricted, dwindled in the minds of many educated Christians at the end of the last century until it only covered the Birth and Resurrection of our Lord, and other miracles of the New Testament. To confine God's miraculous activity to one age and country was found to be rather absurd in face of the many millenniums of human history and the world's great need ; accordingly, those who believe in special miracles have tended, in the last two decades, to include again some of the alleged miracles of Christian saints, and, in modern times, such events as sudden recoveries from disease occurring in answer to prayer. Throwing the net, however, as widely as the modern

mind may dare to throw it, God's miraculous actions in
the world are very few and, for the non-Christian mind,
apparently unimportant in comparison with the great
stream of events whose causes are discoverable. But, as
already noted, the area alleged by the orthodox to be
covered by the supernatural action of God is much larger.
It covers everything that may be considered the result
of the grace of God in the lives of Christians, and
its reality is evinced to the faithful in certain exalted
moments, in their conscious participation in prayer and
worship, and especially through sacramental rites. The
difficulty about this conception of the supernatural
is threefold : (a) the area of what is considered divine
grace in the Church appears small by the total of
human life—as did the area of the miraculous ; and (b)
such results of supernatural grace as can be descried in
the Church by the world do not appear sufficiently
different from, and more important than, natural processes of the same grace outside the Church to vindicate
a religious philosophy based upon the evidence they
afford — for example, to the eye of reason the good
devout person is not, take him all in all, much better
than the good and earnest agnostic, and sometimes not
as good ; or (c) if, as some Jesuit authorities affirm,
God's sacramental grace may build up a supernatural
life in man which has no visible outcome in moral
character, the Author of such grace appears somewhat
indifferent to the harm its subjects commit.

If by "supernatural" we could simply mean that
which, being divine, transcends our finite conception
of nature, while it also interpenetrates that nature, it
would be quite accurate to call our salvation supernatural, for the main and outstanding idea expressed by
the Christian doctrine of the Spirit is that help comes
to man from God—help adequate and efficient from
the Spirit of God, which is other than man's spirit.
An explanation of the way in which God's Spirit may
be thought of as giving help to man's spirit may be

found in another Essay in this book.[1] Our point here
is that the help does not originate in man, nor is it
planted in man, like a seed, and left for him to
develop and increase by his own efforts. Man can
help himself, of course ; he can do a great deal for
himself in every way ; he is a centre of life—which
means, of origination, of the choice of experience, of
purpose, of effort. All this he is by God's initial gift
of life. A sea-anemone on a rock is a definite centre
of life, and has within itself certain powers ; but the
tide which comes twice a day to bring it all that it
requires for life is something other than the anemone ;
and yet, illimitable as is the onrush of the ocean over
the small life, it brings to that small life only just
so much as the creature can or will assimilate. It
puts forth its richly-coloured tentacles in the trans-
lucent flood, and lives by what it can catch of the
water's wealth. So is the action of God's Spirit on
the soul of man ; it is something other than his own
action. Salvation flows over him always—a warm,
illimitable river of life. Man takes from it, if he
will, what he can, and what he can must ultimately
depend upon what he will.

It is this otherness of God, this initiation and carrying out of efficient help by God, that is the valuable
truth in the insistence laid by many on the supernatural
element in our salvation. The term " supernatural " is,
indeed, sometimes used to express this " otherness "
and nothing more. But if this be the meaning of
the word " supernatural," then we require another
word for " supernatural " in its ordinary sense, meaning
something which overrides the order of nature. Unless
we hold the crudest dualism we must believe that
nature is the manifestation of God, and that God
has, by the creative process, produced human nature
" for Himself," as St. Augustine truly preached.
If nature in God's conception and purpose be the

---

[1] Essay V. pp. 162-166.

creaturely existence which develops to its utmost possibility of good by His constant friendship and aid, then such aid is natural in the sense that it is of the very essence of true natural development. To call it supernatural is to confuse it with an incompatible theory of divine grace. Indeed, those who lay most stress upon the supernatural character of the divine salvation do not mean that God works only in natural ways. They mean that God has come, and still comes, in certain times and places, to operate upon man's spirit or body or upon external nature, in ways that cannot be analysed or classified by physical or psychological science. The word "supernatural" is, unfortunately, too deeply dyed with this meaning to be safely used in any other.

On the other hand, there is growing up a school of Christians who believe that the restriction of the area of what is taken to be God's supernatural or miraculous action by our increasing knowledge of natural causes points to the conclusion that God always acts through nature, and that nature at its highest and best is always the manifestation of God's character as He reveals Himself to us, and is also the indication of His will for our further development. If men regard the universe as fundamentally spiritual, they can draw no line between nature and supernature, because all nature is the evidence of something which is above and beyond. If they believe in God they must believe that that transcendent Spirit is personality and intelligence, but need not therefore believe that His action is ever manifested apart from the coherent system of things which we call "nature."

We may perhaps make quite clear the distinction between these two schools of religious thought—*i.e.* those who believe in the miraculous and the supernatural and those who believe God works only naturally—by an illustration. Those who still hold that our faith in God depends upon our belief in His occasional direct interference with nature believe that the Birth and Resurrection of Jesus were unique events in the sense that they happened because He was God, not because He was the ideal man. On the other hand, those who believe that nature is a progressive revelation of God's character and purpose believe, *either* that our Lord's coming into and going out of this world were not physically different from the birth and the entry into eternal life of other men, *or* that, if they were different, that difference was something truly natural to humanity at its highest and best, the triumph of spirit over body, something to which all humanity may one day attain—the first-fruits of what physical existence must become when God's will is done on earth as in heaven. In such a view these events would be thought of as the supreme instance of the power of mind over body—a power increasingly realised to-day.

If we take this "natural" view of God's relation to the world, as opposed to the supernatural, we shall look for the explanation of all that has been called "supernatural" in the action of God evoking latent powers of the human—powers capable of being stated in terms of natural sequence, *i.e.* of psychological law.

What, then, is it that so many religious people fear may be lost by the acceptance of the view that the whole of religious experience is strictly natural from the psychologist's and the biologist's point of view? Clearly they are afraid that, if this view is accepted, God will seem to have left Himself without witness in the world, and that men will deny God's existence and cease to worship Him if they cannot believe that some small special part of their life experience is not natural but supernatural, in the sense in which we have here agreed to use the terms.

There has always been something very good, as well as something foolish and something cruel, in the opposition that we of the Church have shown to any interference with traditional belief. On each occasion the attitude evinced a very real faith in God and in the Christian salvation, and a willingness to sacrifice much in order to bear witness to the truth for the protection of defenceless multitudes and in defiance of any enemy to the faith. Our folly lay in fearing that what was not of God might bring to nought what was of God. There is, moreover, more than folly, there is something really evil, in the complex state of mind which we have often displayed. Like the Pharisees criticising Christ, we have allowed ourselves to attribute moral defect to those who evince a disinterested love of truth.

When Galileo affirmed that the world went round the sun, the Church took upon itself positively to deny the discovery ; and if, with the aid of dramatic insight, we can picture the theologians of that time, we shall see them chatting to each other at street corners, in church porches, and in convent cloisters, deriding the notion, and so entirely convinced that it is absurd that it never occurs to any of them that their derision and righteous indignation will become in future ages a byword for ecclesiastical folly. Very much the same thing is happening to-day with regard to scientific discoveries in individual and social psychology, and, at the present stage of our knowledge, with less excuse. No astronomical discovery is of as much importance to the world as any really forward step in the knowledge of the human mind ; but the ecclesiastical mind, as such, often appears even more averse to the psychological knowledge of to-day than it was to the astronomy of the Renaissance.

In seeking to analyse the psychological aspect of religious experience our question can only be, " What is truth ? " secure in the faith that God, who has begun a good work in the world, will continue to inspire man with faith that is in accordance with truth.

The Psychological Aspect of Religious Experience

II. Both those who claim a special function or manifestation for God's supernatural action and those who claim that God works naturally lay stress on the evidence of the religious experience. It would be well, therefore, to discuss this experience in the light thrown upon it by psychology.

The phenomena of the religious life may be classified thus :

(1) Inward illumination, with corresponding effect on volition.

(2) Inspired utterance, individual and corporate, which may perhaps be defined as the power to express what is received in inward illumination.

(3) Unusual power of (a) resistance to temptation and progress in virtue ; (b) physical or mental effort, endurance of suffering, and power to regulate the health of the body ; (c) influence over the minds of others.

(4) The reception of other benefits for which definite prayer has been made.

I will first give typical and rather striking examples of each phenomenon, reserving discussion and analysis of them till later.

(1) Under the head of "illumination" I would class all experience of vivid enlightenment which comes to seeking souls, whether as to the nature of sin and holiness or as to the nature of God's personal attitude to the self or the world. There can be no question as to the extraordinary reality and productiveness of this experience, nor can any believer in God question that, when increased knowledge of truth or of vital virtue is attained in this way, the enlightenment comes from God. On the threshold of the religious life such enlightenment often takes the form of a vivid sense of God's presence, which, perhaps for the first time, brings the conviction of His existence to the sceptical or the

careless. The conviction of sin, of forgiveness, of vocation, of guidance in perplexity, often comes suddenly as the apparent result of what is figuratively expressed as a flash of light abolishing mental obscurity. Moments of illumination may become habitual in private prayer or in participation in the Eucharist, or in confession and absolution, or in the pursuit of beauty or truth. Many cases of looking for external signs, or opening books at random to find direction, come under this head.

An incident related by Dr. Horton in his *Autobiography* illustrates this. "In my Union time I felt it my duty to invite the Committee to breakfast. . . . It was then the universal custom to bring up after breakfast tankards of college ale. To omit this would have seemed bad form ; and for Oxford in those days 'form' came before both virtue and religion. I was greatly exercised, for I had, on principle, refused to keep wine in my rooms, and the custom of having beer at breakfast was to me revolting. And yet I wanted to show the usual civilities to my guests. The night before the party I knelt in my room and entreated God to guide me. While I waited on Him I opened my Bible, and my eye fell on a text in Isaiah which up to that night I had never heard or seen : 'Woe unto them that rise up early in the morning, that they may follow strong drink' (Isa. v. 11). I could not at first believe my eyes ; it was as if I had seen it written : 'You shall not have beer for breakfast.' The question was at once settled."

(2) Inspiration.—The thoughtful mind demands of Omnipotence, not only enhancement of vision, but power of expression. We may refer to four classes. The artist, be he painter, musician, or poet, with some glimpse of a beauty which he feels powerless to express, reaches out in desire to some universal Power for gift of expression. To the thinker truth is an objective reality which he seeks with disinterested passion. The

social worker, faced with the stupidity or selfish passions of the herd, demands something more than common power of vision and of endurance in order to mould the situation for the betterment of the world. ; In the avowedly religious man this instinctive demand becomes articulate prayer to a Divine Personality who embodies his highest conception of good ; and in the Christian this conception of good or God is moulded upon his interpretation of the life and teachings of Jesus Christ. To all these come moments or hours in which they feel that something other than themselves is expressing beauty or truth or wisdom with eternal authority.

This power to give effective expression to what has come to the soul as a matter of direct personal illumination is not common. It is the characteristic of prophetic literature as well as of the highest poetry. Such expression of individual conviction with regard to the realities of the religious life is always a powerful factor in moulding the religious and moral character of other persons or of communities. It is, therefore, always entitled to be classed as involving a degree of religious inspiration. Words spoken or written, which seem to come without the will of the person producing them and to transcend his mental level, are a not uncommon result of religious fervour. In the individual life it commonly takes the form of teaching or writing, and it is often called "religious genius." The twenty-third Psalm, St. Paul's hymn to Charity, the description of mercy in *The Merchant of Venice*, and Wordsworth's lines on "Tintern Abbey," are outstanding examples.

More rare is the power to express the corporate illumination of assemblies or communities who are together seeking religious truth. Phrases in historic creeds come to mind at once as evidence of such inspiration. So also do certain restatements of Christian belief which reforming bodies have from time to time set forth under the impulse of a corporate revival of spiritual life. Luther's battle-cry, "Justification by faith," and the creed of the French Revolution, "Liberty, Equality, Fraternity," are instances of these.

(3) Again, the experience of unusual power over circumstances which is felt to come direct from God is a frequent element in religious experience.

(*a*) Christian converts have declared that the appetite for some habitual vice to which they were enslaved has been taken from them once for all by the realisation of divine forgiveness. More often, however, the conquest of such appetite is gradual, the pace of conquest being obviously much quickened by deepening religious experience. Again, the development of marked virtues or talents sometimes synchronises with the religious experience, and in missionary effort the power to persuade and convert often receives extraordinary reinforcement after periods of prayer. Many instances of this class are recorded by William James.[1]

(*b*) The increase of power to do and to endure in the Christian life, which by many is commonly experienced after private prayer or after participation in the Eucharist, is an actual experience. I once met a public singer who, having been converted by a band of American evangelists, joined them, and was in the habit of singing sacred solos at their meetings. She told me how, when advertised to sing at a series of meetings in a Western town, she had been attacked by severe laryngitis. Her problem was, whether to go to bed or, as she phrased it, " to go forward, trusting in God." Having decided on the latter course, she found herself, by some accident, turned out of a hot sleeping-carriage in the middle of a winter night, and forced to wait on the platform of a country station for the next train. She described how she went alone to the end of the platform, and there, under the frosty stars, with swollen, aching throat, entreated God to make her extremity His opportunity. The fever left her ; her

---

[1] *Varieties of Religious Experience*, pp. 220-228.

throat became comfortable ; she continued her journey, and found her power of persuasive song at its best.

(c) Power of influence over other minds is illustrated by a story I once heard Moody, the evangelist, tell of how it was borne in upon his mind that he ought to go to a small and inconveniently placed town to hold a series of meetings. He knew no sufficient reason for doing so, and was more than fully occupied with other plans. By degrees, however, the insistent recurrence of the name of this town to his mind, when discussing plans, led him to arrange to visit it. After doing so he discovered that in that town there was a poor cripple who, having heard of his work, had been unceasingly praying that he might come and preach the Gospel to her neighbours.

(4) The reception of other specific benefits in response to prayer.—A friend of mine was one winter concerned for the welfare of a certain poor district of the city of Montreal. A blizzard had visited the place, almost stopping the traffic, and making the price of food prohibitive to the poor. My friend arranged that the women of her neighbourhood should come to a certain chapel kitchen for soup. Early in the day on which it was to be ready she went to the kitchen, to find that the butcher, who with much difficulty had delivered bones, had not chopped them, and no vessel was at hand large enough to cook them whole. She went out, standing to gaze upon a street drifted by almost untrodden snow, and prayed earnestly for a large pot. She immediately felt what she described as an insane desire to visit a certain poor house from which she could not reasonably expect any help. Going there, she found the doorway, to her amused delight, almost blocked by a great copper pot which the family had acquired a few days before for a bad debt, but which was useless to them. In this vessel the soup was easily made.

I give experiences personally known to me, as

well as others, because I wish to insist that such
marvels constantly happen, and happen in connection
with prayer. It would be easy to give chapter and
verse for stories of the same sort in the biographies
of mediaeval saints and modern missionaries.

The question must now be asked, are they open to
psychological analysis, and can they be referred to the
natural order?

The hypothesis of this essay is that God is all-powerful
to produce good in His own way by educating, not by
compelling, living spirits that each have their own
degree of freedom; by using the organising power of
life as His instrument, not by overriding nature. It
is, therefore, for two reasons necessary that we should
learn as much as we can of the *modus operandi* of
religious experience : first, because man is always im-
agining an unreal religious experience which he mistakes
for the real ; and, secondly, because man's humble co-
operation with God must always be furthered by a
better understanding of His ways.

It is from this standpoint that we ask, does our
advance in knowledge suffice to suggest a " natural "
explanation of such experiences as have been cited ?

To this I believe that a well-considered " yes " may
be given. In the last few years we have learned from
the experiments of scientific psychologists, and of late
notably of medical men attending patients suffering
from shell-shock, various facts which throw a flood of
light upon the psychology of religious experience.
These facts go far to explain by known psychological
causes many of the elements in religious experience
that have seemed inexplicable, and therefore warrant a
strong presumption that other facts, which they do
not cover, have a kindred explanation.

To put it quite simply, the mind of man has been
found to be something larger than his consciousness.
One part of that mind is conscious, the other subconscious. From the subconscious mind come im-

pulses to action, or to refrain from action, impulses to think of certain subjects or to refrain from thinking of them, impulses to the encouragement of certain emotions or to their discouragement. This subconscious part of the mind, which cannot be awakened or controlled by any direct effort of the will, can be controlled and educated by what is called "mental suggestion," and mental suggestion is found to work most powerfully when the conscious mind is either quiescent or has its attention distracted.

Such quiescent condition, though a state of mental and physical repose, is not a state of dulness, nor is it always a state of passivity, but is very often rather a state of great progress of thought and insight on any subject on which the attention is focussed. Also in this state certain powers of the mind, unsuspected in former times, come into evidence.

We know this because men often find that during sleep they have formed correct judgements on matters in which they had been wavering and perplexed. Again, the suggestion, under medical hypnosis, that they have the power to do certain things which they have never been able to do before, enables them to do them ; they can remember what otherwise they had entirely forgotten, and under the right suggestion bad habits have been entirely abandoned. Yet again, under medical hypnosis the centres of sensuous impression can be so controlled that negative or positive hallucinations are induced—a fact which bears on cases in which visions are seen, voices heard, etc. Once more, physical functions, such as the circulation of the blood, the action of muscles, respiration, etc., can be affected by mental suggestion—a fact which bears on the healing of disease, and on accession of physical strength to do or to endure.

It is also now recognised that sleep is not necessary to the quiescent state in which the greatest potency of mental suggestion obtains. Such a state can very easily be induced by the mental strain involved in fixing the attention upon one external object or one idea ; and those who have scientific knowledge of such states know that people who fall into them are seldom able to realise their own suggestible condition.

When it is realised that the prolonged effort and emotion of the various phases of "devotional exercises," attention to religious rites or earnestness in private prayer, provide just the strain of attention necessary to produce the quiescent and suggestible state, the candid mind will at once perceive that suggestion, either from some external source or from the automatic movement of the subconscious mind, will be potent in hours of devotion, and that any of the phenomena of the suggestible state may then be experienced, and induce results unexpected by the subject.[1]

Let us then take as a provisional hypothesis the position that the faculties revealed in suggestible conditions, which may be, and are, used by men both for good and evil, are used by the Spirit in the exercise of His beneficent power. We may now take this hypothesis and see how it applies to the various instances already given.

(1) Illumination.—Take the case of Dr. Horton's solution of his dilemma quoted on p. 36. A reviewer in *The New Statesman* remarks on the capriciousness attaching to divine guidance on any such theory, and adds : "No one would mock at the boy who did this, but what is one to say as to the judgement, the intellectual capacity, of the man who, repeating this story, can also admit that he wasted much of his life in thundering against the superstitious errors and the lack of truth among his fellow-Christians?"

But the reviewer is here criticising the magical view of such direction. The natural view would be to take it as a fact of the established order that in every man there resides a greater power of judgement than he

---

[1] See Essay VII. pp. 258-9, 267.

ordinarily exercises ; that in the case of a religious man who, perplexed, cries to God, God enhances his latent natural power ; that when, weary after effort, such a man waits humbly to receive wisdom, the Spirit through this enhancement gives the right auto-suggestion. To put it in other words : the man's mind will then rise to its own highest capacity ; he will see the real issue clear of perplexity ; on that account he will estimate more clearly the probable results of different courses. Just in so far as his whole past life has educated him to see God's purpose for himself and for the world, he will see the right decision. Any oracle that he consults will be useful just in so far as it helps to stimulate and formulate his own best judgement ; it will be misleading just in so far as he accepts what contradicts in any degree his own best judgement. In the case of Dr. Horton's youthful perplexity, it is probable that before this incident arose he had made up his mind on the general principle that conformity to what he regarded as foolish customs was the lower path. In quiet recollection he was able to penetrate below the strong counter-currents that confused his surface mind and apply the deeper principle of his life to the particular case in point. Had he turned up any text which suggested the importance of doing right, even at the cost of temporary misunderstanding, he would probably have found it equally convincing. Had he turned up the text, " Take a little wine for thy stomach's sake and thine often infirmity," he would probably have reflected that it did not apply to his particular visitors. (Whether or not there is, as some think, a latent natural power of what might be called " X-ray vision " or " second sight," which would enable any one in such a case to turn up an appropriate text, must be left to future investigation to decide.) Superstition, in such a case, would be involved in accepting some fiat of the Bible, or other external authority, when it contradicted his own best judgement. In the more important cases in which, as the reviewer points out, he, in later life, admits his judgement erred, the probability is that he took for granted that his course was righteous, went through no searching of heart and mind, and made no candid and humble appeal for help to the Source of wisdom.

Thus interpreted, this trivial instance suggests a clue which may lead us into the heart of every case of apparently supernatural illumination. If God be acting always for our good, the God-consciousness, *ex hypothesi*, is not needed to bring God into a man's life, but it opens a man's intelligence and emotional nature to an awareness of the Spirit's standard of values—a standard transcending any standard of pleasure or of mere expediency—and gives the Spirit opportunity to enhance the natural powers of the mind.

(2) Inspiration.—Again, with regard to inspired expression, many of us know some artist or writer or speaker who experiences the mood of feeling in which he is carried beyond his own powers, and feels enabled to do or say something greater than his natural ability would produce. Frederick Myers called this "an uprush from the subliminal self." He believed this self to be something much greater than the conscious self, but later psychologists believe it to be merely the repository of past experience, subjective or objective, plus such latent powers as the mind may possess undeveloped by exercise or education. We incline to the latter belief ; our sudden memories of things long forgotten, our odd and unexpected impulses, suggest that what is evil and absurd as well as what is splendid may come from this source into consciousness. And that, indeed, is what happens. Words containing sublime messages for the world have risen unbidden in the minds of prophets ; but the same conviction of inspiration occurs in fools and fanatics as in sages and prophets ; and most people who are subject to it acknowledge that they have at times, under its influence, produced what was not worth production. What seems

like automatic speech or art or writing is a perfectly natural process which may or may not be used to interpret the values of the Spirit to the world of sense. How it will be used will depend upon other factors in the life.

We have also to take into account that there is a good deal of evidence of the transference of mood and notion from mind to mind without sense perception, the condition usually being strong or vivid emotion in one or more of the agents and a quiescent condition in the percipient. Of transference of mood we have evidence in many historic corporate manias, chronicles recording that people, even children, living apart in country places, who had heard and seen nothing of the popular commotion, were moved sometimes to dancing, sometimes to beating themselves, sometimes to setting out upon pilgrimage, in the same way in which the populace of the district happened to be moved. We might set aside these annals as false were it not that in our own days we well know that political or military excitement can move people to opinions and actions that they could never rationally infer from what they see and hear, and infection of mood appears to account for the phenomena. There are also very many well-authenticated cases of mental coincidences beyond the possibility of chance and sense perception for the explanation of which we must either accept the spiritualistic hypothesis of the agency of discarnate spirits, or believe that where there is strong emotion in the agent, and quiescence in the percipient, there may be a natural transference of mood and notion which comes as a message from the unseen, and only half a century ago would have been considered miraculous.[1]

In modern accounts of mental coincidence the

---

[1] It will be observed that this statement makes no reference to evidence for or against such thought-reading as has been claimed to pass between people where no emotion is involved. The negative result of the experiments made at Leland Stanford Junior University by Dr. Coover has no bearing upon what we are now discussing under the name of telepathy, as in his experiments no emotion appears to have been involved; nor does there appear to have been any attempt to experiment with percipients in hypnotic conditions.

impression, as interpreted by the recipient, rarely corresponds in all points with the ideas that were transmitted. I may illustrate this from my own experience. One night I dreamed that two friends—a brother and sister —had had a carriage accident. In my dream I saw the brother carried into a garden gateway in a man's arms, and heard his sister say shortly after, in a tone of relief, " There are no bones broken." So vivid was the dream that, although not accustomed to notice dreams, I wrote to inquire, and found the fact to be that the day before the friends in question had been driving out. The brother had seen his favourite dog run over by a cart and carried in the groom's arms into a gateway to be examined ; that, shortly afterwards, his sister had called out that no bones were broken. Neither of them connected the incident in any conscious way with me. Such experiences seem to point to a natural faculty of giving and receiving non-sensuous messages which lies below the level of consciousness. Such impressions, when vivid, urge the conscious mind to find its own fallible interpretation of them.

When we study the religious utterances of minds that the religious world has rightly counted inspired, we find a condition of things closely akin to telepathic impression. Both form and content of the utterance seem so much conditioned by age and nation that they appear to be the prophet's interpretation of some suggestion impressed upon his subconscious mind, rather than anything approaching infallible diction.

(3) Cases of unusual power.

(a) The new personality that may emerge from sudden conversion has been analysed and described by Professor James.[1]

(b) It is admitted[2] that power of endurance may be enhanced, and that disease can often be cured by mental suggestion, as in the case quoted of the public singer.

---

[1] *Varieties of Religious Experience*, pp. 230-237. [2] Cf. Essay III. p. 71 ff.

(*c*) The prayer of the cripple which brought Moody the evangelist out of his way may fitly be regarded as an instance of the working of telepathy.

There should be no difficulty either to faith or reason in accepting these results as the action of the Spirit. If we believe that the Divine Spirit is always, everywhere, acting in the world, we believe, *ex hypothesi*, that He does, by personal influence, exercise a real force of persuasion and instruction upon living spirits that do not shut themselves off from goodness. His working is thus contingent on man's attitude and will. We may grant—what is not yet proven—that all the motions of inanimate nature are predetermined and fixed in a mechanical certainty, but we must still admit that we have, interpenetrating this mechanical system, *life* which is not mechanical, whose motions we do not believe to be predetermined. Now that the biologists are throwing aside the dream of a mechanical system of life which is predetermined, the theologian can with the more confidence repudiate the corresponding conception of the predetermination of all events by God.

(4) The reception of benefits after definite prayer. —The amusing case of the lady and the copper pot may have been both an answer to prayer and entirely natural. The pot was near by, and in the possession of a person who did not want it. The lady who discovered it had previously been the subject of several experiences commonly attributed to " second sight." Whatever natural faculty of the mind such experiences betray had therefore already been quickened by exercise. All that is necessary to place the Spirit's action in this case within the natural order is to say that the subconscious power of this faculty was quickened by Him in response to prayer. Her intense sympathy with the hungry poor, her child-like dependence on God and eager prayer, gave the Spirit opportunity. Had the pot not been at hand we may assume she might have been guided, by means of the same natural faculty, to some other way

out of the difficulty—*e.g.* some one whose mind was open to good and God might have been guided by telepathic impression to come to her aid.

Probably one element in our Lord's vision of the Kingdom was the human community whose many minds should all always be open to such quickening by the Spirit that they would work in harmony, aware of each other's needs. If we say that our antagonisms and dulness have prevented the rise of such a community, we offer a rational explanation of the undoubted fact that many prayers for help in good work as earnest and single-hearted as this one are not followed by immediate relief.

In our present state of knowledge it appears to be just as short-sighted to hold that prayer can only affect the world by elevating the soul that prays, as to insist that God's power overrides natural sequence. Either view appears to entail a moral nemesis that ought to warn us that it is not the track of truth. Those who wed their souls to the first supposition lose in their intercourse with God and man an element of child-like hope in fresh possibilities which, when retained, gives to the mature mind a poise, charm, and influence that nothing else can give. On the other hand, those who believe that God overrides nature on occasion are forced to depict His way as cruel or entirely incomprehensible because of the great multitude of cases in which there is no marvellous response to prayer. This last is the ethical difficulty of the belief in miracles that override natural sequences. A world awakened to ask "the reason why" can never be reconciled to a God cruel or wholly arbitrary ; it can understand a God self-limited by creation.

On this question of whether, and how, God responds to definite petitions we often hear the argument that because man, by free will, can interfere in the course of nature it is absurd to suppose that God cannot. But man cannot interfere with nature in the sense of abrogating natural laws; he can only control their working. It has been said that a man who catches a cricket-ball in its flight neutralises the force of gravitation, by which law, without his wilful action, the ball would fall to the ground. But his whole action is conditioned by the force of gravitation; without it he could do nothing. By that he stands his ground and exerts the force necessary to catch the ball. The will and skill to catch the ball are the contribution of the man's mind, but he effects his purpose in strict co-operation with all the laws that govern matter and motion. As far as reason differs from folly, so far does the belief that man can only perform what he wills in accordance with natural law differ from the assumption that man's choice is predetermined by mechanical sequence. There is the same difference between the belief that God's action will always be in accordance with natural sequence and the assumption that He cannot act in the world in direct response to man's desire. We may accept the hypothesis that God acts only through natural means while at the same time we retain the fullest belief in His personal freedom to answer prayer by shaping natural events in the line of our desire. There is much evidence encouraging the belief that God evokes our faith by using prayer as a factor in the construction of the immediate future. It is unquestionable that without the calculable properties of matter man could carry out no purpose. What we call natural law is his instrument, his tool, his weapon. It is the instrument of life in all its forms, from the smallest germ of vegetation to the greatest human genius. Our hypothesis is that all life, culminating in man's free spirit with its intelligence, is, in turn, God's instrument, by which he will accomplish the desire expressed in every true prayer.

What then, we ask, is the value of religious experience as an evidence of God's action in the world? The only evidence that has really convinced religious men of

E

God's action is the correspondence of the religious desire with its satisfaction. It is not the appearance of magic in the method of its satisfaction that is convincing. The religious instinct demands from God the security of mutual love and the enhancement of life. If God does not satisfy these demands of those who seek Him, then, as the Apostle said, "religion is vain." Every godly mind rises to corroborate the truth of the cry, "Herein is love, not that we loved God, but that he loved us" (1 John iv. 10); or this, "Thou hast been a strength to the poor, a strength to the needy in his distress, a refuge from the storm, a shadow from the heat, when the blast of the terrible ones is as a storm against the wall" (Isaiah xxv. 4); or this, "My soul shall be joyful in my God, for he hath clothed me with the garments of salvation" (Isaiah lxi. 10); or again, "As far as the east is from the west, so far hath he removed our transgressions from us. Like as a father pitieth his children, so the Lord pitieth them that fear him" (Ps. ciii. 12-13). It is the discovery that the godward appeal is a valid cheque upon the bank of reality that convinces those who make it of the reality of God's action. If a man pray for bread his faith that he is answered does not depend on his seeing the bread brought by a raven instead of a baker. If he seek direction from God he does not turn atheist because he gets it through a neighbour's advice. Though it be proved to us that all response to our prayer and aspiration comes through natural process, our faith will not fail as long as we are sure of response.

NOT ALL THAT HAPPENS EXPRESSES GOD'S MIND

III. If, then, we agree that God is a Spirit and works in the world through natural process, are we to believe that whatever happens is God's will—that whenever disaster occurs it is a divine judgement? Theology has often taught this, but in seeking thus

to enhance the divine glory it has really detracted
from it.

Man's judgements with regard to truth, goodness, and
beauty certainly exist ; and these realities are in sharp
opposition to human error, ugliness, and cruelty, and
their results—which also actually exist. Both, however,
cannot equally be the work of the Spirit ; we cannot
read the divine character equally in both. And we
cannot believe that God is divided ; that as God the
Father He does one thing, and as the Holy Spirit
opposes His own act. He cannot by His sovereign
will drive men mad in order to destroy them, while by
His Spirit He seeks to save them.

And if human action can oppose God, what right
have we to suppose that all other creatures that make
up the biological system of which man is a part always
act in concert with God? The power which controls
the world is *either* a non-moral power, and therefore
despicable in man's judgement, *or*, man's judgements
of value show the influence of the Spirit upon his
spirit, and it is to them that we must look to discover
God's character. The Holy Spirit cannot both be the
divine power of Christian experience and the divine
power of the fatalist who cries, " Whatever is, is
right."

We need more clear thinking in this respect than
religious teachers sometimes give. Many men, looking
back on their past lives, see that good has come to them
out of misfortunes ; and history presents cases when
national disasters, and even national crimes, have in-
augurated new eras of higher development. This
proves that the Spirit may inspire men to meet evil in
such a way as to attain a higher good than was theirs
before they encountered the evil. It does not prove
more than this. A mariner whose ship is struck by a
storm may set his sails so as to be sped upon his way while
at the same time he is in peril from the blast. This
does not prove that he would not have made a better

voyage by a steady, favourable wind. Our imaginations are feeble ; whenever we try to conceive another past than that which has actually happened, they wave in nothingness as the tendrils of a young climbing plant, unsupported, wave in air. We comfort ourselves for our feeble-mindedness by falling back upon what we call " real life," and pointing out that whenever men or nations have enjoyed monotonous prosperity they have degenerated. We are like a mariner who, reaching his port by a skilful use of storms, does not picture the voyage that might have been with the steady, favourable wind, but points to ships that are becalmed and thanks his lucky stars. The fact that men and nations often deteriorate when they enjoy monotonous security is undeniable, but such security has had its source in the temper which hedges itself about with safety, and refuses, in this present evil world, to " live dangerously." That temper carries within it the seeds of degeneration. Such fact does not prove that the disasters which men of noble endeavour frequently meet are of the Spirit's contriving, or even that the disasters which befall notorious evildoers are His work. In fact, if we will but interrogate our own beliefs strictly we shall see that we none of us believe the fatalist creed that on occasion we recite. We do not believe the Holy Spirit inspired the Jerusalem crowd to cry for the crucifixion of Jesus. The spirit that urged this crowd to this national crime was not the spirit which urged a crowd in the same city to repentance on the day of Pentecost. The spirit that urges a mob to lynch a criminal is not the spirit that urges prison reform. The spirit that urged the pioneers of modern science to seek the truth of things is not the spirit which urges ecclesiastics to their persecution. The spirit that urges men to the subjection of the weak and the atrocities of war is not the spirit that urges them to true brotherhood and true bravery, to the heroism of the magnanimous victor and the heroic nurse, to balanced thought and good statesmanship. The miseries that come to man through men do not come to them because their opponents are inspired by the Holy Spirit.

Or if we take the disasters that befall men from the forces of what we call lower nature, we are all ready to admit that the spirit which urges men so to observe and co-operate with these forces that they may avoid destruction from them, and even make them their servants, is not the spirit that inspires men stupidly to acquiesce in the recurrence of such evils.

Curiously enough, while popular theology often ascribes calamity to God, it never ascribes it to the Holy Spirit. But orthodox theology has never countenanced tritheism. No one would assert that God the Father urges men to rob or murder their neighbours while the Holy Spirit is striving with them to resist the temptation. Yet this is implied if we say that disasters brought about by the wickedness of men are the will of God. Nor can we suppose that God the Father has foredoomed men to destruction—let us say, by earthquake—while the Spirit of Wisdom, working through science and sanity, is prompting them to quit the area of danger. The God of the fatalist is not the God of the Christian ; and the effort of Christian thought to combine these two characters in one Being is the chief cause of the practical atheism widespread in all ranks of society and among nominal Christians.

It is unavailing for the advocates of this combination-God, who builds and destroys, afflicts and consoles, to cry that God is so great that He transcends the opposition in a way the finite mind cannot understand, because God only enters into man's field of vision at all in so far as man can understand His character.

If we interrogate religious experience as to the character of the supreme Spirit, we find it has always claimed to possess the mutual understanding involved in kinship. Thus the religious mind claims always to be " His offspring," to be " made in his image " ; it cries, "His spirit beareth witness with our spirit that we are the sons of God"; "Whereby we cry Abba Father"; "Our father, which art in heaven." All these are ways of expressing the conviction of kinship or a mutuality of comprehension which implies that human judgements of good are God-implanted and reflect—feebly indeed, but still reflect—God's intenser knowledge of good and evil. And as the religious mind rises to apprehend the more universal obligations of goodwill, it realises that the forces and animosities which cause all that is dire cannot be the action of a good God.

The Goal of the Spirit

IV. If, then, we are agreed that the Divine Spirit is at work in the world of men in ways that are natural to the world and to men, and also that in that world good and evil are really opposed to one another, the Spirit working on the side of good and against evil, we have still to discover (*a*) what is the nature of the good for which the Spirit works, and (*b*) how we may co-operate with the Spirit for the realisation of that good.

(*a*) What do we to-day understand the universal good to be? Science tells us that it is correspondence with environment; Jesus Christ calls it "the kingdom of God" or "of heaven."

We are accustomed to realise that the welfare of any living thing depends upon correspondence with its environment. It only lives in so far as it corresponds; it only lives perfectly by perfect correspondence. Taking humanity as a whole, it is clear that man will not correspond perfectly with his physical environment until the knowledge and skill of all applied science render him no longer in any degree the sport of the elements but their master. As the old tradition had it that God brought the animals one by one to Adam to receive their names, and gave him dominion over them, so science is bringing to mankind the forces of earth, air, fire, and water to receive their names, and giving men dominion over them. An Abraham or a Hesiod may correspond better with local and temporary environment than does a modern man of science, but while the race has failed, and fails, to deal rightly with plague, famine, and war, genius seldom gets its chance and successive nations prematurely perish. What has that to do with Jesus of Nazareth and His kingdom of God? Does not one glance at our world to-day show us that as long as man uses each small advance in knowledge and skill to subject and destroy his fellow-man he is not in correspondence with his human environment, nor forwarding the universal knowledge of constructive arts? The utilisation of the forces of earth for human welfare can only be achieved by brotherhood and co-operation. Peace, which is the jumping-off place for the great adventure of catching and harnessing the elements for the world's welfare, can only be obtained by learning how to sympathise with our fellows, learning how to like and befriend and correspond with them. Man is the greatest factor in man's environment. If, then, what we call nature is working for man's correspondence with his environment, it is working through every effort that tends to endow the coming race with kindly and good-humoured impulses, with a store of skilful methods of righting wrongs and governing the wrong-headed by friendly means instead of by grim disapprobation or cruel suppression, by laughter rather than by tears.[1]

To correspond with his environment, man must learn not only to be ready if need be to die rather than compromise with falsity, but also to forgive to seventy times seven, and to love his enemies. If the push of life be for the survival of those who can best

---

[1] This subject is more fully dealt with in the present writer's essay in *God and the Struggle for Existence* (published by the Student Christian Movement).

correspond with their environment, universal brother-hood and goodwill is the far-off event towards which evolution moves. The movement, as we have seen, is not mechanical, for the mere process of the ages does not bring wisdom. It must always depend on the right choice of free creatures. The character of God the Spirit, as revealed by this divine purpose of universal goodwill, is the same as that revealed by Christ, and also by every prophetic soul that has had glimpses of the truth. To put it more adequately—Jesus Christ gave forth definitely the good news of the harmony toward which the historic process tends, and explicitly declared the method by which it should come. This method was the response of man to the saving processes of the Holy Spirit—processes of forgiveness and heal-ing, helpfulness and goodwill, of passion for truth and reality, and a true comparison of man's tawdry notions of glory with the beauty of nature whenever it is receptive to the care of God. The harmony of human wills, when attained, will be a new starting-point for unrestricted racial development ; but to us it is the mountain-peak which we must reach before we can see further.

Thus our question, What is the good for which the Spirit works? would find an easy answer if we could be satisfied by a far-off future event and a future culmina-tion of our race. We cannot be satisfied with what is future, except as it explains and justifies the present and the past. Such a culmination would justify the past and present of the race as a whole, but it could not justify the mistakes and sufferings of the individuals in each generation.

The great difficulty in recognising the Spirit's work in the process of development arises from the fact that the individual, and the single generation, is constantly crushed in the process, without apparent opportunity of escape. The great armies of Humanity march on to victory, but on every yard of the advance lie the wounded and the dead. The course of evolution, considered in itself, seems wholly careless of the individual.

Yet, in apparent opposition to this there is the striking paradox that, considered as an educative process, it has educed, and does educe, in men, not greater contempt for the individual in comparison with the whole, but ever-increasing respect for every individual of every generation. This fact—that the claim of the individual on society has everywhere through long ages become more and more clearly recognised—points perhaps to a solution of the difficulty. The value set upon the individual life, its well-being, freedom, and education, which has become the criterion of higher and lower in our estimate of national progress, reveals, if anything reveals, the character of the Spirit's work, for it is here discovered in the efflorescence of the great principle which no less conspicuously penetrates the struggle for existence, showing itself in parental affection, family devotion, and the tribal bond—the principle of the sacrifice of the strong for the weak, the wise for the ignorant, the righteous for the lawless. If, then, we can accept this principle—which is, indeed, the shadow of the Cross projected by the level light of sunrise across all the ages of evolution—as indicating the character of the Spirit, we may reasonably suppose that the Spirit has His own ways and means of compensating the individual for whatever of failure or misery has been thrust upon him.

In what way can this compensation be given? We cannot believe a good to be all-inclusive unless it represents the fruition of the desires of all men and women who have lived, and must still live and die, before the era of human triumph which we may descry on the horizon of this world's future. It is on salvation for the individual that Jesus laid His emphasis, and we must inquire how far we have reason to believe that the Spirit gives to each living soul ample opportunity to enter into a process of development which will both bring it to such fruition of all its permanent desires as will compensate it for all suffering and will make it a co-operator in realising the universal good.

As any process must be estimated by its outcome, let us first consider the case of those souls who are most vitally Christianised, frankly admitting that vital Christianity is different from nominal Christianity. The Gospel of Christ teaches us that full salvation depends upon the soul setting forth to save the world in the experience of being himself saved by the Spirit. Salvation is offered freely, and must be experienced as a gift. This is no missionary cant, but a psychological fact. The result of the experience is that the saved soul so loves the world that it gives its all that the world may be saved. Both these elements are interdependent, and both are a process. Yet from the moment that the soul really sees God in Christ, *i.e.* sees that the Spirit's character and action on the world may be interpreted by the character of Christ, it knows the fruition of all its desires to be secure. It *is* saved perfectly and ideally in prospect, and yet it will for ever continue to be raised to fuller vision. Likewise, the moment the soul really sees God in Christ it also sets forth to save the world. It can no other. It sees the divine character giving to the utmost for the world's salvation, and by that sight is transformed into a life-centre whose main and most permanent desire is to live for the perfecting of all things, realising the prospective joy of God therein. But many a transient and lower desire may temporarily intervene and be followed—as a child may chase butter-flies hither and thither while still proceeding in the direction of home. The giving up of all by the soul for the world's salvation is a process, as the ex-perience of being saved is a process. Yet from the moment the soul really sees God in Christ, its most permanent and abiding desire is to speed further and further in the great adventure of world-saving, whether by the avenue of truth, of beauty, or of moral right. Irreligious it can never again be, for the universe has become a fane, and the love of God its light.

There are very many who see this vision reflected in the best thought of their age, and are themselves inspired by it, yet, misled by the blind guidance of His nominal exponents, they deny Jesus Christ to be its source. These, because really inspired by Him, though only indirectly, are at one with Him in the Spirit's power. On the other hand, undoubting acceptance of the most correct of creeds may leave the soul without the vision, still working for its own salvation, still repulsive in its zeal for what it holds to be the salvation of the world. The unthinking acceptance of religious tradition, the docile obedience to a religious rule, may each have a value of a different sort for different souls, but they are not the vision of God in Christ. That vision is the realisation that the supreme Spirit at work in all life has the character of Jesus Christ. The realisation of this fact may be sudden or gradual, but it is an experience which transforms any self-regarding effort to attain salvation into an other-regarding effort to show forth the beauty of God to whatever coterie of souls, little or large, may form its world. Can it be said that this adventure of world-saving, and the future toward which we believe it tends, will afford the fruition of all desire?

Before answering we must clear away any narrow or grotesque pictures of world-saving that we may have formed. There are as many ways in which the world of men may be effectively helped forward into co-operation with the Divine Spirit as there are men and women ; and that of itself is sufficient evidence that the Spirit has for each a unique mission, and that that mission will best conserve and develop all the powers and faculties of each soul. Human good is a trinity of truth and beauty and social welfare ; and while none of these qualities can really exist without the others, the vocations of men can roughly be put into three classes, according as men exercise their enterprise and ingenuity to augment the world-stock of any one of these. Heretofore the phrase " soul-saving " has been too exclusively associated with strictly pious effort ; it is along all the avenues opened by this trinity of God that the Spirit urges and inspires us to link up men in trust and fealty to the Source of Love and Life.

Can we, indeed, think of any other or greater fruition of our desires than the exercise and development of all our powers in making some unique and lasting addition to the good of the whole ? What artist, what patriot, what self-seeker even, can ask for more ?

But, granted that this creative work can satisfy those who may become vitally Christ-like in giving themselves as instruments of the Spirit for the world's salvation, can we infer from their satisfaction anything which will justify the suffering of those innumerable lives that seem to have been, and still to be, crushed in the process of race education ? Yes, for their case proves that nature, when she urges to correspondence with environment, is the instrument of the Spirit urging the race to inexhaustible goodwill as well as to all scientific enterprise ; and if we see reason to believe this, and further to believe that the individual who enters into conscious communion with the Spirit is not only led into the fruition of all his own permanent desires, but led into a constantly increasing carefulness for the welfare of every other individual life, then we are bound to believe that the character of God is indicated by this double testimony. Because God is God, each life will some way find its compensation and development. " He is not the God of the dead but of the living " ; life's opportunities do not end on earth.

(*b*) The Christian Church should be the nursery of all free souls, but, like the rest of creation, it has shown forth no transcendent and flawless perfection. It is hardly reasonable, however, on that account to deny it to be a characteristic school of the Spirit, unless we are prepared to set aside the claim of all nature to be the manifestation of God because of the chaotic elements of harm and destruction and consequent misery that still exist in the world as it now is. But it is vital to distinguish between the inspiration of the Church and the chaotic evils within it that still frustrate that inspiration.

The man who sees God the Spirit in the world or in the Church must bring forward his tests of good and true and beautiful, and claim as divine in the whole system only what tends toward the good and true and beautiful, holding that such tendencies alone point in the direction in which the whole must move for the accomplishment of the divine purpose. We shall make mistakes, but we cannot escape the responsibility of exercising our own discrimination. We naturally desire to be saved the trouble of search and discovery ; we passionately desire that some visible finger from heaven should point out to us the track of the Spirit ; but if it is God's way that we should find out in what the holiness of the Spirit consists by the faithful exploiting of our own values for beauty and goodness and truth, this end could not be attained by infallible external revelation. Our values are within our own souls. Jesus taught that we must first find *within* us the kingdom—the purposes and works of the Spirit—before that kingdom can be realised in the complex harmony of the external life. In the Church we must fix our aspiration upon increase of religious insight rather than upon any repetition of the past.

The great tragedy of human life has been the amount of religious force that has been expended in vain efforts to obtain the help of God. The word religion is commonly used to mean all human activity that is in intention directed Godward ; but if God's

Spirit inspires, not everything, but only what is good, we must recognise that much of man's religious activity has been and is directed toward something merely imagined to be God. While our sense of justice constrains us to believe that every man who thinks of God as his own highest ideal of good comes into touch with Him when he tries to worship or pray, and thereby gives the Spirit opportunity to enhance his own nature and the natures of those for whom he prays, it by no means follows that when men worship and entreat a Being of character morally inferior to themselves they will come by that means into touch with Creative Power. A population visited by plague might quite innocently believe that the disease could be moved magically by the fiat of God. As long as their prayer was offered to a God as good—*i.e.* as kind and compassionate—as they themselves would like to be, we must, on our hypothesis, believe that the prayer would be answered by some enhancement of the life of the community ; that hope, observation, understanding, and physical vitality would be quickened, with consequent result upon health. Jesus Christ constantly averred that it is faith in God's fatherliness that makes the human spirit accessible to Him ; but, if so, then the more men wailed out entreaties to a hardhearted God, the more they performed penances to propitiate Him, the more they would be actually turning away from the proffered help of Heaven. For men, although faulty and ignorant, know not only how to give good things to their children, but how to give them kindly, without waiting for the child to grovel and wail and torture itself. A normal standard of kindness was never far to seek : even in very primitive communities the claim of a sick child on the utmost kindness of its parents is recognised. A sense of sin need not confuse human judgement in this respect, for very degraded is the parent who refuses to help a suffering or dying child because it has previously been naughty.   Prayer and worship directed to a God conceived as acting on the level of such a degraded parent would naturally tend to shut the soul against the Spirit with His recreative power.   If, therefore, men seek to obtain either spiritual or physical good from God by such a method, they are sinning against the light that lighteth every man coming into the world.   The same may be said of attempts to propitiate God by ritual exactions or by the use of relics and mascots, practices that no father or kind man would require from the needy before giving aid.   The single or simple eye, of which Jesus Christ speaks, sees goodness as one both in God and man, and is therefore the avenue of light and life.   The father in the parable of the Prodigal Son shows God seen by this simple eye.   If we believe that the Spirit works according to psychological law and awaits this child-like simplicity in man, the failure of much religious prayer and effort can be explained.

But in admitting this we must not overlook the fact that human experience is always complex.   In so far as men are kind to each other, even while they worship a hard-hearted notion of God, they come unconsciously into touch with the Spirit by their kindness.   The poetic insight of the Christ depicts the virtues of pagans in the story of the sheep gathered from all nations. Again, good people whose unchallenged traditions have led them to believe in a false notion of God are often, after performing propitiatory rites to an unkind God, in a frame of mind to turn with simple faith to the notion of true goodness in God, and thus come in the end, and intermittently, into touch with the Creative Spirit.   The result of such worship we should expect to be a combination of power and weakness, insight and superstition, common sense and folly, magic and science, cruelty and love.   Religious history certainly bears out our hypothesis here.

In turning from the imperfect historic actual to the better thing which might have been, we are bound to question again the mind of Christ. What concerns us here is the discovery made by Jesus Christ of the power of the Spirit and the conditions under which that power could be received, not as the occasional afflatus which men had recognised from all time, but as the very warp and woof of the web of man's social life, the daily food by which men, women, and children could be satisfied and empowered for the greater enterprise—dowered with the inward resourceful wisdom that can make the liberty of each harmonise with the good of all. A community thus inspired was to be the new reign, or what we might call the new civilisation, of Heaven or of God. Whether realised on earth, or in some new plane of being mystically conceived, what was essential was the power of the Spirit. "Neither be ye called masters, for One is your master." "It is not ye who speak, but the Spirit of your Father that speaketh in you." "The kingdom of heaven is within you." "Unto you it is given to know the mystery of the kingdom."

It was not a new idea that divine wisdom might be a quasi-personal emanation from God, and live in intimate fellowship with man ; but Jesus saw that this Spirit *was* God, and cared with creative purpose for despised field flowers and sparrows, for the body of man as well as the soul. He saw that this Divine Spirit was at the same time the emotion that surges up into the practice of parental kindness, the instinctive wit of all true love, and also the eternal source and goal of all.

This discovery of Jesus—which He called the mystery of the kingdom—was nothing less than such insight into the very heart of the relation of life to its environment as enabled Him to see the goal from the starting-point, to see the divine, far-off ideal toward which the whole race must move. He saw the way in which men, while still in a false civilisation, must live so as not only to bring about the true order, but in the midst of the old to grasp at once the joy and liberty and fellowship of the new.   This was a fetch of genius—the genius at once of the poet, the prophet, and the statesman ; yet Jesus seems to have drawn in this wisdom as simply as He drew His breath.   To Him the method was, in truth, very simple ; it was the opening of the heart to the creating Spirit which could not only teach that all things in the universe are held together by attraction, not compulsion, but also, at every step of the way, could show how this great principle of animation by love may be translated into life.

F

III

THE PSYCHOLOGY OF POWER

BY

CAPTAIN J. A. HADFIELD, M.A. (OXON.), M.B. (EDIN.)

ASHHURST NEUROLOGICAL WAR HOSPITAL, OXFORD

ANALYSIS

THE PSYCHOLOGY OF POWER.

    The urgency of the problem of energy and fatigue.
    The view of the physicist, and of the religious.
    The psychological view.

EVIDENCE OF EXTRAORDINARY POWERS.

    Illustrated from various fields.
    Conclusions from these illustrations :
        (1) Existence of an ample re-supply of strength.
        (2) Not attained by power of will.
        (3) Originate in the instinctive emotions.

THE MENTAL FACTOR IN FATIGUE.

    I. Mental origin of fatigue demonstrated by—
        (a) Experiments in hypnotic suggestion.
        (b) Experiments in physiology.
        These prove the importance and priority of mental fatigue.
        Biological reasons why mind is fatigued before the body.
    II. Forms of fatigue :
        (1) Physical fatigue.
        (2) Over-sensitiveness of mind to physical fatigue.
            Application of this to everyday life.
        (3) False interpretation of mental fatigue as physical.
        (4) Purely mental fatigue, due to mental conflict.

THE INFIRMITY OF THE WILL.

    Power does not originate in the will.
    Illustrations to prove impotence of will against conviction and
        suggestion.
    Evil habits unconquered.
    Will requires power of the emotions.

THE INSTINCTS.

    The force of ideas : will : emotions.
    Instinctive emotions the real driving force of our lives.
    The importance of instincts in modern life.
    Policy of suppression a false one. Passion necessary in
        morality and religion.

THE INSTINCTS AND MORALITY.

    Is power derived from the instincts moral ?
        (1) Many instincts in themselves beneficent, *e.g.* maternal.
        (2) Instincts apparently anti-social may be directed to useful
            ends.
        (3) In the long run the maximum power is gained when
            instincts are harmonised and directed by the reason
            towards worthy ends.

THE CONFLICT OF INSTINCTS.

    Of will and emotion : of emotion with emotion.
    Illustration.
    Minor conflicts exemplified in worry and anxiety.

THE CONVERSION OF THE INSTINCTS.

    Living beings raise the potential of energy.
    Illustration of the conversion of the instincts and instinctive
       emotions.
    Hunting : curiosity : pugnacity.
    Fear : necessary fear ; morbid fear ; fear that stimulates.
    Sex : its overflow into the parental instinct.
    Self-assertion : aggression ; submission ; confidence.

CONFIDENCE AND FAITH.

    Derived from instinct of self-assertion.
    Essential to success and power.
    Illustrations.

THE EXPENDITURE OF POWER.

    Damming up the flow of energy leads to stagnation and fatigue.
    The inspiration of a purpose.
    Strength comes to those who expend it.

ENERGY AND REST.

    The cause of fatigue in mental conflict.
    The remedy is mental quietude.
    The characteristic neurasthenic.
    Physiological law of alternation of activity and rest.
    The art of resting.

THE SOURCE OF ENERGY.

    Physiological, psychological, and philosophical theories.
    Summary.

THE DYNAMIC OF RELIGION.

    The power of the Christian religion in abolishing conflict
       and directing the instinctive energies to high purposes.
    Power characteristic of primitive Christianity.
    Restfulness and peace also characteristic.
    Christianity as a moral healing force.

CONCLUSION.

III

THE PSYCHOLOGY OF POWER

THE increasing pressure of modern life, with its anxieties and cares, constitutes an ever-augmenting tax upon our strength. It is hardly surprising that nervous breakdowns are common, and that neurasthenia, or nerve fatigue, is the most significant disease of the age. Yet while, on the one hand, we see men and women so ill-adapted to face the demands of life that the slightest exertion produces fatigue ; on the other, we are called upon to witness exhibitions of power which fill us with wonder. The increasing demand for the power and energy requisite to face the strain compels us to investigate the sources of their supply. The purpose of my study is to direct attention to the problem of the sources of human energy and power.

It is commonly supposed that in each of us there is a reservoir, as it were, containing a certain supply of energy. This energy is said to be derived from the food we eat and the air we breathe, and to be, therefore, strictly limited in amount. When our expenditure is excessive our supply of energy runs very low, and we consequently suffer from a feeling of fatigue. Such is the theory of the physicist. The natural consequence of this belief in the physical character and the limited supply of our energy is that we are careful to economise our little store of strength, to husband our resources, lest by excess of expenditure we find the springs of our life run dry.

70

In contrast with this view, there have been men, and chiefly among them religious men, who have held that if our powers seem to fail, it is not because all the energy available is used up, but because its flow is checked, either by the channel being blocked up or by our inability to use it aright. The chief cause of fatigue is not exhaustion but stagnation. The way to power, therefore, is not to harbour our resources and store up our strength by inactivity, but to find the way to tap the resources of power at our disposal, so that they may flood our life and fill us with energy.

Of the two theories above stated modern psychology tends, on the whole, to support the second. At least the fact that (whatever their ultimate origin) there are resources of power, whose existence we do not ordinarily recognise but which can be made available for the purposes of our daily life, is one which has been firmly established by the scientific researches of recent years. In this Essay I propose, in the first place, to produce evidence of the existence of resources of power normally untapped; secondly, I shall show that these are psychic rather than physical in character; and, after discussing their relation to the instinctive emotions and to the will, shall consider the means by which they can be made available.

Evidence of Extraordinary Powers

I cannot do better than introduce the subject to the reader by one or two illustrations. A patient of mine, a tailor by trade, was buried by a high explosive shell in France. One of the striking features of his case was extreme weakness, the slightest exertion or a short walk producing fatigue. In the course of the treatment I induced him under hypnosis to remember the details of the incident, and made him live through it all again—the terrifying explosion, the débris burying him up to his neck, and a great baulk of timber tottering

above his head in act to fall. By the recollection
of these things he was thrown into a condition of
extreme terror, and began to fight like a madman,
flinging himself on the floor and dragging the bed
down over him, seizing a heavy armchair and flinging
it across the room, and generally putting forth such
extraordinary strength that it required four men to
hold him down. The strength he exhibited appeared
almost superhuman, and it was quite beyond his
voluntary power, for when he was awake his greatest
exertion of will served only to emphasise his weakness and impotence. Furthermore, when he was
wakened from the attack, far from being fatigued, he
was relieved and refreshed, and spontaneously told me
how much better he felt.

Similar exhibitions of strength are quite common
in men swayed and mastered by a great emotion.
Such strength is typical also of madness, in which
strong bonds are broken, iron bars are wrenched loose,
and extraordinary feats of endurance are performed.
What is the secret of such power ? In all these cases
men seem to be tapping resources of strength, whether
from within or from without, which, if we could discover
and use, would rescue us from feeble ineffectiveness
to a life of untold possibilities. We look upon such
an exhibition of strength with much the same feelings
as when we behold the lightning rend the heavens and
tear up oaks by the roots—if only we could seize
and store up such energy and devote it to the uses of
our daily life !

The endurance and strength of men fighting against
fearful odds when they are " up against it " is notorious,
and many instances could be given from the war.
Another of my patients had suddenly found himself in
a trench containing six Germans. Realising that he was
cornered he fought with fury, and succeeded in killing
three of them before he was stunned by one of the
survivors. A corporal, whose courage won the V.C.,

was for several days cut off from our troops, was exposed the whole time to bombardment (subsisting meanwhile on the barest rations), and yet, in spite of the awful strain, he came out feeling cheerful, elated, and without fatigue. Several men with him had the endurance to pass through the same experience, but at the end were exhausted and broke down. The corporal had evidently discovered sources of power which were not exhausted by the terrible strain he underwent, but provided an ample re-supply.

One of my patients, suffering from an obstinate neurasthenia, asked for leave one day because his wife, the mother of six little children, had fallen ill with pneumonia consequent on influenza, and, owing to the epidemic, could secure no doctor except for the one visit in which her condition had been diagnosed. He had been a most despondent and depressed individual, scarcely ever speaking to any one else in the ward, and left, still suffering from the tiredness and exhaustion typical of neurasthenia. He returned some days after, looking bright and cheerful, and almost his first words to me were, "I shall never doubt the power of prayer again, sir." In addition to the worry with the children, he had had the great anxiety of nursing his wife through a very serious illness without the aid of a doctor, and had been up day and night in his devoted labours. It is only those who have passed through a strain of that kind who know what it means ; but it is equally true that they alone can know the mighty resources that come to our aid in the time of extremity. In this case, his keenness to bring about the recovery of his wife, and the conviction of divine assistance, buoyed him up during the time of anxiety ; and after the strain was over, the exhilaration of triumph saved him from the relapse that people too often bring on themselves by their lack of confidence.

Four years ago, at midnight, I witnessed an explosion at a great munition factory, and afterwards heard that a woman, after her day's work, had risen from bed and, in anxiety for the safety of her husband and son, had run practically the whole distance of seven miles to the scene of the explosion in an incredibly short time.

William McDougall quotes the case of a boy who, being chased by a furious animal, leaped a fence which he could never afterwards scale even as a grown man, and after continuous athletic training. The emotion of fear liberated powers which his strength of will could never equal.

The reader will be able to add many, and perhaps more striking, cases than those I have mentioned. Most men, indeed, have experienced the invigorating effect of an overmastering emotion whose power is expressed not only in mental vigour, but in *physical* manifestations — the hot rush of blood in the veins, the quickening pulse, the deep strong breathing, the quivering nerve, the tense muscle, and the inrush of power which fortifies the soul and renders it quick to act and brave to endure.

Glancing over these illustrations of extraordinary powers, we are struck with three outstanding facts.

(1) Under certain conditions *extraordinary expenditure of energy can take place without equivalent fatigue.* It is generally assumed that such outbursts of power must end in a relapse leaving the exhausted man or woman broken in health. This undoubtedly often occurs, but is by no means necessary, and did not in fact occur in the cases that I have quoted from my own experience. The fatigue consequent on great exertion seems to bear no necessary relation to the amount of energy expended. One can become fatigued, like the neurasthenic, on very slight exertion ; but, on the other hand, as in these cases, men, essentially no different from ourselves, are seen to exhibit extraordinary powers without any apparent fatigue. The successful issue of a great endeavour causes the gladness of victory to refresh the soul. This fact suggests to us the hypothesis that,

while our energy is being used up, there is an ample store of energy to take its place if we could but discover and conform to the law of its supply : " the barrel of meal wastes not, neither does the cruse of oil fail." The power which can sustain us during the trial can renew our strength when victory is won.

(2) We observe that *these powers are greater than any at the disposal of the conscious will.* The most strenuous efforts to walk made by the soldier who had been buried ended only in weakness ; the athlete could never leap the fence again ; the patient who has passed through the time of anxiety and strain with his wife's illness felt that, though his will was feeble, some other power laid hold of his life and gave it strength.

(3) As to *the origin of these powers*, those who experience them can give no more account than the onlooker. In olden times such outbursts of strength were looked upon sometimes as being due to possession by evil spirits ; at other times, as in the story of Samson, the amazed beholders exclaimed, " The spirit of the Lord came mightily upon him." To the scientific observer, however, there is one very significant phenomenon. In every case these powers are associated with one of the *fundamental instinctive emotions*— whether of fear in the buried soldier and the athlete, tenderness in the husband and the wife, or in the other cases, the instincts of self-preservation and pugnacity. It would look as if it were only when instinctive emotions like these are aroused that energies are liberated adequate to sweep away all obstacles and take complete mastery of our lives.

These points we shall discuss in order, taking up first the question of fatigue, then illustrating the infirmity of the will, and, lastly, the ower of the instinctive emotions.

The Mental Factor in Fatigue

If we are to discover the sources of strength we must first investigate the causes of fatigue. There is a fatigue that comes from the body, and a fatigue that is of the mind ; and these two forms of fatigue are very closely associated, although they are separable in origin. A mile walk with a bore is more fatiguing than twenty miles with the lady of your choice. Disappointment will leave us tired out. The desert traveller is about to fall exhausted, when the sight of an oasis will revive his spirits and give him energy to plod on for miles.

We have already observed in the illustrations of extraordinary powers—the endurance of men fighting with their backs to the wall, or buoyed up by a great hope—that great emotions can endow men and women with almost superhuman strength. On the other hand, the neurasthenic, tired with the slightest exertion, is suffering from a fatigue due sometimes to despair or stagnation of the mind, rendering the body lifeless and inert, sometimes to discouragement resulting from a conviction of bodily debility. This is the type of fatigue from which most of us normally suffer. It may take the form of a feeling of boredom, of *ennui*, of the want of ideals and ambitions, which makes the soul limp and exhausts the body ; or it may express itself in a helpless inability to cope with work in which we are really interested. In all these instances it can be shown that it is the mind that has flagged and become fatigued ; when the mind is revived it finds the body ready and prepared to answer to its call.

The mental origin of fatigue may be illustrated by two experiments—the one psychological, the other physiological. (*a*) In the first, an experiment in hypnotic suggestion, we shall see how either fatigue or strength of body can be brought about purely by a mental attitude. (*b*) In the second, an experiment first devised by Mosso, we shall see that of all the functions that come into play in the performance of any action, the mind is the first to be fatigued; and it is therefore with fatigue of the mind that we have to concern ourselves most.

(*a*) Before describing the experiment in hypnotic suggestion it is, perhaps, well to say that the old view that in hypnosis some virtue, fluid, or power goes out from the hypnotiser to the subject, is now completely discredited. The essential feature of hypnotic suggestion is the communication of an idea to the mind of the patient; by hypnotic suggestion we inhibit for the moment the critical powers of the mind, and get the mind into such a condition of receptivity that any idea introduced into it is accepted without question and, for the time being, holds complete sway. The hypnotist does not, as is sometimes supposed, impose his will upon a reluctant subject; he merely suggests an idea to the mind of the patient, under conditions which predispose the patient to accept and appropriate it as his own.

To illustrate this point I may be pardoned for quoting the words of a patient. "When I came," he writes, "I thought I was going to be doped; that you were going to put something in me, perhaps something I did not like. Now I know that I have lived for years in a cellar; you have lifted me out and liberated what was in me." [1]

To return to my experiment. I asked three men to submit themselves to test the effect of mental suggestion on their strength, which was measured by gripping a dynamometer. I tested them (1) in their normal waking condition; (2) after suggesting to them under hypnosis that they were "weak"; (3) after suggesting under hypnosis that they were "very strong." In each case the men were told to grip the dynamo-

---

[1] For a fuller discussion of the nature of the state of hypnosis, I may refer the reader to my article on "The Mind and the Brain" in *Immortality*, pp. 32 ff.

meter as tightly as they could—that is to say, to exert
the will to the utmost.   Under hypnosis the mind
is very suggestible, and the response to the suggestions of weakness and strength gave very remarkable results.   In the normal waking condition the men
gave an average grip of 101 lbs.   When, under hypnosis, I had given the men the idea that they were very
weak, the average grip was only 29 lbs., one of them,
a prize-fighter, remarking that his arm felt " tiny, just
like a baby's."   My suggestions of strength produced
an average grip of 142 lbs. as against the 101 lbs.
which was the best they could do in their normal
waking conditions.   A second test, measured by
the time occupied in holding out a weight, gave
similar results.   In brief, when I suggested " weakness,"
the full flood of energy was checked and the men were
capable of only one-third of . their normal strength,
whereas by suggestion of " strength " latent powers
were liberated and their normal strength increased by
half as much again.

Such an experiment shows us that, when our minds
are depressed with the idea of weakness, our strength
may be diminished by two-thirds ; whereas if we have
the stimulus of a great inspiration our strength may
thereby be increased by one-half.   It is a conclusion of
the utmost importance for practical life.   The weakness
that overtook the men when they felt they were weak is
exactly what we observe in those suffering from neurasthenia.   In these men there was produced an artificial
neurasthenia.   The neurasthenic, whose tiredness makes
him a burden to himself and to every one else, is in
the same case as these three men when their minds
were obsessed by the idea of weakness so that they
could grip only 29 lbs.   He, like them, is physically
strong, but he is overmastered by the feeling that he
has no strength, and therefore is easily fatigued.   The
radical defect, both in the neurasthenic and in these
three men when weakness was suggested, is in the

mind.   They *believed* they were weak and fatigued, and this belief produced the reality.   According to their faith was it done to them.   Once let the mind lose confidence in its strength, and its energy flows away like water.

On the other hand, the condition of the three men when, being obsessed with the idea of strength, they could grip 142 lbs. illustrates the cases of men of whom we have given examples, who were possessed of an abnormal energy for which they themselves could not account, but which made them capable of almost incredible feats of strength and endurance.

It would seem, then, that the limits of possibility in our daily lives are defined less by the body than by the mind, and that the resources of power are psychic rather than physical in character.

(*b*) Mosso's famous experiment proves that, of all the factors involved in the performance of any action, the mind is the first to be fatigued.   In an ordinary voluntary action, say, the moving of an arm, the impulse passes from the mind and will by means of the cells of the brain, down the nerves, passing through the nerve-endings to the muscle.   By stimulating the nerve with electric shocks, one can produce contractions of the muscle, but after a time these contractions cease, owing to fatigue; but if the muscle alone is then stimulated, the muscle continues to contract.   That is to say, it is not the muscle that has been fatigued.   By similar experiments it is proved that neither is it the nerve nor the nerve-cell that first is fatigued, but the nerve-ending; indeed, the nerve-cell and the nerve are found to be almost unfatiguable.   But press the experiment a stage further and the more important question then arises, whether the fatigue may not be psychic rather than physical in origin.   *Is it the mind or the nervous system that is first fatigued?*   Mosso's experiment helps to decide this question.   A man's fatiguability is tested by tying a weight to his finger and making him flex and extend the finger until the onset of fatigue prevents him moving his finger any more. If the nerve to the finger is then immediately stimulated by a weak electric current, without giving time for the fatigue to pass off, the finger continues to flex and extend. In other words, the fatigue does not originate in nerve, nerve-ending, or muscle, which are all still quite active, but in the will.[1] The mind is fatigued, whereas the body is prepared to go on : the flesh is willing, but the spirit is weak.

The deduction that we draw from this experiment is that *the mind is exhausted before the body*. And this fact, strange as it may seem at first sight, is explicable on biological grounds, and that for two reasons.

The first reason is obvious. The mind is the latest part of the human organism to have developed in evolution, and is therefore the least completely adapted to its environment. In the face of the chances and rebuffs of life it frequently finds itself nonplussed : it cannot live as it would because of the limitations surrounding it ; it turns away sick at the problems it has to face. From time to time we actually get cases from the seat of war of men who have "regressed " to childhood, behaving almost exactly as children of two or three years old. In these cases the mind, unable any longer to endure the strain of living under such conditions, becomes tired out and reverts once again to the golden age of a protected infancy.

The second biological reason would appear to be that the body may be protected from exhaustion. The susceptibility of the mind to fatigue is valuable in warning the body of its approach to the danger zone, and so preventing the body from going too far. If it were not for this warning we might sometimes be carried away by our enthusiasm. The man of genius has, indeed, an extraordinary capacity for

[1] It is possible, of course, to hold that toxins formed in the body poison the brain (see below, on Physical Fatigue) and thus produce the fatigue, but it is inconceivable that the amount of waste products from the exercise of one finger could have such wide-reaching effects.

work, because his mind is inspired by a great enthusiasm ; but his inspiration might urge him to deeds too strenuous for his outworn body, and the world would perhaps be poorer for his loss. Thus nature determines that the mind shall normally be fatigued first, so that he will not put too great a strain on the body. But in the majority of men (if we may assume that the majority are not men of genius) such mental fatigue occurs long before we get anywhere near the danger zone of bodily fatigue, and the body is rarely given the opportunity of showing the extent of its endurance.

The discussion so far has put us in the position of being able to affirm the dominant influence of the mind in the production of fatigue, and to sum up *the four main forms of fatigue* : (1) Purely physical fatigue ; (2) Over-sensitiveness of the mind to physical fatigue ; (3) False interpretation of mental fatigue as physical ; (4) Purely mental fatigue, chiefly due to the conflict in the mind itself between will and emotion, or between the different emotions themselves.

(1) *Physical fatigue.*—I would not have it assumed that, in emphasising mental fatigue, I am denying there is such a thing as *physical* fatigue. During the exercise of the muscles there are formed certain waste products which are supposed gradually to poison the nervous system ; and after a great physical effort changes are seen to take place in the nerve-cells. There are, again, cases in which the mind's activity outstrips the body in strength. This has been observed in birds flying across the continent, in whom the instinct of migration is so strong that it outdoes the body and the birds fall dead with exhaustion. This also occurs occasionally in men whom some great enthusiasm or passion for reform drives on to reckless neglect of their strength, till they are compelled to rest their bodies in eternal sleep. But the psychological experiment in hypnotic suggestion, as well as the physiological experiments quoted above, show that at

G

any rate the greater part of the fatigue from which we suffer is of mental origin ; in fact, exhaustion of purely physical origin is rare.

(2) *The over-sensitiveness of the mind to physical fatigue.*—In the course of our daily life we more often feel fatigued because we are too sensitive to this physical tiredness ; we take notice of its symptoms when we ought to neglect them. Normally there are thousands of impressions and sensations in our body which ought never to reach consciousness but should be dealt with and responded to by the lower brain centres, such as the beating of the heart, the movements of the stomach, the sense of position of our limbs, and the sensation of normal fatigue in our body. But sometimes, owing to some exceptional experience—palpitation through fear, indigestion, or extreme physical exhaustion—these sensations force their way into consciousness, and, having once gained a footing, continue to claim the conscious attention of the mind. The mind begins to pay undue heed to these sensations, and pseudo angina pectoris, nervous dyspepsia, and neurasthenia with its over-sensitiveness to fatigue result. Even with reasonably healthy people the mind may at certain times be responsible for the fatigue felt in that it may be over-sensitive to the tiredness of the body and, by forcing it into consciousness, may exaggerate what should be a trifling and transient sensation into a feeling of complete exhaustion. Normal fatigue of body, like all the other thousand routine sensations of the body, should never reach consciousness except under very exceptional circumstances. The healthy individual comes in from a long, pleasant walk, and, though his body may be tired, he takes no notice of it and is quite happy. The neurasthenic, perhaps owing to some exceptional experience of over-fatigue in the past, but more often through introspection, becomes over-sensitive to these sensations. The same amount of waste products are probably formed in each of the men after the same

length of walk, but, while the healthy man neglects, the neurasthenic notices his tiredness, and therefore suffers from exhaustion. Under hypnotic suggestion a pin-prick can be made to feel like the stab of a dagger, and the lifting of a book can cause complete exhaustion, because the mind is made over-sensitive. Similarly the man who is always expecting fatigue will find what he looks for. The slightest thing tires him, but only because he is sensitive to the slightest thing. He turns the molehill into a mountain, and this mountain goes into labour and brings forth neurasthenia.

(3) Meanwhile we need to point out that *fatigue of purely mental origin is often misinterpreted and is attributed to a physical origin.* Man has not yet learnt to discriminate clearly between mental and physical sensations. Hence mental pain tends to express itself in terms of physical injury. Thus when we receive bad news the shock is primarily mental, but our mind subconsciously finds a physical expression for the pain and localises it in the head, with the result that we get a nervous headache ; but this is because our mind has no other way of finding for a mental pain "a local habitation and a name." This is the explanation of not a few apparently physical, but really functional, diseases. For this reason, when the mind is itself fatigued by worry, anxiety, depression, or fear, this fatigue, though purely mental, is often *felt* to be physical, and we have the same sensations as if it were the body that was tired out.

(4) *Purely mental fatigue* is chiefly due to the conflict in the mind between the instincts and the will, or between the instincts themselves, and is of the greatest importance not only in the study of the causes of fatigue but for the acquisition of power. The powerful instincts crave for free expression ; the will attempts to hold them down ; the house is divided against itself and cannot stand. The instinctive emotions conflict with

one another, and the struggle for mastery robs our lives of strength and leaves us prostrate. This inner conflict, the chief cause of fatigue, and its cure, we shall study in a later section.[1]

To call fatigue mental rather than physical is not to suggest that it is "unreal." Mental fatigue is the *most* real and the most important for our lives. It follows that those who would live lives of energy must look to the resources of the mind rather than to those of the body, and must study the laws which condition mental energy and mental fatigue.

The Infirmity of the Will

It is generally considered that it is only by force of will that we exercise power; and in recent years the glorification of will power has been characteristic of certain philosophers, mainly of Teutonic origin, and has been exploited by advertisers in pictures of square-jawed, clenched-fisted supermen. But is the will in point of fact as potent as popular theory would have us believe? My own hospital ward, as well as those of every physician of the mind, is full of examples of will that fails to accomplish what it wills. We are constantly dealing with cases where a man tries his utmost to perform certain actions and fails to do them; and yet they are perfectly possible to him.

I had a patient, a healthy lad of twenty, who had been engulfed in the marshes of the Piave and was invalided home paralysed in both legs. When put on his feet he was absolutely terror-stricken, and was with the greatest difficulty supported by two men. He frequently attempted to walk, exerting his will and determination to the utmost, but his attempts all ended in failure and distress. As there was no actual disease of the nervous system I treated him by hypnotic suggestion, and a few weeks later he was playing

[1] P. 94.

football. The desire to walk was there; the effort of will to walk was there; but these could not cure him—the will was impotent to save.

Another lad, whom I treated only a few days ago, suffered from a bullet wound through the shoulder, which, however, did not injure any important nerve, but paralysed his whole arm. I hypnotised him, and in less than two minutes had restored the power which had been lacking for months. His greatest effort to move it had resulted in failure; yet movement proved to be possible. Again, where the will was impotent, some other power succeeded.[1]

To revert back to my illustrations: the man who in fright leaped the fence, the patient who struggled so violently that four men were needed to keep him down, the man fighting with his back to the wall, were all able to do things which by the greatest effort of will they could never have accomplished. On the other hand, I have been in my ward speaking casually with the men when suddenly I have told one man that he could not rise from his chair but was stuck to it; another that he could not move his arm; another that he felt compelled to stand on one leg; and it was ludicrous to observe the strenuous efforts they made to act contrary to my suggestions. They exercised their wills, but to no effect. The performances of public hypnotists abound with such experiments; my only excuse for doing them is that I may convince men whom I want to heal of the power of suggestion, even in the absence of hypnosis.

Let me refer again to my hypnotic experiment in fatigue. As each man gripped the dynamometer I told him to do so " as hard as ever he could." Yet a man would one minute be able to do only 29 lbs., and a few minutes after he could manage 142 lbs. It is quite

[1] It is only right that I should mention that " shell-shock " cases are more dramatic in their symptoms and in their cure than we can hope for in civilian patients, where the disease is often of long standing, its cause difficult to expose, and its cure proportionately more difficult.

obvious that the difference in power was due, not to the exercise of the will, which was strained to the utmost in each case, but to some force that the will was impotent to affect. We shall observe, later, that this obstacle to the full exercise of the will was *the belief that the thing attempted was impossible*.[1] This break-down of the will accounts for a large number of the nervous ills and morbid habits with which the physician has to deal. Sometimes it takes the form of perversion. I have a patient who, when trying to move his right leg, invariably moves his left leg. He observes his mistake but cannot correct it. There is a want of co-ordination somewhere: the couplings have gone wrong.

But I have only to appeal to the reader to look into his own life to realise how futile is the will to help us in many of our difficulties. Our attempts to prevent blushing produce only a deeper crimson; the effort to be at our ease produces a strained attitude; and in moral actions how often does our greatest determination to do right end in failure? It was long ago that one discovered "what I would, that do I not; but what I hate, that do I." One thing is willed, another is performed. The victim of a moody or irritable temper, or of some evil habit, spends days and nights in vain endeavour to master it. What more pathetic sight than that of a confirmed drug-taker affirming with a sickly smile that he can easily give it up. A vulture was seen to be feeding on a carcase as it floated down the Niagara river above the Falls; when the danger-point came it doubtless expected to spread its wings and fly off; but when, in fact, it spread its wings, it found that it could not rise; its talons were frozen to the carcase on which it fed, and so it was carried over the Falls to its doom. So the victim of evil habit tells you, "I am all right, you don't need to bother about me; I can give it up when I want to"; but when he rises to shake himself and put on strength,

[1] See section on "Confidence and Faith."

he finds his will power has gone. The freedom of the will may be a doctrine which holds true of the healthy, and, indeed, the exercise of will and determination is the normal way in which to summon the resources of power ; but the doctrine that the will alone is the way to power is a most woe-begone theory for the relief of the morally sick—and who of us is whole ? Freedom to choose ? Yes ! But what if, when we choose, we have no power to perform ? We open the sluice-gates, but the channels are dry ; we pull the lever, but nothing happens ; we try by our will to summon up our strength, but no strength comes.

> We cannot kindle when we would
> The fire that in the soul resides.

Will and determination are, of course, essential to moral endeavour, and without them the instincts would run riot. When we say " I will," we feel an accession of power that enables us to conquer, and we attribute that power to the will. But the futility of looking to the will *alone* for our source of strength is obvious, and those who rely on it are running the risk of disaster : for practical action the will is dependent on some other power. As long as it acts in conformity with this power all is well. Under these circumstances the more strenuous the will, and the greater our resolution and determination, the greater will be our strength. But if it conflicts with this power, as in our illustrations, the will is impotent. The energies which give the driving force to our lives are not derived from the will, but from another source ; they will be found to have their origin in the instinctive emotions. As we shall observe later, the function of the will is to direct and work in conformity with the potent forces derived from the instinctive emotions, and to regulate the release of these forces waiting ready for action.

This view of the will suggests two conclusions of great importance for religion. (1) An evil deed is not always due to an "evil will" for which one is to be held responsible, but may be due to impulses over which the will has no control, or to distortions of character which the will is unable to set right, and it is only just that the offender should be treated as sick rather than sinful.[1] (2) We cannot rely upon the will alone to deliver us from evil habits. Modern psychotherapy confirms the old religious belief that to give power to the will, confidence and faith in the possibility of victory are essential.

THE INSTINCTS

The great driving forces of life are the Instinctive Emotions.[2] The Will may open the sluice-gates, but the Instinctive Emotions constitute the flood which sweeps through the channel. Great Ideas may sway masses of men, as when the cry of "Liberty, Equality, and Fraternity" called thousands to rise in revolution ; yet it is only when associated with an emotion, and particularly an instinctive emotion, that the idea is charged with compelling power.

The instinctive emotions give driving force to the will and put life into great ideas, and, being liberated like the winds from the cave of Aeolus, burst forth, either to do their work of destruction or, if rightly controlled, to speed us, with full-bellied sail, on the voyage to the harbour of our destiny.

When we look back on our previous illustrations of extraordinary powers we see that the *main* forces acting in and through these men were the instinctive emotions. Fear, the expression of the instinct of self-preservation,

[1] I would suggest that the "cure of souls" is a practice too seriously neglected by the modern Church.

[2] On the subject of the instincts and their practical bearing on human life, I would urge the reader, if he has not yet done so, to study W. McDougall's *Social Psychology*, for it is to Dr. McDougall that we owe the recognition of the paramount importance of the instincts in social life. That book shows how intimately connected are the instincts and certain great emotions, and I use the term Instinctive Emotions to indicate such emotions as Fear, Tenderness, Wonder, which are racially inherited and primitive, and therefore can dominate our whole human life and conduct.

gave the soldier, buried in the débris and fighting for his life, almost superhuman power. The instinct of pugnacity gave one desperate man surrounded by the enemy the strength of five. The instinctive emotion of fear enabled the athlete to make a spring which he could never afterwards accomplish by power of will alone. In these cases the driving force obviously comes from the instinctive emotions; and they are none the less at work in great reformers, statesmen, and industrial monarchs. Wilberforce could never have induced Britain to make so great a sacrifice in hard cash for the liberation of the slaves had he not appealed to an instinctive emotion which could sweep away thoughts of prudent economy. The emotion aroused in his own soul, and which he quickened in the soul of others, was the feeling of pity, an emotion characteristic of the parental instinct.[1] The instinct of constructiveness combined with the instinct of self-assertion and the ambitious desire for power drives one man from the seclusion of a village to control the affairs of an empire, and another to organise a trust. It is when our feelings are aroused, when passion is awakened in the breast, when the approach of danger makes us alert to strike, when the sight of brutality to a child kindles our indignation, or when we are possessed by some soul-satisfying ambition,—it is then that we feel most deeply the sense of power. Not in the cold, deliberate choice of the will, but in the passion of the soul, is to be found that flood of energy which can open to us the resources of power. Mastered by such a passion the soul will admit no defeat.

The strength of the instincts has not yet been fully appreciated, nor is it fully realised how great a part they play in common life. They have been boycotted by the cultured as brutish survivals, and even now some regard them as little more than a power that makes the birds migrate and the bees

---

[1] "Like as a father pitieth his own children."

furnish the hive. Hardly do these people realise that society itself exists in response to an instinct of the herd, that their desire to travel is a response to the instinct of migration, and the impulse to build great cities and empires is the same impulse as compels the beaver to build the dam. The sociologist is most concerned with the gregarious instinct, so lucidly demonstrated by Trotter in *The Instinct of the Herd.* Yet it is only recently that adequate recognition has been given by sociologists to the instincts. Fortunately we have now ceased to ignore them, and we realise that the instincts are the raw material upon the direction of which depends most of our individual and social life, and we now regard them for the most part as healthy. But even to this day many moralists adopt the prevailing attitude towards the instincts in advocating a stern suppression of them. Such an attempt is doomed to failure, for two reasons. Because, in the first place, it is practically impossible to suppress such deep-rooted hereditary predispositions ; and, secondly, because the suppression of them would only dam up the channels of power which nature has provided. If we attempt to suppress our instincts, will is divided against instinct and the house cannot stand.

Religious teaching has sometimes been guilty of this mistaken suppression in two ways. The one is exemplified by those who would suppress the instinct of curiosity on which, as will be shown later, intellectual inquiry is based, and advocate that so-called "asceticism of the intellect" which would ultimately stifle truth. The other, with which we are more concerned here, is the suppression of emotion. In their dread of emotionalism—the unruly debauch of unrestrained feeling—and its consequences in conduct, they have attempted to abolish all emotion as a thing either dangerous or vulgar. In so doing they have failed to appreciate that the Christian religion is founded on an emotion—the all-embracing emotion of love.

To rob the soul of emotion is to deprive it of its driving force and leave it lifeless. Matthew Arnold's description of religion as being morality *touched* with emotion is a delightful though unconscious satire on what religion actually is at the present day, but certainly not what it should be. A "touch" of emotion is not the kind of thing to turn the world upside-down. "No heart is pure that is not passionate ; no virtue is safe that is not enthusiastic." If religion means anything at all, it ought to mean the full and harmonious display and exercise of all our powers, emotional and intellectual, so that we present our whole selves a *living* sacrifice to God.

The Instincts and Morality

But if we accept the thesis that the instinctive emotions are, humanly speaking, the sources of our human energies, the question arises—Are these forces moral ? Revenge and lust, as well as heroism, bring an enhancement of strength. If the instinctive emotions are the springs of power, can the sexual libertine lay claim to it as justifiably as the devoted mother ? The blind rage of instinctive passion can scarcely be called moral, and yet it fills beast and man with extraordinary power.

The following observations are therefore necessary to a true estimate of the moral value of the instinctive emotions.

(1) In the first place, it must be recognised how many of the instincts have naturally a truly moral tendency. The tenderness of a mother for her child, perhaps the most perfect example of virtue in the whole of human life, is at the same time the most perfect example of a beneficent instinct. It is found not only in the human mother but in the lioness, the tigress, and the bird. Again, in the herd instinct, which makes the individual surrender all his personal claims to the demands of the

pack, lie the germ and source of most of the social virtues. The instincts are not brutal because they are shared by brutes, and, indeed, it might be urged that the noblest deeds of man have sprung from the altruistic instincts which originate in mother-love and loyalty to one's fellows and can be traced far back into the animal kingdom. But even such beneficent instincts need to be wisely directed. In the case of the maternal instinct, for instance, there comes the time when the child must no longer rely upon the mother but win independence. The lingering care of the mother for the grown-up daughter is certain at some time to clash with the impulse to independence in the daughter, and is the cause of that misunderstanding and consequent friction which so often brings unhappiness to both mother and daughter. They are both guided by instinctive impulses that are right and necessary—the one of maternal care, the other of independence. The friction which so often results would frequently be avoided were both mother and daughter to realise the causes of their misunderstandings. A wider knowledge of the influence of the instincts would materially assist in bringing about peace and harmony in everyday life. As soon as both mother and daughter *realise* that the opinions and desires of the other are not due to "sheer cussedness," but understand that such desires are instinctive and natural, so soon will this understanding bring about peace and forgiveness.[1]

(2) On the broadest definition, morality is that which is found to be valuable for social life. In the animal world all the instincts are, in this sense, moral. And, as we have seen, some of them, such as the tenderness of the mother for her young, or the loyalty

[1] The need for such understanding is most felt in regard to the instincts in growing children, whose impulses towards the expression of the instincts are so often treated as "naughtiness." The child naturally feels unjustly treated, for the impulse to obey the instincts, a perfectly beneficent impulse if wisely guided, is stronger than the impulse to obey the injunctions of the parent, whose business it ought to be to make the instincts amenable to the control of reason.

of the individual to the pack, can, with but a little sublimation, become the basis of all that is best and highest in human life.   Others, however, like the instinct of pugnacity, may seem in human society to have outlived their day.   At an early stage of human evolution such an instinct was valuable in the struggle for existence.   But this struggle, at least in its cruder form, is, or ought to be, a thing of the past; with the result that the instinct of pugnacity may easily lead to anti-social conduct.   Nevertheless, every instinct, however ill-adapted to the requirements of present-day civilised life, has had its value in its day in that it worked for the good of the species as a whole, and should be regarded, so far, as moral, or capable of being moralised. I shall deal with the question of the transformation and moralisation of the instincts in a later section.

(3) The moral potentialities of the force manifested in the instincts may be judged also from another point of view.   The source of power lies not in instinctive emotion alone, but in instinctive emotion expressed in a way with which the whole man can, for the time being at least, identify himself.   Ultimately, this is impossible without the achievement of a harmony of all the instincts and the approval of the reason.   An evil man has access to the same instinctive emotions as the good man, and may use them for wrong ends—as a Napoleon for his ambition, or a murderer for his hate. The man who gives vent to blind rage may feel the same satisfaction and relief as does the man who shows his indignation at some moral wrong.   Yet in the long run those who misuse their powers destroy themselves by their very passions.   It may be true that the man who takes personal vengeance on another may satisfy his instinct of revenge and feel elated, but he is apt to be so ostracised by his fellows that, quite independently of any practical inconvenience their consequent action towards him may entail, the herd instinct in him rises up in opposition to the instinct of revenge and sets

up an internal conflict which soon robs him of that harmony of the instincts which I shall show later on to be essential to power.[1]   Thus the greatest and permanent power comes to him who uses it not for his own personal ends, but for the good of his fellows ; for only by such a use of it does he achieve the maximum inner harmony.   We may therefore assert that, while it is open to the evil man to give vent to a particular instinctive emotion, and thereby to lay claim for a moment to the power that nature lavishes upon those who use her gifts, it is only to those who use them aright that the greatest powers are given.   Thus the powers at our disposal are not so neutral and non-moral as they seem, but tend to favour those who will use them for the noblest purposes.   Revenge, pride, and passion destroy the permanent inner harmony of the soul, even though they may temporarily energise it into activity.   Chivalry, honour, and love, devoted to the service of others, tend to produce a transformation of instincts and a living harmony of the soul which can permanently keep open the sluice-gates of power.

We shall proceed, then, to deal with the questions which have just arisen, and show how the crude forces which reside in the instinctive emotions can best be utilised for human endeavours and ideals.   We shall first show how the instincts of the baser sort, if focussed on some dominating purpose or idea, may be transformed ; after which we shall demonstrate the necessity of expending our powers as a pre-requisite of receiving more power, and finally we shall deal with the question of the conflict of instincts, the abolition of which conflict is necessary to unity and to power.

THE CONFLICT OF INSTINCTS

The presence of conflict in the soul drains it of strength, and is one of the main causes of weakness.

[1] See section on " The Conflict of Instincts."

" I see another law in my members warring against the law of my mind." The conflict may be of instinctive emotions with ideas, as when a man is feeble because he is obsessed with intellectual doubt. At other times the weakness is due to the conflict of instinctive emotions and will, one of the most common forms of which is the attempt to suppress the instincts by the will, already referred to. But chiefly our powers are sapped because the instincts are divided against themselves. Let *one* instinct sway the mind and there is the sense of power. But the instincts are often opposed and turn many of our best endeavours into failures. We are ambitious to succeed, but we are checked by the fear of making fools of ourselves. We never learn to skate, because we think of the ridiculous figure we should cut if we fell. Thus the desire to excel in any accomplishment (the instinct of self-assertion) conflicts with the possible feeling of shame and self-abasement.

The following case illustrates my point so well that I shall give it in some detail. I have recently been treating a lady who, when she came to me, was so neur-asthenic and easily fatigued that she habitually slept for sixteen hours out of the twenty-four. After a good night's sleep from 9 P.M. till 7 A.M. she would rise and have breakfast, but the effort caused her so much fatigue that she would retire to bed again at 9 A.M. to sleep till 12. Now this was not laziness in the ordinary sense ; she was an affectionate mother, and was anxious above all things to be able to work and play with her children, but she had not the strength. It was purely a case of mental fatigue, produced by a conflict of instinctive emotions.

Her cure could only be effected by discovering the cause and eradicating it from the mind. This process of discovery was conducted largely under hypnosis, since the patient could give little assistance in her waking state. It was discovered that the cause was the long-continued strain of nursing a very delicate child, when on more than one occasion it seemed that it must be a question of whether mother or child should be sacrificed. In her, then, two most powerful instinctive emotions had been at war, namely, the instinct of self-preservation and the maternal instinct. The result was a complete breakdown, several phobias, and a fatigue lasting some years, even though the original cause of anxiety was happily at an end. These were in turn removed, the instincts readjusted, the phobias explained, and the last account I have received from her husband, some months later, is to the effect that she is perfectly well.[1]

Fortunately most of us are not called on to suffer from such conflicts, but conflict is nevertheless represented in everyday life by anxiety and worry. Anxiety is essentially a conflict of emotions. Anxiety about the future, about one's children, about the dinner one is giving, about the destiny of one's soul, about a railway journey or one's health, are all conflicts of opposing emotions. By such worries and restlessness of spirit we waste our strength and sap our vitality. By facing our conflicts and deliberately making our choice, by directing all our endeavours to one great purpose, confidently and fearlessly, the soul is restored again to harmony and strength.

The Conversion of the Instincts

Perhaps the most characteristic feature of a living being is, that it can raise energy from a lower potential

---

[1] Other cases of conflict leading to nervous breakdown which have lately come under my notice may be briefly indicated. The sense of duty to her mother clashed with the instinctive desire for independence in a grown-up daughter, and a feeling of restless discontent resulted. Fear and the impulse to run away conflicted in the mind of the soldier with his sense of duty, and ended in a condition of paralysis of the legs, unconsciously produced, which solved the immediate problem but brought about a breakdown in health. The eagerness to please a master, with whom a patient of mine was in love, together with the constant sense of failure in this attempt, brought about a conflict between sexual instinct and self-pride, and produced a neurasthenia of many years' standing. A man's desire to live a clean and pure life was hampered by the shame of a past sin.

to a higher potential, *i.e.* its efficiency for a given purpose is increased.   In all *in*animate things energy, such as heat or motion, tends to be dissipated instead of being raised to a high potential.   The human being can raise the energy contained in food and transform it into nerve energy, and by so doing he raises the potential of this form of energy.   William James probably had in mind this difference of potential when he says : " Writing is higher than walking, thinking is higher than writing, deciding higher than thinking, deciding ' no ' higher than deciding ' yes.' "   It is the intellectual and moral privilege of the human being that he can similarly raise the energy contained in the instincts, the radical fault in most of which is their selfish and egocentric character, to higher potentials ; that is to say, by transforming the *quality* of this energy he raises its power to accomplish his ends, as sexual passion has been transformed into love ; and by changing the *direction* of the energy he endows it with a greater effectiveness of *purpose*.   By doing so he retains the power or force of the instincts, but directs that force to greater purpose.   Furthermore, directed to altruistic ends, these individual instincts will no longer clash with the social instincts and thereby be deprived of strength, but co-operating and working in harmony with the social instincts they will be magnificently reinforced and their power multiplied.

The *hunting instinct* affords an obvious illustration of this principle.   We see its evolution in the transformation from the child's game of "hide and seek," to the keenness of the boy scout, until finally it assumes the form of exploration and discovery, its original object having been almost entirely forgotten.

Again, the instinct of *curiosity* is one the potentialities of which are not sufficiently realised.   We often use this term in a derogatory sense, as when one is said to be "inquisitive out of mere curiosity."   Curiosity often takes the form of prying into other people's affairs ;

H

it has driven more than one medical student I have known into morphinomania, and it leads many a young man and woman to sample those "thrills" which constitute "seeing life." "It is in their blood," we say, by which we imply that this impulse is instinctive. But this instinct of curiosity also gives the impulse to all true scientific pursuit. The instinct of curiosity directed towards human nature makes of one person a prying gossip, but leads another to search, like the psychologist, into the hidden depths of the human mind with sympathetic insight. Nothing short of a fundamental instinct could urge on the scientist to the researches which he pursues year after year, regardless of result or reward, to the great good of mankind.

The combative instinct.—We often hear it maintained that the instinct of pugnacity which in the past has led to war must *necessarily* do so in the future, and that those who look for a permanent peace are therefore doomed to disappointment. This is a most unjustifiable assumption. Granting that the emotional element of every instinct must always remain, it is not necessary either that the same stimuli should awaken that emotion, or that the emotion should express itself in the same action—in this case, in slaughter. The instinct for combat finds expression in games such as football and in the rivalry of sport ; and it is probably for this reason that the English people are less aggressive than other nations we know, though when the instinct is directed to war the Englishman throws himself into it with no less energy and zest. Long ago, William James pointed out the possibility of finding a moral equivalent of war in social service, from an egocentric to an altruistic and chivalrous end.[1] We can take up arms for others even though we refuse to do so for

---

[1] In the Great War men in this country were largely divided into those who fought because they hated the Hun and those who fought in chivalrous defence of the Belgian nation. The resultant action was the same, yet the motive for the impulse was very different, being the expression of a selfish instinct in one case and of an altruistic one in the other.

ourselves. Then our instinct ceases to be aggressive, and becomes protective. So ultimately we shall learn that we can fight with other weapons for truth and purity, we shall join a crusade against oppression and vice—and this kind of combat will employ for social ends those emotions and instincts which at present we use for war and destruction. So we may confidently hope that the pugnacious instinct will find scope in fields of social service in the fight for justice, purity, and right.

It is often said that instincts are blind. It is rather we who are blind to their potency and to the purposes for which they exist. The abandonment of that false doctrine which would have us suppress them, and the substitution for it of an understanding of their proper uses, would open up to us resources of power which would give us in abundance energy and life.

Fear : Sex : Self-assertion.—The instinctive emotion of fear and the instincts of sex and self-assertion deserve more detailed description on account of their great power—a power derived from their primitive character, their origin dating back to the earliest forms of animal life, but one far greater than the circumstances of modern life necessitate. Abolish these instincts and their effects in individual and social life, and the problems of mankind would be well-nigh solved. But abolish them we cannot ; to suppress them is to deprive ourselves of their forces. To convert them and to redirect their forces to higher purposes is the work of beings possessed of intelligence, of will, and of an ideal.

The *instinctive emotion of fear*, so intimately associated with self-preservation, is one very necessary to our existence ; without it we should soon be run down in the street. But the strength of this instinct is far greater than the uses of our civilised life require, for modern life is comparatively safe. There is a great deal of the primitive fear that is left over, as it were, which we cannot use. The consequence is that the excess of fear tends to flow into wrong channels, or we fear excessively things which should rightly be objects of fear. Our surplus fear produces fear of poverty, fear of sickness and pain, fear of the future, fear of what might have been, fear of ourselves, fear of death, fear of life, fear of failure, and, perhaps most paralysing of all, fear of fear. If fear were abolished from modern life, the work of the psychotherapist would be nearly gone. It was not without cause that the Master of the soul so often reiterated "Fear not," "Be not afraid," "Be not anxious."

Is this, then, an instinct we should suppress? That is both impossible and undesirable. The effects of fear are of two kinds : there is the fear that paralyses and the fear that inspires. Nothing paralyses our lives so much as fear, depriving them as it does of that abundance of power which is our birthright. But there is also the fear that nerves and inspires and expresses itself in the effective avoidance of imminent disaster. Now, we ask what constitutes the difference between the fear in these two cases ? The answer is that fear paralyses when it offers no way of escape ; it inspires when it is associated with hope. A hare, suddenly surprised, is either temporarily paralysed by fear, or stimulated to its topmost speed. It has been conjectured that the paralysis is probably a protective mechanism to enable the animal to hide when it cannot escape. If escape is possible the fear no longer paralyses, but is expressed in that tension of muscle, that alertness of mind, which make swift and effective action possible. Fear which includes a large element of hope passes into confidence, and this, as we have seen, is the first essential of power. If we apply our principle to what we have said concerning morbid fear, we can see that our problem is to turn the fear that paralyses into the fear that inspires. The fear of poverty inspires us to greater efforts, the fear of the future saves us from indolence, the fear of accident makes us alert; but this transformation takes place only when we have confidence that we can come through, and that the struggle will issue in victory.

Those who have raised discussion as to whether we should "fear God" have, I think, failed to appreciate this difference between the fear that paralyses and the fear akin to hope that urges us to active service. To fear God may mean that we are afraid of God because He may punish us, and in this case the fear is paralysing and brings forth no good result—" I knew thee, that thou wert an austere man . . . and hid thy talent in the ground." But the fear of God may mean that, indifferent to ourselves, we are filled with reverent awe (in which emotion there is an element of fear), combined with a conviction of His willingness and power to help. This shifts the fear from ourselves, turns it into hope, and fills us with a confidence which stimulates us to great endeavours, and gives us that inspiration which only comes to those who humbly devote themselves to a noble cause.

The *sexual instinct* at first sight appears to be incapable of being raised to higher uses. It is an instinct which is necessary to the race for the purpose of reproduction. But, like fear, it has a far greater " affect " or emotional tone than we need for this purpose, and therefore its lavish expression apparently needs to be suppressed. On the other hand, the suppression of this instinct causes a very large number of the nervous ills to which men, and still more women, fall victims. But the sexual instinct, which naturally expresses itself as admiration for personal beauty, is probably at the basis of all the higher forms of art and may well be sublimated to this end. Further, this instinct is very closely associated with the maternal and paternal instincts, and seems almost to form a harmonious complex with them. The true lover is not only moved by the sexual instinct, but almost always associates with it the maternal or paternal instinct, and desires to "have some one to care for."[1] Many a woman has married an invalid man simply in order to gratify this maternal instinct in caring for him. Unmarried women, in whom the sexual instincts are strong (and let them never be ashamed that these instincts *are* strong), may transform them into the maternal instinct in caring for children, "mothering" the lonely, or nursing the sick. The sexual instincts, debased to the uses of fleshly lust, kill the soul and stifle all noble thought and feeling ; but from the same soil there may spring the stainless flower of love, whence comes all that is pure and holy in human life.

The *instinct of self-assertion*, when directed to purely individual ends, produces that aggressive character which is as offensive as it is anti-social. Nevertheless the opposite emotion of submission, if over-emphasised, results in a lack of practical initiative and independence. The virtue which corresponds to these excesses is not to be found in the "mean" between them, as Aristotle would say, but is the right direction of them both to altruistic ends. There is room for a new ethic on these lines. A self-assertion which forgets itself in the pursuit of a noble end is the truest humility. Submission that is self-conscious may be egoism disguised. True humility consists not in thinking little of oneself, but in not thinking of oneself at all. Thus both self-assertion and submissiveness are harmonised, and so lend the force of two combined instinctive emotions to the accomplishment of a noble end.

But more than that, the instinct of self-assertion is at the basis of the *sense of confidence* which I shall proceed to show is so essential to a life of power. Besides the intellectual acceptance of the idea " this is possible," confidence consists in the emotional reaction arising out of the instinct of self-assertion, " what is possible *I*

---

[1] The intimate connection between the sexual instinct and the maternal instinct is demonstrated by the physiological co-operation between the physical organs corresponding respectively to these instincts.

can do," whether the confidence is based on the belief in my own power or in some other power on which I can rely.

CONFIDENCE AND FAITH

Confidence, deriving its power from the instinct of self-assertion, turns weakness into strength and failure into success.

"Somehow, when I started, I knew I was going to succeed." This is a phrase we often hear on the lips of a man flushed with success. He hardly realises that it was his confidence in success, his belief that he would succeed, that gave him the power to surmount his difficulties and win his way to victory. All round us we see men failing simply because they lack the confidence that they will succeed, while men with far less ability and talent, but with greater daring, carry off the prizes that life has to offer. It is not that the others do not try, but that they do not expect to succeed.

In the section on the will I quoted cases of men paralysed in arms and legs whom the will was quite impotent to restore to health : yet there was nothing organically wrong with such patients. Why, then, were they paralysed? Why did not their strenuous efforts enable them to walk? Because they believed they could not move their limbs. They could say " I will," but *they had not learnt to say* " *I can*." The man paralysed in both legs would cling to me with such vigour that he nearly pulled me down with him—simply because he had not the confidence to trust himself to walk. In the hypnotic experiment on fatigue the subject could only grip 29 lbs. because he said " I am weak, I cannot grip it any harder." When he said, and believed, " I am strong and powerful," his strength was multiplied fivefold. I suddenly told another man that he could not talk ; he tried, but found that he was dumb—simply because, being suggestible to my words, he lost confidence in his power to speak, and believed what I suggested to be in fact true. In all such cases we have seen that the will alone does not ensure success. " To will is present with me, but how to perform I know not." That which is lacking is " confidence."

I have spoken of the paralysing effects of fear. Confidence removes this paralysis and turns belief into a mighty impulse to act. It fills men with the strength which makes the soul master of its fate. It possesses the timid who cling to the shores of life, who have toiled all night and caught nothing, and bids them launch out into the deep, where endeavour is crowned with overwhelming success. Want of belief in its possibility is always the main obstacle to the performing of any mighty work. Faith in its possibility—a faith not necessarily founded on evidence but one that dares to take the risk—is the greatest asset to success in any task. " If thou canst ? " " All things are possible to them that believe."

THE EXPENDITURE OF POWER

Nature is economic in her gifts : she will not give strength to those who will not expend it. These remain uninspiring and uninspired. She is lavish in her gifts to those who will use them, and especially to those who devote them to nature's altruistic ends, for such ends harmonise the soul. Life demands expression. If the life-stream that flows through us finds the channel blocked by a life of inactivity, we inevitably suffer from staleness and boredom, or a sense of physical debility. A purposeless life is a life of fatigue. We all know from personal experience how tired we may become while doing nothing, but let us once find an outlet for our energies, some object upon which to expend them, and our instinctive powers awake us to life. The Sea of Galilee is fresh and blue, and gives life to living creatures within its sunlit waters—not because it receives waters, but because it gives of them freely. The Dead Sea is dead, not because there is no supply of fresh water, but because it permits no outlet. It is therefore stagnant and deadly ; no fish lives in its waters, nor is any beast to be found upon its shores. It is a law of nature—a law of life—that only by giving shall we receive. None is so healthy and fresh as he who gives freely of his strength, and thereby liberates his impulses and instinctive powers into quickened activity. This is of immense practical importance. In the treatment of neurasthenia, the chief symptom of which is fatigue, it is often found that the "Weir Mitchell" treatment of inactivity and isolation is the worst a physician can prescribe. Already is the patient suffering from too much self-consciousness and introspection. Some disappointment or sorrow may have taken all the life out of him : the zeal and keenness of his life has suddenly gone. In popular language, what he needs is "something to take him out of himself" ; something to interest him, some object which will liberate the forces pent up in his soul. Give such a man " something to live for," that awakens his interest, and his ambition will arouse his instinctive emotions till the heart that was sluggish palpitates with the joy of life once more, the nerves tingle with eager expectation. Life's demand for expression will be satisfied.

How wonderful is the way in which, with quite ordinary folk, power leaps to our aid in any time of emergency. We lead timid lives, shrinking from difficult tasks till perhaps we are forced into them or ourselves determine on them, and immediately we seem to unlock the unseen forces. When we have to face danger, then courage comes ; when trial puts a long-continued strain upon us, we find ourselves possessed by the power to endure ; or when disaster ultimately brings the fall which we so long dreaded, we feel underneath us the strength as of the everlasting arms. Common experience teaches that, when great demands are made upon us, if only we fearlessly accept the

challenge and confidently expend our strength, every
danger or difficulty brings its own strength—" As thy
days so shall thy strength be."

ENERGY AND REST

In considering the causes of fatigue we found that
the mental factor played a very prominent part. The
main causes of such fatigue were over-sensitiveness to
ordinary physical fatigue, the conviction of weakness,
and the conflict of will and emotions or of the emotions
with themselves. A life of purposeful and altruistic
activity will rid us of that habit of introspection which
produces the first form of fatigue ; the sense of confidence will drive away thoughts of weakness ; and we
have now to deal with the third form, conflict within
the mind, the most characteristic form of which is worry
and anxiety. This is to be met, firstly, by discovering
and bringing into consciousness the latent cause of our
worry, which normally tends to elude consciousness.
Modern practice in psychotherapy confirms the old
belief that confession, more especially confession of fears
and anxieties, is good for the soul. The "letting out"
of the "repressed complex" is itself often sufficient to
cure ; secondly, by converting the instincts and directing their energies towards useful and harmonious ends ;
and, thirdly, by cultivating a *restfulness of mind* which is
the counterpart of a life of energy.

Weakness results from the wastage caused by
restlessness of mind ; Power comes from a condition
of mental quietude. The secret of energy is to learn
to keep the mind at rest, even in the multitude of life's
activities. Look at this patient suffering from neurasthenia. He complains that he is suffering from fatigue ;
but there is another symptom you notice about him—
he is irritable, cannot stand noises, cannot bear to be
crossed or disturbed. The fatigue and the irritability
are part of the same trouble. It is a characteristic of

nervous patients that they are always restless : they tell you that they must always be doing something, always be " on the go." They cannot concentrate, they cannot remember. They are in a state of perpetual motion. They are worried and anxious, fret and are irritable, until, through sheer exhaustion of mind, they drift into the most characteristic condition of the neurasthenic, that of fatigue. And it is not surprising that such men become fatigued. The average neurasthenic is ordered to take a rest in the afternoon, but he spends the time in reading the paper ; he goes to bed early at night, but sits up reading a novel. He gives his body more rest than it needs, failing to realise that what the body needs is not relaxation but re-invigoration. At the same time he never permits his mind that rest which alone can enable it to invigorate the body. It is characteristic of the neurasthenic that in the morning, possibly after a long night's sleep, he wakes up more fatigued than he went to bed ; for though his body has had many hours' rest, his mind has been restless and perturbed even in sleep.

This art of resting the mind and the power of dismissing from it all care and worry is probably one of the secrets of energy in our great men. It is generally said that Edison, the inventor, finds four hours' sleep sufficient for his needs and that he works for eighteen hours. If that is the case, I can conceive him as a man whose mind, in spite of the nature of his work, has the power of banishing all the problems and difficulties of the day. This, I understand, was also one of the secrets of the energy of Gladstone, and probably also of many other great men who have the power to free their minds entirely from the business of the day in dreamless sleep. Look into the face of Napoleon and, besides the cruelty there, you will see that perfect composure and calm which stamps him as a man of great reserve power.[1]

[1] It is interesting to note that, even physiologically, Napoleon was constructed with a power of rest shared by few men, for he had a pulse rate of only about 50 compared with the normal rate of 75.

The mental and moral strain that some men have to undergo seems incredible. In the course of a day a Prime Minister, for instance, guides the counsels of state, directs wars, settles industrial disputes, and conducts diplomatic relations with other nations, all in addition to the ordinary cares of his private affairs. Compare his output of energy with that, say, of his barber, whose anxieties are confined to his little shop, whose disputes are concerned only with his two assistants, and whose diplomacy reaches its height in his attempt to persuade you to buy his hair lotion without suggesting that you are bald. Yet, if you observe these two men at the close of day, probably the Prime Minister is the less fatigued of the two. The thing that strikes us is that, however much energy such a man expends, there always seems to be an ample re-supply which keeps him vigorous and fresh.

At the present time I am treating each morning about twenty neurasthenic patients at once by hypnotic suggestion. I always commence treatment by suggestions of quietness and calmness of mind, of freedom from anxiety and the passing away of all nervousness and fear. To attempt to stimulate a restless and worried mind with energetic suggestions is as futile as whipping a dying horse. When the mind is quiet and rested, only then do I suggest thoughts of vigour of mind, strength of body, and determination of will. Inspiring, stimulating thoughts, falling on a mind calm and receptive, draw from its silent depths ample resources of strength which produce calmness and peace. The confidence and happiness with which these men rise from their half-hour's rest is a proof that this rest, unlike the neurasthenic's ordinary night's "rest," has brought them into touch with untold resources of power.

The art of alternating rest and activity is an art well worth acquiring. Some people have the power of putting themselves to sleep for five or ten minutes at any time of the day. This carries with it the power of dismissing from the mind at any time all cares, which forthwith

> fold up their tents like the Arabs
> And silently steal away.

Night-time should be reserved for sleep, and no thoughts of the day should be permitted to break into the preserves of sleep.

I once put into a short hypnotic sleep a patient, tremulous, anxious, sleepless. When he awakened he spontaneously remarked that that was the best sleep he had had for months, and on being questioned replied that he thought he had slept for several hours, whereas, in point of fact, he had slept only a few minutes. During those few moments he had had a perfect control over a mind worried with anxious thoughts.

That the life of energy is dependent on the art of resting is one of the fundamental laws of physiology as well as of psychology. The alternation of rest and work is necessary for the activity of life. Even the heart is not always active, as is sometimes supposed ; it has its periods of repose at the end of each beat when there is a rest and relaxation, which, though it lasts only the fraction of a second, is sufficient to refresh it for the next beat. In the last section we mentioned the fact that a nerve was practically unfatigable. That fact is not due to there being no wastage, for the nerve tissue is always being used up ; as Waller says, the nerve "is inexhaustible, not because there is little or no expenditure, but because there is an ample re-supply." The nerve rests for only a very small fraction of a second between the electric shocks which pass along it, yet in that moment of rest it is able to draw upon that ample re-supply which reinvigorates it to renewed activity. These physiological principles point the way to find refreshment of the mind. There are ample resources of power at our disposal, but in the course of our life we need moments of mental rest when the

soul can go apart and rest awhile.   Life, like music, has
its rhythm of silence as well as of sound; it has its
crests of surging energy, and its quiet calm in the trough
of the wave.   Life has its moments of throbbing energy,
but needs also its moments of relaxation.   The restful
life does not demand that we withdraw from the world
in ascetic retreat ; but it demands such a control of our
thoughts and feelings that, even when active in body,
we can have that quiescence of mind which is itself the
most perfect rest.

> And out of that tranquillity shall rise
> The end and healing of our earthly pains,
> Since the mind governed is the mind at rest.

THE SOURCE OF ENERGY

This Essay has raised the question as to whether our
strength comes from within ourselves, in which case we
may be conceived as a reservoir of energy, or whether
it is derived from an outside source, using us as a
channel for its activity.   (1) It is true that we do store
up a certain amount of energy derived, physiologically
from the nutriment of food and air, psychologically
from the myriads of impressions of sight, sound, and
touch, which are continually falling upon our senses
and being recorded and stored, probably in the lower
brain centres.   (2) But what we have been specially
considering are not these acquired energies, but the great
hereditary instinctive powers which have borne down
like a wave through humanity from generation to generation.   (3) Several of the greatest psychologists, and,
in particular, those clinical psychologists who have to
deal with the actual diseases of men, have tended towards
the view that the source of power is to be regarded as
some impulse that works through us, and is not of our
own making.   What Janet calls " mental energy " is
a force which ebbs in the neurasthenic and flows in
the healthy man ; Jung speaks of *libido* or *urge* as

a force which surges through our lives, now as an impulse towards nutrition, now as the sexual instinct; there is also the *élan vital* of Bergson. These views suggest that we are not merely receptacles but *channels* of energy. Life and power is not so much contained in us, it *courses through* us. Man's might is not to be measured by the stagnant water in the well, but by the limitless supply from the clouds of heaven. These descriptive theories represent man as borne on the crest of an impulse which he can only partially control. Whether we are to look upon this impulse as cosmic energy, as a life force, or what may be its relation to the Divine immanence in Nature, it is for other investigators to say. It is the business of the philosopher to speculate upon the ultimate nature of reality. The scientist has merely to study the laws of its manifestation in concrete expression. I merely wish to point out that the view expressed above as to the derivation of our human energies from the instinctive emotions does not exclude the foregoing or any other theories as to their *ultimate* source, which is yet a matter of speculation.

The Dynamic of Religion

While it has not been the purpose of this Essay to deal with questions of theology, I cannot help pointing out that our discussion of the psychology of power has a very direct bearing on the question of *the dynamic of religion*, and especially on the power possessed by the Christian religion of liberating energies which can transform the living soul into a quickening spirit. In its fundamental doctrine of love to God and man, Christianity harmonises the emotions of the soul into one inspiring purpose, thereby abolishing all conflict, and liberating instead of suppressing the free energies of men. In its doctrine of the Spirit it emphasises the element of power in religion. No reader of the New Testament can fail to be struck by the constant reiteration in different forms of the idea that the normal experience of a Christian at that epoch was enhancement of power—"I can do all things"—an enhancement attributed by them to the operation in and through them of a divine energy to which the community gave the name of the "Spirit"—"Ye shall receive power." Pentecost, the healing miracles of the Apostolic Age, the triumphant progress of the religion through the Roman Empire, the heroic deeds of saints and martyrs,—all these point to the sense of a power newly discovered. In contrast, looking at the Church of to-day, one cannot but be struck with its powerlessness. It contains men of intellect; it produces a type of piety and devotion which one cannot but admire; it sacrifices itself in works of kindness and beneficence; but even its best friends would not claim that it inspires in the world the sense of power. What strikes one rather is its impotence and failure. This want of inspiration and power is associated with the fact that men no longer believe in the existence of the Spirit in any effective practical way. They believe in God the Father, and they are reverent; they believe in the Son, and the Church numbers amongst its members millions who humbly try to "follow in His steps"; but for all practical purposes they are like that little band at Ephesus who had "not so much as heard whether there be any Holy Ghost," and, lacking the inspiration of such a belief, they are weak and wonder why.

In this place I need only indicate the close connection between restfulness of mind, so essential to the cure of nervous ills, and that characteristic of religious devotion. "They that *wait* on the Lord shall *renew* their strength." There is the alternation of repose and work, and the insistence on the source of strength being of a psychical and not a physical character. Christianity also teaches that to learn to rest, not only in moments snatched from our work but by keeping a mind free from worry and anxiety, neither caring for the morrow nor fearful of the forgiven past, is to give ourselves the opportunity of drawing on that "ample re-supply" which comes to those who do not fear to expend their energy for others. Life will throb within and through us, but our souls will be in repose.

The religious writings of men of old constantly emphasised confidence and cheerfulness as the keynote to strength. "In quietness and confidence shall be your strength." "Let not your heart be troubled." "Be not anxious." "Be of good cheer, I have overcome the world." "Say unto them of a fearful heart, 'Be strong, fear not.'" Such words as the following are literally fulfilled before our eyes in a shell-shock hospital of the present day. "The eyes of the blind shall be opened, and the ears of the deaf be unstopped. Then shall the lame man leap as an hart and the tongue of the dumb shall sing. They shall obtain gladness and joy, and sorrow and sighing shall flee away." Accurately and wonderfully these words describe both the treatment by the suggestion of confidence and its effects, as well on the body as on the mind.

This power which the Church has lost is being re-discovered, but along different lines. The psycho-therapist, who is a physician of the soul, has been compelled to acknowledge the validity of the practical principles of the Christian religion, though he may or may not accept the doctrines on which they are said to be based.

Speaking as a student of psychotherapy, who, as such, has no concern with theology, I am convinced that the Christian religion is one of the most valuable and potent influences that we possess for producing that harmony and peace of mind and that confidence of soul which is needed to bring health and power to a large proportion of nervous patients. In some cases I have attempted to cure nervous patients with suggestions of quietness and confidence, but without success until

I have linked these suggestions on to that faith in the power of God which is the substance of the Christian's confidence and hope. Then the patient has become strong.[1]

I have tried to show that the experience of applied psychology, and especially psychotherapy, points towards the conclusion that we are living far below the limits of our possible selves, and that there are open to us resources of power, available through the right use of our instincts, which, if directed to noble purposes, will free our minds from those worries, anxieties, and morbid fatigue which spoil our lives, and will free us for a life of energy and strength.

In the course of my argument I have indicated directions in which this line of investigation cannot but affect the theory and practice of religion : to have done more than indicate directions might have seemed presumptuous in one who speaks as a student of science rather than as a philosopher or theologian. I hope, however, that I have made it clear that few things would be of more value, whether for medical science, for everyday conduct, or for religion, than such a reinterpretation of some of the fundamental beliefs of Christianity as would

---

[1] Lest this should be considered a prejudiced view I quote from Jung (*Analytical Psychology*) : " I have come to the conclusion that these religious and philosophical motive forces—the so-called metaphysical needs of the human being—must receive positive consideration at the hands of the analyst (physician) . . . he must make them serve biological ends as psychologically valuable factors. Thus these instincts assume once more those functions that have been theirs from time immemorial." Again in a volume entitled *The Christian Religion as a Healing Power* (E. Worcester and others) I find quoted some weighty opinions. Möbius, the neurologist, says : " The consciousness of being within the hand of Providence, the confident hope of future righteousness and redemption, is a support to the believer in his work, his care and his need, for which unbelief has no compensation. If we consider the effect of irreligion as increasing our helplessness to resist the storms of life, its relation to nervousness cannot be doubted." " Religious faith," says Dubois of Berne, himself an agnostic, " would be the best preventative against the maladies of the soul and the most powerful means of curing them, if it had sufficient life to create true Christian stoicism in its followers. Feeling himself upheld by his God, he fears neither sickness nor death . . . he remains unshaken in the midst of his sufferings, and is inaccessible to the cowardly emotions of nervous people." Dr. Clouston of Edinburgh, the specialist in mental diseases, says, " to treat of the hygiene of the mind, without including a consideration of the religious instinct and its effects, would be to omit one of its most powerful factors."

make them intellectually possible of acceptance to the modern man.   And Psychology has opened up lines along which one may look to see effected that reconciliation between science and religion, the attempt to procure which led to an impasse a generation ago because " science " was taken almost exclusively to mean Physics. The main object, however, of the Essay has been practical —to show that there are resources of power at the disposal of all.   But the fact that so many seek for power and yet do not receive it suggests that piety is not the only requisite of power.   To obtain it we must obey the higher laws of nature, and in particular make use of the forces we already find at our human disposal ; and fearlessly expending them in a spirit of confidence for the fulfilment of our ideals, we shall harmonise mind, will, and emotion in one throbbing impulse of life and power.

Taking, then, the instincts in their cruder form as handed down to us by our brutish ancestry, we should seek not to suppress them, but to use the powers which lie latent in them.   We may transform where we cannot suppress, and, by aid of reason and the higher emotions, redirect the lower instincts to nobler purposes.   We need not obstruct, but press into our service, the passions of the soul ; we can fill our sails with the very winds and gales which threaten the shipwreck of our lives ; tap the resources of the lightning which ruthlessly destroys, and turn its electric power into the driving-force of our enterprises.

IV

WHAT HAPPENED AT PENTECOST

BY

C. A. ANDERSON SCOTT, M.A., D.D.

PROFESSOR OF THE NEW TESTAMENT AT WESTMINSTER COLLEGE, CAMBRIDGE
AUTHOR OF "DOMINUS NOSTER," COMMENTARY ON REVELATION
IN "CENTURY BIBLE," ETC.

SYNOPSIS

INTRODUCTION.—Current answers may be true, but are not adequate—origin of conception of spirit. Specific contribution of Hebrew mind, the idea of the Spirit of God. Functions assigned to the Spirit, especially that of inspiration. Operations sporadic and discontinuous. Ethical connotation of the idea but slightly developed in the Old Testament. Profound change in the conception of the Spirit due to the teaching of Christ, and the experience of Pentecost.

THE UPPER ROOM.—The persons present were taking up a common faith attitude to Jesus—the miraculous features of the narrative are capable of explanation along the lines of psychological phenomena and traditional accompaniments of the Spirit. The speaking with tongues was not comprehensible : its true character. The narrative is not the result of mythical accretion. There has been a converse process of clarification of the experience through the application of the ethical criterion. The "founding of the Church" not an adequate explanation.

THE NEW THING : EMERGENCE OF THE FELLOWSHIP.—Significance of the *Koinonia*. Illustrations of its importance from the Acts and from St. Paul. The power of the Spirit was first manifested in permanent form in the emergence of the Fellowship, with Agape for its connecting tissue. Nature of the Fellowship.

THE SYMBOL OF THE FELLOWSHIP: THE LOAF.—There is a symbolism attaching to the Loaf even prior to the breaking—and a symbolism in the breaking. Further, the Body represented by the Loaf was there to be offered up.

THE FELLOWSHIP THE ORGAN OF INSIGHT.—The intense vitality of the new community was manifested alike in thought and in diversity of organisation. A clue to the meaning of St. Paul's formula "in Christ."

THE ETHICAL CONFIRMATION.

FURTHER RESULTS : GIFTS AND POWERS.

WHAT A NEW PENTECOST WOULD BE LIKE.

IV

WHAT HAPPENED AT PENTECOST

THE coming of the Spirit? But was there any time when the Spirit was not at work among God's people? Was there any people in whom God's Spirit did not continually seek to operate or "rule" (Gen. vi. 3)? Was there any people that did not show some results of the Spirit's working in intellectual and moral progress?

The birth of the Church? But was there not already "a Church" existing in some real sense before the day of Pentecost? Was it not present as a Christian Church from the day when Jesus first gathered round Himself a band of permanent disciples —not to speak of the existence of a Church of God under various aspects from the time that God called His people out of Egypt? What was afterwards described as "the fruit of the Spirit" was not a new phenomenon in any of its parts; no generation had been without some witness of the response of man to the ethical ideals of God.

Neither the presence of the Spirit, nor the recognition of that presence, nor yet some results of it, had been lacking prior to Pentecost. What then happened that was so epoch-making? It is plain that though most of the answers which are commonly given to this question are correct, few, if any, of them penetrate to the heart of the matter as an experience which produced such stupendous results.

To find a true answer to the question we must first examine the origin of the conception of "the Spirit," and then the limitations under which prior to Pentecost the Spirit was understood to work.

The origin of the conception lies far back in the history of human thought. Earlier than any written record, it is nevertheless not obscurely indicated by the history of human speech. This testifies that the fundamental idea underlying the word "spirit" is that of invisible force. The earliest form of invisible force of which men became aware was undoubtedly the wind without, the breath within, themselves. And there is great significance in the fact that in many languages the same word has stood for "wind," "breath," and "spirit." The spectacle of the leaves being whirled over the ground, or of the trees shaken by the gale, was impressive evidence of an invisible force. A similar invisible force within man himself was somehow connected with his being "alive." When man "whose breath is in his nostrils," "breathed his last," the power that animated him departed. He ceased to "live"; but what about the power? Did it cease to be, or to be invisible force? If it did not disperse, if it continued to exist, it was natural to think of it as still his "breath," his "spirit," invisible but not wholly unknown, seeing that the man himself had been known. And to it came to be ascribed not only a continuance of existence but a continuance of force or influence. To human beings in almost total ignorance of the "natural" causes of phenomena which affected them, perhaps the readiest explanation of such happenings would be the influence still exercised by the "spirits" of the departed—more especially when the event corresponded to their disposition when alive, malevolent or otherwise. Thus for men at a certain stage of development the unseen world, the air or the sky, came to be peopled with invisible spirit-forces, manifesting in the experience of those they affected characters of good or evil.

By a converse process it was natural to ascribe to other invisible forces of Nature, as they were successively discerned, entity and character corresponding to what was observed in men. And so to unseen forces of human origin were added "super-human" forces, what St. Paul calls "the spirit-forces in the unseen" (Eph. vi. 12).

Upon this basis of speculation common at least to most primitive religions the Hebrew mind developed a conception which appears to have been peculiar to itself, part of its specific contribution to human thought about God. Alone among the races of which we have record the Hebrews conceived of the "Spirit of God." They thought of their God Jehovah as having a "Spirit"; and increasingly, as time went on, they traced the effects of the Divine Will, especially those which were startling or abnormal, to the agency of this Spirit. This was partly due to the increasing reluctance to ascribe such things to the direct operation of God, the increasing tendency to feel a necessity for intermediaries between God Himself and man. The old frank and simple anthropomorphism had not felt that necessity. God conversed directly with men. But a change had followed the revelation which came through the prophets, of the "holiness" and the universality of God. To the attribute of ritual "holiness" or separation was added that of ethical separateness: "Thou art of purer eyes than to behold iniquity." At the same time the discovery was made that the God of Israel was "the Lord of all the earth." In both ways, through the moralising of His "holiness" and the increase of His majesty, it became increasingly difficult to think of God entering into immediate communication with men. Human sinfulness and the Divine "holiness," human littleness and the Divine "majesty"—to account for

communication or intercourse between these wide extremes it seemed necessary to posit the operation of
intermediate agencies.   Sometimes these were represented by " spirits," " messengers," or " angels " sent
" from the Lord " : ." who maketh his angels spirits,
his ministers a flaming fire."   But even more commonly
the agency was ascribed to some specific energy of the
Divine being—God's Word, God's Wisdom, or God's
Spirit.

It does not appear that the writers of the Old
Testament drew any exclusive distinction between
these forms of the Divine activity in respect of the
functions which were assigned to one or other of
them.   The place of Agent in Creation, for example,
is assigned by different writers to each of the three,
to the Word, the Wisdom, and the Spirit (Ps. civ. 30)
of God.   Nevertheless there are certain functions
which are assigned to the Spirit as peculiarly appropriate to its activity.   These include the enhancement
in certain men of their natural gifts and powers,
such as wisdom, judgement, skill, and craftsmanship.
But there is one function which is specially assigned to
the Spirit in the Old Testament, that of " inspiration."
It was the Spirit that took possession of men, and
became the organ of Divine communication through
men to other men.   It is the Spirit that inspires men to
" prophesy," that is, primarily, to give ecstatic utterance
to religious emotion and conviction.   Possession of and
by the Spirit was sole and sufficient authority for speaking the truth of God in the name of God (Is. lxi. 1).
In the Old Testament this operation of the Spirit
is both sporadic and discontinuous.   It was recognised
from time to time in certain individuals or in certain
groups.   It was not part of the general and continuous
endowment of God's people.   And we have a measure
both of the value attached to the manifestation, and of
the wistful desire for its extension, in the fact that part
of the promise held out regarding the Messianic period

was a wide extension, if not a universalising, of the gift:
" I will pour out my spirit upon all flesh ; and your
sons and your daughters shall prophesy " (Joel ii. 28).

It is only very rarely in the Old Testament that the
Spirit appears as agent in the sphere of physical nature :
" The Spirit works on man and through man." And
still more rarely is its influence represented as affecting
the moral nature of man.

The modern reader is apt to take the contrary for
granted. It is natural to assume that throughout the
Bible the specific influence of " the Holy Spirit " is
and must be towards " holiness," " sanctification,"
in the meaning which we attach to the words to-day.
The fact, however, is that we owe it to the teaching of
Christ that we give an ethical meaning to these words
to-day. Only twice in the Old Testament does the
phrase " holy spirit " occur (Ps. li. 11, Is. lxiii. 10). And
prior to the revelation through Him there was at most
only a rudimentary trace of ethical meaning in the
words " holy," " holiness." In the Old Testament
they signify primarily, and almost exclusively, " separated " or " dedicated," and so " belonging to God,"
whereas in the Epistles of the New Testament the
ethical significance of the words has established itself,
and is rapidly advancing to a position of predominance,
though not to the entire exclusion of the earlier " ritual "
meaning.[1] If we find in the later portions of the Old
Testament the beginnings of the idea that he who is
" holy " as belonging to God ought to be and is on the
way to be " holy " in the sense of conformity to His
character, it is to Christ that we owe not only the
confirmation of the possibility but the full contents of
the conception.[2] " Holy Spirit " in the Old Testament
is best represented to our minds by " Divine Spirit."

[1] To realise the change it is sufficient to compare Lev. xi. 44 with 1 Pet. i. 15,
16, where the same precept evidently involves different conditions of fulfilment on
the two occasions. Cf. also Ps. lxxxvi. 2.
[2] That the other conception has not disappeared from the New Testament is seen,
for example, in 1 Cor. vii. 14, where it forms the basis of Paul's argument.

Even in the Old Testament, therefore, God in His active relation to man was conceived in terms of "spirit." The revelation "God *is* Spirit," with all its implications, was still in the future. But already a discovery or revelation (the two words describe the same thing looked at from opposite ends) had been made that God reached the minds and wills of men through His "Spirit." This discovery was to prove of momentous importance in the history of religion. It opened the way for the development of religion on a new plane, for all that is properly described as "spiritual religion"; in other words, for a religion which involves and expresses reciprocal intercourse and fellowship between God who is Spirit and the spirit of man—one in which law and ritual, authority and observance, fall into a subordinate and ancillary position, as valuable but not indispensable — one which can be universal because it postulates no other condition than the activity of the Spirit, "the ultimate expression of the unity and communion of God and man."[1] The men who first spoke of "the Spirit of God" were unconsciously preparing for the revelation that "God is Spirit," and that religion in its highest form is the cultivation of the reciprocal bond between God as Spirit and man made a living spirit by the Spirit of God, even as redemption is the restoration of that bond suspended or destroyed by sin.

But before Pentecost "the Spirit was not yet, because Jesus was not yet glorified." So did one, writing after fifty years' experience of the Spirit's influence within the Church, express the immeasurable difference between its power and its character as apprehended before and after Pentecost. After Pentecost the effective presence of the Spirit within and among men had become so indubitable, so revolutionary, and so central to religious experience, that, by comparison with what went before, it was as though the Spirit had then come into

---

[1] Pringle-Pattison, *Idea of God*, p. 410.

being. Of course the writer of the Fourth Gospel
neither meant nor expected that his statement would be
taken literally. It was not likely that he would deny
the existence of the Spirit, even under the earlier
dispensation, or its influence in former generations on
certain persons and in certain directions. Neither were
any of his fellow-disciples, who had been nourished on
the Hebrew Scriptures, in ignorance on the subject.
Just as the mind of God in His relation to the world
of men and things had been there described as His
"Wisdom," so His Will in effective contact with men
had been described as His Spirit. It was not in the
Spirit that any change had taken place, but in men,
who had become fully receptive of the Spirit through
the experiences that culminated in, and those that
started from, the Upper Room.

THE UPPER ROOM

The Persons.—The gift of the Spirit under the new
conditions came first to a company of men and women,
some hundred and twenty in all, numerous enough to
include many widely divergent types of character and
experience. The Apostles (their number restored to
twelve) were apparently all present, though the narrative does not call attention to the fact, and still less
gives any ground for supposing that the gift was
bestowed on them alone. What had brought this
company together, what was holding them together,
was a common attitude of mind and will to Him who
had been known as Jesus of Nazareth. This was an
attitude of the whole personality ; that is to say, it
involved not only the feelings—admiration, affection,
sorrow at His removal, wistful longing for His
return—but also the intellect, in the recognition of
Him as the Messiah, the One in whom the age-long
expectation of Israel was at last realised. And it was
an attitude involving not feeling and intellect alone,

but also will. In Jesus they had yielded to the authority of a unique personality, a character wholly inspired by love. Through Him and in His fellowship they had discovered God as a supreme force of love and righteousness that really counted in their lives. And though they were not yet able to construe the implications of their submission to Jesus and to God in Him—any more than they were able to express the total impression He had made upon their minds in propositions regarding Him—they had accepted His yoke; they were, as in the Acts they are frequently called, His "disciples." Their confidence in Him as the Messiah had been restored by the Resurrection. They had not yet perhaps been led to give to Him "the name that is above every name," the name of "Lord." But all the motives and dispositions for so "sanctifying Christ as Lord" were already present, except the experience of His gift of the Spirit.

And for that they were waiting. It was "the promise of the Father." And they believed that the fulfilment was imminent. Their recognition of Jesus as the Messiah, their conviction that the Messianic Age had begun, or was just about to begin, would quicken the hope that the promise which went back to Joel would now be fulfilled, and that God would "pour forth of His Spirit upon all flesh." It was to the disciples of Jesus taking up this attitude to Him, and gathered together in one place, that the Spirit in the first instance came.

The Event.—As they waited the Spirit "came." There were elements of emotional tension and strained expectation, as well as elements of assured faith and joyful thankfulness, in the psychological situation. And it would be small wonder if all of these have contributed to the account which was afterwards given of the events of Pentecost. Our interpretation of the narrative must take account of modern research in respect of what was physically or psychologically abnormal.

It takes but little heightening of well-authenticated psychological phenomena to account for the impressions, whether of hearing or seeing.[1] And the things heard and seen, the wind and the flame, were, it is not unimportant to notice, phenomena that were traditionally associated with the Spirit.[2] They were therefore the kind of thing which people profoundly convinced of the Spirit's coming would be likely to feel and see, or think they felt and saw. So that whether we think of this company of believers in Jesus as Messiah, intensely preoccupied with the thought of His function and His promise, exalted by a high emotional tension, and then "receiving the Spirit," or whether we think of one of them who had shared with the rest in the wonderful "baptism," afterwards describing what happened, it is not difficult to understand how the hearing of wind and the seeing of flame came to be the form in which the central fact was expressed.

The other external phenomenon, which is specially emphasised in the account of Pentecost, is the glossolalia or "speaking with tongues." This was reproduced on other occasions of the "descent" of the Spirit, and was reckoned as one of the charismata or normal manifestations of the Spirit's presence. It appears to have been widespread in the Church, and persisted certainly for twenty years, and probably for much longer in certain areas.

Here also the narrative in the Acts bears marks of heightening due to emotional excitation, and possibly to traditional association. There can be little doubt, however, that the glossolalia of Pentecost did not differ in character from that which was afterwards a familiar feature in the worship of the Church at Corinth. That is to say, so far from it being speech intelligible to those who spoke a different language from the speaker, it was speech or utterance which was intelligible to no one.

[1] Cf. William James, *Varieties of Religious Experience*, p. 478.
[2] According to Justin Martyr and also the Gospel of the Ebionites, the Spirit appeared at the Baptism of Jesus in the form of fire. Cf. also Ps. civ. 4.

"He that speaketh in a tongue edifieth himself," but if
he is to edify others, he must either interpret for himself
or find an interpreter (1 Cor. xii. 2-13). So it was in
Corinth twenty years later; and we may be sure it was not
otherwise at Jerusalem on the day of Pentecost. There
it is important to observe the different witness borne by
different sections of the crowd. Some, possibly those
on the outskirts, or possibly those who had no religious
interest in the scene, were content with the explanation,
"these are filled with sweet wine." To their ears the
utterances were incoherent, just as St. Paul assumed
that the "tongues" at Corinth would be: "If outsiders or unbelievers come in, will they not say you
are insane?" (1 Cor. xi. 23). Others again, possibly
those who stood nearer, or possibly those who were
less "outsiders" in a religious sense, were deeply
impressed, and are reported to have said, representative though they were of many nationalities, "We
do hear them speak in our tongues the wonderful
works of God." The crowd was not, however, so
heterogeneous as is suggested by the list of nationalities.
It was made up for the most part, if not wholly, of
"Jews and proselytes," the racially miscellaneous yet
religiously homogeneous crowd brought together in
Jerusalem by the attraction of a religious festival of
the Jews. What they heard need not have been coherent or even intelligible speech, but such utterances
as quickened in their minds a sympathetic response.
Their own stored-up recollections of the "wonderful
works of God" were set loose by the ecstatic, though
it may have been unintelligible, utterances of men with
whom they were to some extent *en rapport*.[1]

The situation may be illustrated by something which
occurred at Westminster just before the war. There
was then held a world-wide conference of the Salvation
Army, at which were present representatives of nations

[1] The expression given to the experience, and possibly the psychological
character of the experience itself, may find illustration in John iv. 29, "Come see
a man that told me all things that ever I did."

even more numerous and more heterogeneous than those tabulated in Acts ii. A report of one of the meetings contains the following striking sentence : " Each time the theme (the saving love of God in Christ) was touched upon, it brought forth from the pent-up feelings of the vast assembly a sort of half-sigh of appreciation. Yet many in the audience knew no English, but they felt that the one great truth to them was being announced at this particular moment. Indians, Chinese, Canadians, Peruvians, Swedes, all of them gave the deep emotional response." It would not be difficult to believe that when the speaker on that occasion had finished, representatives of these various races would be found saying, " We heard him speaking in our tongue the mighty works of God." [1]

Ecstatic utterance, requiring, but on the occasion of Pentecost lacking, interpretation to make it comprehensible to the hearers, but utterance which at the same time quickened in those who had some religious feeling in common with the speakers a sympathetic response, an excitation of religious emotion and insight—such appears to have been the phenomenon of glossolalia as manifested at Pentecost and after.[2]

Subsequent chapters of the Acts record cases both of individuals and of groups in which the taking up of the same faith-attitude to Jesus (expressed by calling upon Him as " Lord ") was followed by a similar reception of the Spirit. In one instance (which may possibly embody another tradition of the initial experience of Pentecost) we find allusion to accompanying phenomena in the physical order. " The place was shaken where they were assembled together " (Acts iv. 31). Similarly there is more than one case where we are told that the reception of the Holy Spirit was followed by the gift of glossolalia (Acts x. 44-48, xix. 6) ; but had it not been for the long discussion of the subject

[1] *Church Times*, June 26, 1914.
[2] See Bartlet, *Apostolic Age*, pp. 13, 14 ; also *Comm. on Acts of the Apostles*, p. 384.

K

in 1 Corinthians we should not have known how wide and how enduring was the experience. But meanwhile other "charisms" had begun to manifest themselves, for which there was no opportunity in the Upper Room— "gifts of healings," "working of miracles," as well as "prophecy" and "discerning of spirits" (*e.g.* 1 Cor. xii. 9). The striking thing about the allusions to these gifts is the way in which they are taken for granted as phenomena with which every one was familiar. They were valued not as evidence, say, of the truth of the Gospel, but for the contribution they made to the common life of the community. No appeal is made to such manifestations as evidence of anything else than the effective presence of the Holy Spirit. The nearest approach to an argument based upon the possession of such powers is found in Paul's claim to be recognised as an Apostle on the ground that he showed "the signs of an Apostle," "by signs and wonders and mighty works" (2 Cor. xii. 12). "Miracles" were commoner in those days, and less significant, than many have supposed.

This comparatively subordinate position assigned to "miracles" in the defence or presentation of the Gospel is very remarkable. We may see not only a singular correspondence between the attitude and method of the primitive Church and those adopted by our Lord Himself, we see also a clear indication that it is not in phenomena of this class that we are to find the really significant results of the Spirit's working. And there is a further indication of their minor importance in the fact that St. Paul foresaw regarding "prophecies" that they should "fail," and "tongues" that they should "cease." Neither does the Apostle appear to have been disturbed by the anticipation. But nothing that was transitory can give the true differentiation of what happened at Pentecost. We have to look for something that was lasting and revolutionary, something that underlies and accounts

for the experience along its whole length. We may
well be guided by the criterion employed by St. Paul.
The Apostle never displayed his spiritual insight more
conspicuously than in his analysis of the group of
"charisms" or "spiritual gifts," which were in fact
forms of the Spirit's action (1 Cor. xii.-xiv.). He
arranges them in a definite scale of comparative value.
There are among them good, better, and best. The
best of all is Love, with its correlates (which indeed
it includes) Faith and Hope. And the criterion by
which its supremacy is primarily confirmed is its
permanence. It "abides." Prophecies, tongues, even
knowledge, fail or disappear. "Love never faileth."
The same criterion of comparative value is to be
applied to the whole range of phenomena connected
with Pentecost.

Some have sought to explain the marvellous features
in the narrative of Acts ii. as due to mythical accretion.
But this is not necessary, nor even probable. Such
accretion may take place around a person or movement
the circumstances of whose initial appearance have been
obscure or unimpressive. In such a case an internal
experience or impression of a striking kind has been
the first thing to be distinguished. And "mythical
accretion" is due to the attempt to objectivise it, to
give the experience a concrete form adequate to the
impression. To this we have a parallel in the growth of
the "legend" of St. Francis. But here we are presented
with the converse process. When the initial impulse has
been externally startling in its character and immediate
in some of the results, the tendency of an approximately
contemporary account is to enhance the attendant circumstances, but for subsequent reflection, penetrating
through the circumstances to the real phenomenon, to
reduce the emphasis on the externally marvellous and
concentrate on the essential facts.

It is this latter process of which we see evidence when we compare successive stages in the record of the Spirit's influence in the primitive community. In the first stage attention is concentrated on the marvellous accompaniments which attended the original outpouring of the Spirit, but were not, so far as we are told, repeated. A vivid description is given of external phenomena culminating in the disciples " speaking with other tongues, as the Spirit gave them utterance," and the consequent amazement on the part of the bystanders. In the second stage the phenomena belonging to the physical order no longer appear. The Spirit comes upon men, but no reference is found to any " rushing mighty wind," or to the appearance of " tongues as of fire." The glossolalia or " speaking with tongues " continues, but as a manifestation which requires to be regulated. On the other hand, it is now found to be accompanied by a group of exceptional manifestations also belonging to the psychological order, such as gifts of healing, prophecy, and administration. In the third stage, while the physical phenomena continue to be absent, the importance of the psychologically abnormal is markedly diminished ; they tend to die out, because the ethical consequences of the Spirit's presence are now clearly observed and estimated at their superior value. First glossolalia, and afterwards prophecy, falls into discredit. The ethical results assert their supremacy.

This is not a process of " mythical accretion," but of progressive clarification, through the application of an ethical criterion.[1]   And the way in which the record

---

[1] A good parallel to the process suggested in the text (which might be described as " decretion " of mythical material) is furnished by a comparison between the three narratives of St. Paul's conversion which we find in Acts (ix. 1-19 ; xxii. 6-16 ; xxvi. 13-20), to which may be added, as representing a further stage, Gal. i. 15-16. In this series the first is plainly characterised by special emphasis on the marvellous. The details are elaborated with the obvious desire to enhance the certainty of the wonder by dwelling on the attendant circumstances. The later accounts differ in consequence of a shifting of the emphasis on to that internal experience to which the speaker could testify. And the latest, from the pen of

in the Acts preserves the features that marked the
earliest stage is a point in favour of its historical character. Luke reproduced the story as he got it from
some one who may have been in the company, or
present at the subsequent scene, regardless of the fact
that the coming of the Spirit was no longer evidenced
by the same physical phenomena. He laid himself
open to the challenge : How do we know that the
Spirit really comes now, seeing that these things do
not happen now ? He trusted the consciousness of the
Church to dismiss such a challenge with an appeal to
religious and ethical experience.

If, however, neither any nor all of the physical or
psychological phenomena which accompanied or followed
the descent of the Spirit provide a sufficient answer to
our question, and if, as will be generally agreed, we
cannot be content to say "The Holy Spirit came,"
what was it that happened ? Many have been content
to answer, "The Church." Whereas some have
regarded the Church as "founded" on that day, others,
holding it to have been founded by the Master in the
Galilean days, would see the Church coming to self-
consciousness and taking shape before the eyes of men
on and immediately after Pentecost. There is no
doubt a true fact lying behind this answer ; but while
it is certainly not an exhaustive account of what
happened at Pentecost, it is doubtful whether, even so
far as it goes, it is a satisfactory one.

Much depends upon the significance which we attach
to the word "Church." If we allow our thought to be
guided by anything bearing the name which has come
under our own observation, or by anything that is

the subject of the experience himself, touches the heart of the matter, and that
only ("It pleased God to reveal his Son in me"). The process becomes even
more striking (and more intelligible) if, according to Professor Torrey's theory,
the series represents three different authorities—(1) an Aramaic source, (2) Luke,
(3) Paul.

described for us subsequent to the first weeks, we are
in danger of going far astray. For one thing, the
narrative in Acts (chapters ii.-iv.) is strangely silent as
to any such phenomenon appearing as an immediate
result of Pentecost. St. Luke, or more probably the
source which he is using, gives no hint of anything which
can be said to characterise the Church as an externally
visible and organised institution. And he rather
markedly refrains from using the word " Church " itself.
Even in v. 11, where it occurs for the first time, he may
be using it, as Dr. Hort suggests, " by anticipation."[1]
And in the preceding chapter he rings the changes on
descriptive phrases, such as " they that believed," " the
brethren," and the like. Indeed, it is difficult not to
feel that he (or his source) is actually at a loss for a
word to describe the new community : " the Lord
added . . . thereunto." Later copyists, recognising
the ambiguity, substituted the word " Church " for
Luke's ambiguous phrase, and so we find " added to
the Church " (Acts ii. 47) in our A.V.

Further, we must note the fact that in these chapters
the increasing body of believers, though positively distinguished from their surroundings by their common
faith-attitude to Jesus as Messiah, are not yet negatively
delimited by separation from the Jewish Church. The
Temple is still for them the natural place for meeting
and for worship : " day after day they resorted
thither," and " they were looked on with favour by
all the people." Moreover, the speech of St. Peter in
Solomon's Portico (Acts iii.) is remarkable for its tone
of mildness and consideration towards the Jews : " I
know, however, that you acted through ignorance, like
your rulers." It looks as though down to the appointment of the Seven—the first definite step in organisation—the new community was not conscious of essential
distinctness from the Church of the Jews ; and even as
though down to the subsequent martyrdom of Stephen

[1] *Christian Ecclesia*, p. 49.

it was not beyond hope that the people as a whole might be swept into the movement.[1]

It is sometimes suggested that, either during His ministry or during the forty days following the resurrection, Christ had given to His disciples, or to the Apostles, instructions for the organisation and administration of such an institution as the Church, and that these instructions were carried out immediately after the coming of the Spirit. But apart from the serious difficulty arising from the fact that the record is silent as to any such instructions, the suggestion is untenable because inconsistent with that expectation concerning the future which was dominant in the Christian consciousness of these first weeks. "The first disciples believed that they had their Master's authority for expecting the end of the existing world order in their own lifetime. Whether they understood Him or not, clearly they could not have held this opinion if they had received instructions for the constitution of a church."[2]

Such considerations—the absence of recorded instruction, the incompatibility with the dominant outlook on the future, the absence of evidence in the opening chapters of the Acts, and the evidence pointing to a community as yet imperfectly differentiated from the Jewish Church—seem to preclude the possibility that there was, at least during the first weeks, anything to which we should give the name of "Church," an institution present to the eyes of men as a distinct and organised society. How, then, are we to describe the common consciousness of the disciples during the interval?

There is, moreover, an interval of another order which cannot but be felt. It is the psychological gap

---

[1] St. Paul's remarkable phrase in Gal. i. 20, "the churches of Judaea which were in Christ," appears to distinguish the "Christian" Churches there from the Jewish (cf. 1 Thess. ii. 14) ; and, if so, it is an echo, perhaps the latest, of this consciousness of sharing a common status with the Jewish Church ; it would also be a point in favour of an early date for the Galatian Epistle.

[2] Dean Inge in the *Quarterly Review*, 1918, p. 33.

between the action of the Spirit upon the spirits of the Apostles and any external result of man's reaction to the Spirit's influence. Modern psychology would rule out categorical instruction by the Spirit ; even the quickening of memory as to earlier instructions is precluded by what has just been said. Some intermediate result of the Spirit's influence seems to be called for, as well as something to fill the interval of time, some form of consciousness which on the one hand had been quickened by the Spirit, and on the other led to the organisation of the Church.

The conclusion seems to be that neither in the manifestation of supernatural phenomena, nor in those " gifts " and " powers " which were subsequently traced to the Spirit's presence, nor yet in " the foundation of the Church," do we find an explanation which is at once adequate and penetrating of what happened at Pentecost.

The New Thing : Emergence of the Fellowship

All types of explanation emphasise the descent of the Spirit as the significant happening at Pentecost, but none of them explore its dynamic meaning. Whereas for one class of explanation this coming of the Spirit remained the unexplored fact which the supernatural phenomena serve to attest, for the other it remained the unexplored starting-point for the development of an organisation. The question still remains, What was the real, primary, and enduring result of the Spirit's coming ? And the answer here suggested is that the primary result which was permanent, and that which filled the interval, was what was recognised and described as the " Fellowship " ($\dot{\eta}$ Κοινωνία) ; that the symbol of the Fellowship (to which the highest importance was attached) was " the Loaf " ($\dot{o}$ ἄρτος) ; that its religious efficacy was found in " intuition of truth " ($\dot{\epsilon}\pi\dot{\iota}\gamma\nu\omega\sigma\iota\varsigma$), and that its demonstration to the world, which was found in the first instance in "mighty works," was ultimately and permanently discovered in what St. Paul called "the fruit of the Spirit."

Among the many meanings or shades of meaning which may legitimately be assigned to *Koinonia*, it would seem as though the primary and most important one has been seriously overlooked. There is reason to think that in the Acts and the Epistles the word not infrequently bears an absolute significance which corresponds to a specific element in the primary consciousness of the nascent Church. The earliest instance of its use is found in connection with the narrative of Pentecost, in Acts ii. 42, as now read by the critical editions : "They were steadfastly adhering to the teaching of the Apostles and to the fellowship, to the breaking of bread and the prayers." The old rendering following the Received Text ran : "continued steadfastly in the apostles' doctrine and fellowship" : and our Revisers have not thought it necessary to alter the translation. But most, if not all, modern commentators recognise that the introduction in the critical texts of the article before the word Κοινωνία justifies, if indeed it does not require, the recognition of the phrase as an independent one. *It is not the teaching and fellowship of the Apostles to which the community adhered, but the teaching of the Apostles and the Fellowship.* It was a new name for a new thing, community of spirit issuing in community of life :[1] that was the primary result of the coming of the Spirit.

Consistent with this view is the emphasis which in these opening chapters is laid upon the fact of "togetherness," where the external coming together and being together so frequently referred to is the expression of that inward sense of oneness indicated by Koinonia. The intense reality with which this

[1] Cf. "Inward Fellowship and its outward Manifestation" (R. J. Knowling) : "Used in connection with the Christian Society to express the idea of the fellowship in which it is united, and the acts of fellowship in which the fellowship is realised " (J. Armitage Robinson).

oneness was felt is indicated in Acts iv. 32 : "the multitude of those that believed had but one heart and one soul." It was something approximating to a corporate personality that had come into being. The persons of whom it was made up were conscious of a "oneness" with one another which was spiritual, and anterior to any of the more or less external forms in which it proceeded to express itself.

The first indication of this inward bond was seen in their "togetherness" ("the believers all kept together") ; the next in an eager readiness to treat the possessions of each as belonging to all : "they shared all they had with one another ; they would sell their possessions and goods and distribute the proceeds among all, as any one might need" (Acts iii. 45 ff. ; cf. v. 32, 34 ff.). To describe this as "an experiment in communism" is seriously to misconceive the situation. The conduct described was rather the spontaneous expression of the spirit of fellowship, in those first moments when it welled up in each individual member at the touch of the Spirit of Christ. The attitude of the individual towards the things he had called his own was a measure of the completeness with which he had been merged in the Koinonia.

This is thrown into high relief by the story of Ananias. His offence was not simply falsehood, but treachery, treachery to the Koinonia to which he professed allegiance. He had acted falsely to its inherent character, and in so doing he had "cheated the Holy Spirit." It was a gross case of failing to "discern the Body,"*i.e.* to act loyally in accordance with its nature.[1]

Turning to St. Paul we find that both the reality and the importance of this new thing were clearly apprehended by him. And he gives it the same name, Koinonia. He reminds the Corinthians for their comfort that it is a "faithful" God who has called them (with an "effectual calling") "into the Fellow-

[1] See my article in *Expositor*, VIII. x. 182.

ship of Christ." [1]   And by this he means not the
"companionship" of Christ, but the Fellowship belonging to and named after Him.   And the same may
also be described as "the Fellowship of the Spirit"
(Phil. ii. 1).   The Spirit has called it into being, and
by the indwelling of the same Spirit it is sustained.
"If Christ has any appeal, if love carries any sanction,
if the Spirit has really created a Fellowship, if affection
and tenderness are really its atmosphere," show it in
word and deed.   A third case is found in 2 Corinthians
xiii. 13, where the same idea appears in the Apostolic
Benediction—"the communion of the Holy Ghost be
with you all."   There Paul prays not for the companionship of the Spirit with individual believers, but that the
Fellowship which has been created by the Spirit may
continue, even as he prays for the continuous manifestation of the grace of the Lord Jesus and of the love
of God. [2]

The power of the Spirit was manifested in this way
first in the experience of a company of men and women
who belonged to the same race, and were already united
together by earlier religious affinities.   But it was
subsequently displayed not only in bringing into one
Fellowship those who belonged to non-Jewish races and
religions, but, greatest miracle of all, in combining
within one such Divine Society Jews and Gentiles,
between whom there had been an impassable gulf.
This was in truth for St. Paul the supreme miracle,
paralleled only by the miracle of Reconciliation between
God and man, of which indeed it was for him an essential
part (Eph. iii. 9-11).   This was the mystery that had
been concealed from previous generations, the secret

[1] The thought is the same as that which finds very different expression in John
xv. 16 : "Ye have not chosen me, but I have chosen you."
[2] It has been said that "no exegetical skill can give us certainty as to the
meaning of this phrase."   But one thing it cannot mean, and that is what in all
probability it is usually supposed to mean—"the companionship of the Holy Ghost."
And there is at least high probability that all three genitives are subjective, and
signify respectively the grace, the love, and the fellowship, of which Father, Son,
and Spirit are severally the source.

purpose of God now illumined by Christ.   It was "the mystery of Christ," "the mystery of the Gospel" (Eph. iii. 4, vi. 19).   This indeed was the specific element in Paul's teaching which he called his Gospel, and which, as distinct from those elements of his preaching which reached him from older disciples, he traced to direct revelation by God to himself (Gal. i. 12 ; Eph. iii. 3).   The Gentiles were eligible for the Fellowship, and on the same terms as the Jews ; they were σύσσωμα, *i.e.* participators in the life of the same Body.

This is the true theme of the Epistle to the Ephesians, which is quite inadequately described as "the unity of the Church."   The august act of God which Paul here celebrates is rather the unification into one Body of those sections of humanity—Jews and Gentiles—which had hitherto been as poles asunder, held apart by prejudice, misunderstanding, hostility (Eph. ii. 16), and even, as it appeared to the Jew, by divine ordinance (Col. ii. 14).   This removal of "the middle wall of partition," the cancelling of "the feud of the law" (Eph. ii. 15), the unification into "one new man" of these hitherto antagonistic elements, was what filled the Apostle's mind with wonder and adoring praise.   It was for him a factor in the work of Christ so vast in its import, and so contributory to the glory of God, that to do justice to his thought we have to set side by side the two phrases : "He is our peace" (*i.e.* the source and ground of peace between us who were previously alienated) and "We have peace with God."

Another name for the Koinonia is the Unity (ἑνότης).[1]   Under this name also Paul traces its existence to the work of the Spirit, and urges the duty of maintaining it (Eph. iv. 3).   It is the "Unity of the Spirit." In Ephesians iv. 13 he indicates its primary sources within the human personality ; it is the unity brought

[1] Cf. Ignatius, *Phil.* 4, εἰς ἕνωσιν τοῦ αἵματος αὐτοῦ.

about by faith and knowledge of the Son of God. In
his eyes it is a sacred thing, and he strives to make
those to whom he writes realise its sacredness. When
he warns them not to " grieve the Holy Spirit of God,"
he is really summing up the various precepts which
he has just laid down—" lie not one to another " ;
" be angry and sin not " ; " let your speech be not
destructive of the moral coherence " ($\sigma a \pi \rho \acute{o} s$) but
" unto upbuilding." All these find their sanction and
appeal in the sense of corporate unity, and in the
sacredness of its claim. Whatever denies or injures
that corporate unity offends the Spirit who has
created, and now maintains, the Koinonia (Eph. iv.
25-30 ; cf. Acts v. 3). The same principle is further
illustrated by the appearance in the catalogue of
" deeds of the flesh " (Gal. v. 19, 20) of such
things as exhibitions of rivalry, sectarianism, party
spirit ($a \acute{\iota} \rho \acute{e} \sigma \epsilon \iota s$). Such sins against the body corporate
are treated as equally heinous with those against the
individual body.

Further light is thrown upon the conception by
the relation which St. Paul postulates between the
Spirit and that Love which is the connective tissue
of the new man. This " love " is part of the " fruit
of the Spirit " (Gal. v. 2). And the same thought
underlies the striking collocation in 2 Corinthians vi. 6 :
" by kindness, by the Holy Spirit, by unaffected love."
The remark " See how these Christians love one
another " was not originally made in irony.

The emergence of the consciousness described as
Koinonia, not only at the first in Jerusalem, but
elsewhere and subsequently as successive new groups
of believers " received the Spirit," points to the fact
that the primary function of that Spirit was the removal
of " diffinities," and the bringing into existence of a
sacred Fellowship in which " there was neither male nor
female, bond nor free." And this Fellowship became in
turn the organ of the Spirit, and so an extension of the

Incarnation, to which it was only natural, ere many years had passed, to give the description "Body of Christ." With almost incredible boldness Paul seems in one passage (1 Cor. xii. 12) to identify this, the corporate body of believers, with Christ Himself. Certainly he had before his mind the vision of a redeemed humanity growing up into "the measure of the stature of the fulness of Christ"; and the vision was no baseless dream, but rested on his observation of what had already been accomplished through the Holy Spirit in creating the Koinonia.

The word in this specific sense would appear to denote a fellowship which was not merely a fellowship of believers *inter se*, nor yet a fellowship of the believers individually with the Spirit, but a complex experience which included both. It was in relationship with one another that men continuously realised their relation to Christ and to God through Him. Indeed, they found in this reciprocal fellowship the convincing proof of their own salvation : "we know that we have passed from death unto life, because we love the brethren" (1 John iii. 14). The "Fellowship" was, in fact, the sphere within which this complex experience was realised, the reciprocal interaction of moral and spiritual forces divine and human. And this Koinonia, called into being by the Holy Spirit, was prior to the organised Ecclesia : it was related to it as the life to the organisation.

The Symbol of the Fellowship : the Loaf

Of this Koinonia the primitive community recognised that it possessed a symbolic representation, which played an important part in the devotional life of the early Christians. This was the loaf, or "bread," as it is translated in our English versions. These disciples of the first days were known by the fact that they adhered not only to the teaching of the Apostles and the Fellowship, but also to "the breaking of the loaf." [1]

The investigation of this initial stage of Christian worship has tended to overlook this symbolism of the loaf, and the symbolism of its breaking apart from, and anterior to, the partaking of it. The commentators are probably mistaken who consider themselves justified in reading back into this and similar allusions in the Acts what they believe to be St. Paul's interpretation of the Eucharist. As a synonym for the Eucharist, or for the Eucharistic element in the Agapé, "the breaking of bread" has certainly an antiquarian sound. And if Luke wrote with Paul's teaching before his mind, it is all the more necessary to account, if possible, for the use of a phrase which emphasises the breaking, and passes over in silence the partaking, not to speak of other features of the Eucharist. It seems at least equally probable that in this, as in other matters, the writer of the Acts has preserved with marked fidelity the recollection of a stage of thought anterior to St. Paul, and that here also the work of the Apostle was to develop or add to the primitive conception.

Paul himself does not use the phrase "breaking of bread," though he describes the action in the institution of the rite. But the usage in the Acts suggests that there was a time when alongside the symbolism of partaking, and possibly overshadowing it, there was a symbolism attaching to the loaf itself and to the breaking of it. Of this we seem to have the latest surviving evidence in the *Didaché*, and in the designation there given to the Eucharistic rite or to part of it : "The Breaking" or "the thing for breaking." And the prayer which is there prescribed in connection with the rite is remarkable no less for what it omits than

[1] According to the accepted critical texts, as well as the Textus Receptus. But the Western text has a very interesting variant, according to which they adhered to "the fellowship of the breaking of the loaf." Blass appears to think that the original form may have been "the fellowship of the loaf." See Add. note p. 158.

for what it emphasises : " Concerning the Breaking. We thank Thee, our Father, for the life and knowledge which Thou hast made known to us through Jesus Thy servant. . . . As this broken bread was scattered upon the hills and being gathered together became one, so let Thy Church be gathered together from the ends of the earth unto Thy kingdom." [1] According to this prayer the loaf of the Eucharist was the sacred symbol of the unity into which believers had been kneaded, that corporate unity of common life, compact of all the individual lives, which was also expressed as Koinonia.   But this was always understood to be more than the sum of these personalities.   For it was the " Koinonia of the Spirit " : it had a life of its own, created and sustained by Him.

From this we may infer the significance which in the Acts is attached to " the breaking of bread."   The loaf represented the fact that the new life was held and enjoyed in common.   It was the symbol both of the Koinonia and of the " bread from heaven " by which it was nourished.

In this symbolism pertaining to the loaf itself we may find the key to the right interpretation of the difficult passage in 1 Cor. x. 16 : " The loaf which we break, does it not represent a fellowship of the Body of Christ ? " [2]   The loaf represents His corporate Body, the Church.   And what is the Body there for ?   In the first place, to be broken ; in the second place, to be offered up.   The breaking may possibly have symbolised the spiritual participation of Christ's followers in His death, that " death to sin " of which the Apostle speaks elsewhere, and in His sufferings, participation in which belonged both to the anticipation and to the experience of His Church.   In any case it would symbolise

---

[1] The Paulicians who preserved so many primitive features of doctrine and practice laid great stress on the oneness of the loaf ; see F. C. Conybeare, *Key of Truth*, pp. xlix, 123, etc.

[2] The reasons supporting this translation will be found in my article, " The Communion of the Body," in the *Expositor* for August 1919.

participation by the individual member in the common (heavenly) life of the whole.

The Body represented by the loaf was there also to be "offered up." The Church itself was the subject of a sacrificial offering to God. It is the proud consciousness of being the agent in such an offering, and in that sense a "sacrificing priest," which rings through Paul's words in Romans xv. 16. He acts as a priest for the Gentiles, when he leads them in the act of worship which consists in the offering up of themselves, of the sacred Body of Christ, which has been "consecrated by the Holy Spirit."[1] This was their "spiritual worship," before whose intense moral reality every other form of sacrifice withered into irrelevance.

This again may have been symbolised in the "breaking"; and when the people proceeded to partake of the loaf thus broken, they set forth to themselves their several dependence on the common sacred life of the Body. It was the "Body of Christ," inhabited and consecrated by His Spirit; and they drew from It, from the Spirit, and from Christ, whom it represented, the nourishment necessary for the growth and strengthening of the "new man."

The Fellowship the Organ of Insight

The presence of the Spirit in the Koinonia was attested by an extraordinary measure of what we can only call vitality. And the vitality manifests itself in many ways, in the spheres of intellectual insight, of administration, and of character.

The Fellowship was recognised as the organ of spiritual insight. In writing to Philemon, St. Paul prays that "your faith-fellowship (the fellowship founded on your faith) may be effective unto the recognition of every good thing that is ours in Christ." That is to

---

[1] It is to this conception that we are to trace all the allusions to "sacrifice" in connection with the Eucharist down to the end of the second century.

say, the Fellowship is to have its proper and expected
result in the progressive discovery of spiritual truth.
This is the only passage where such a result is traced
expressly to the Koinonia ; but precisely the same idea is
illustrated by the close connection which for the Apostle
exists between " love " and "knowledge," or "intuition."
Writing to the Philippians (i. 9), he prays that their
love " may more and more abound in insight and all
manner of perception." For the Ephesians he prays
in like manner (iii. 18) that, " being rooted in love,
they may be able to comprehend with all God's people
what is the breadth," etc., and for the Colossians that,
" being knit together in love," they may have all the
wealth of conviction and insight into the mystery of
God (ii. 2). It is in the company of God's people,
" with all saints," that the fulness of spiritual insight is
attained. And the " Love," which is the atmosphere
of the Fellowship, is the condition, the stimulating
medium, of spiritual knowledge.

In Ephesians iv. 20 ff. we find a striking illustration
of the process as observed and understood by the
Apostle. He reminds these Ephesian Christians that
they had " learned Christ," had been " taught Him,"
had been "instructed in Him." What they had learned,
the " truth as it is in Jesus," was in the first place what
we should call doctrine, the possibility and the necessity
of " putting on the new man " ; but also morals, the
details of Christian duty. And this knowledge, this
instruction, had come to them " in Christ," that is, in
that sphere of intensely realised faith, hope, and love,
which looked at from its divine side was " Christ," but
looked at from its human side was the Koinonia. Instruction both on faith and on life, with the spiritual
insight which made it vital, was due to reciprocal action
within the Koinonia. Within that sphere every faculty of
the Christian personality was quickened, and along with
others that apprehension of ethical and spiritual realities
which St. Paul describes as Epignosis or Knowledge.

This experience of the Fellowship as the organ of insight was that which finds classical expression in the promise regarding the Holy Spirit which appears in the fourth gospel : " he shall lead you into all truth." It has long been recognised that what is meant by " truth " here and elsewhere is not rightly represented by any collection of truths however complete, or even by the totality of relevant truths. The " truth " is the living reality, the eternal which lies beyond and behind the changing phenomena of experience. One function of the Spirit was to conduct men into this whole region of reality. Under His influence (and that was supremely experienced within the Fellowship) they saw things of time and of eternity as they are, and saw them in their right proportionate value.

The New Testament as a whole bears witness to the working of the same vitality with similar results. Everywhere we find the same paradox of independent variation combined with conformity to a general type. When we compare, for example, the three Synoptic Gospels, we are almost baffled by the oscillations between conformity and variation. The variations are due, not so much to the influence of conscious presuppositions or literary motives, as to the working of creative minds on plastic material ; and yet they are held in check by loyalty to a common type, or what Plato would have called $\iota\delta\epsilon a$. We find the same when we compare either the three groups of Pauline epistles with one another, or the work of Paul, Peter, and the author to the Hebrews. The difficulty which has been found in establishing the literary relations between these is due to the fact that these relations are not so much literary as psychical. It is a common experience still hot from the crucible which is run into these various moulds. And here again the variations are not more striking than the general conformity to type ; the diversities of operation are as conspicuous as the oneness of the Spirit.

And the penetrating insight (ἐπίγνωσις, αἴσθησις, σύνεσις), which is claimed as the product of the Koinonia, or of love its animating temper, finds conspicuous illustration in the case of St. Paul, and that in at least two directions. By his searching examination of the history of his own conscience, he became the pioneer for European thought in the moral analysis of self. And he penetrated deeply into the meaning of Jesus, both as an ethical teacher and as a religious personality. In both connections he seized what was central, and in both connections it was the same, namely, Love (1 Thess. v. 9 ; Gal. ii. 20). And from that centre he drew in each case a circle, the ethical contents of which prove to be what was in the mind of Christ, whether of ideal for humanity or of purpose for Himself. A portrait of an ideal Christian drawn from material provided by the first Epistle to the Thessalonians would not be easy to distinguish from one constructed out of the Synoptic Gospels. And yet the one is not a copy of the other. They are portraits of what is seen by two different persons from practically the same point of view. It was not without reason that Paul said, "We have the mind of Christ."

These manifestations of "life," intellectual, ethical, spiritual, and practical, could be described indifferently as taking place "in Christ," "in the Spirit," and "in" or "through the Fellowship." These three conceptions mutually support and explain one another. They are really different ways of contemplating the sphere of Christian experience. And, indeed, it is here that we shall find the clue to what is called the "mysticism of St. Paul." "The Lord is the Spirit," wrote the Apostle in a sentence of profound significance. The epoch-making discovery was due to the observed identity in the working of the Spirit with the recorded influence of Jesus. It was a discovery as important in its bearing on the conception of the Spirit as on the conception of Christ. If Jesus, who was the Christ, is now thought of in terms of " the Spirit," *the Spirit is now understood in terms of Christ.*   Previous to Pentecost it had been regarded as the divine energy in its operation especially upon men—invisible, potent, somewhat unaccountable. Henceforward, through being discovered to have character, the Spirit is conceived as " personal."   It, or as the writers of the New Testament now begin to call it, " He " operates along lines which can be foreseen, because they have been observed already as guiding the activities and the influence of Jesus.   And the Koinonia, within which men could count on feeling the full pressure of their influence, might be described indifferently as the sphere that was " Christ," or the atmosphere that was " the Spirit."   If " Messiah " connects " the Spirit " with history, the " Fellowship " connects them both with experience.

The Ethical Confirmation

It has become the fashion with some to label much of what has been here set forth as " Pauline mysticism," and to dismiss it as subjective, or esoteric, or incomprehensible.   But if the view which I have tried to expound and support be correct, this line of thought runs back behind Paul ; [1] it is rooted in the experience of the days immediately following Pentecost ; and it is redeemed from the imputation of being only " mysticism " by the attestation it receives from the ethical standards and achievements of the primitive Church.   An ἀγάπη or "love " which embraced Gentiles as well as Jews was as new to the Jew as other parts of the Christian ideal were to the Gentile.   And neither the ἀγάπη nor any part of the ideal remained as ideal only.   Members of the Koinonia manifested distinct approximation to it in all its parts.   Paul's demand for further achievement, even his criticism of

---

[1] There is some reason to think that even the phrase ἐν Χριστῷ and the significant use of it were pre-Pauline.

failure, must not blind us to the evidence that he assumed, and must have had ground to assume, a firm foundation of purpose and of achievement on which to build further. He is found perpetually rejoicing over the alliance between religion and morality, between the experience of the Spirit and the fruit of the Spirit. Already in the opening of the first Thessalonian Epistle, in what are probably the earliest written words of Paul that have come down to us, we meet the triad of Christian virtues—faith, love, and hope ; and these not as requiring to be inculcated or extolled as ideals, but as already distinguishing, and known by the outer world to distinguish, the Christians of Thessalonica. And further, by the phraseology which the Apostle here adopts we may clearly see these virtues not merely passive or dormant. We see faith at work producing achievement (ἔργον) ; love undertaking, and manifesting itself in, toil ; and hope issuing in patient endurance, apparently of the disabilities and persecutions incident to the profession of faith in Christ. And in these facts, before him, the Apostle finds ground for the assurance that his message had been " not in word only, but in power and in the Holy Spirit."

For the acceptance of this ideal and the partial fulfil-ment of it was not due to the adoption of a new law or code for the regulation of life. The Christian had a law, in the sense that he knew what was required of him ; but it was no external code ; it was the law, the regulative influence, of the Spirit, who was the source of the life he lived in Christ Jesus (Rom. viii. 2). The effect of it was to emancipate him from any system of positive law ; and at the same time the same Spirit was at work to do in him and through him the things that " the law could not do." For the Spirit was recognised as the source of those inward conditions realised by the believer alone, the " love, joy, peace," and also as the source of those ethical qualities and tempers which distinguished the internal relations of the new community, the " long-temperedness, kindness, goodness."

But these things again had been characteristic of the Christ in the days of His flesh (2 Cor. x. 1), and they were found developed within the Koinonia established by His Spirit. The new life, the life of the " new man," had transcendence and a divine quality secured to it by its being " in the Spirit " ; its norm and goal were set for it by its being " in Christ " ; it discovered the experimental confirmation of its reality and the pledge of its perfection in the ethical power and progress generated within the Koinonia.

The immediate and essential result of Pentecost was the creation of this Koinonia : "a community of sacred love which frees humanity from all limitations of natural egotism." The primary work of the Spirit had been to sweep away or to submerge diffinities, to combine men and women of many different types into this Divine Fellowship, which became in turn the organ of the same Spirit in deepening the knowledge of God and in purifying and ennobling the character of those who were at once partakers in the Fellowship and contributors to its life.

FURTHER RESULTS : GIFTS AND POWERS

We need not extend our survey of what happened at Pentecost far beyond the early days before we meet evidence of another phenomenon which should not be overlooked. The "life" which pulsed through the Body and its members was not life of a kind which had to do only with the world to come ; and it showed its presence and its energy in the rapid differentiation of functions within the community, functions which ministered to its own well-being and to its extension in the world. The Koinonia displays marked capacity both for analysis and for synthesis.

Its power of synthesis is seen in the real coalescence

of the several groups in which the Koinonia was successively embodied. They flowed together spontaneously,
with the result that there emerged the consciousness of
a catholic Koinonia. They stretched out hands to one
another, hands containing that "collection" for the
poor Christians at Jerusalem which Paul valued so
highly as the symbol of this all-including unity (1 Cor.
xvi. 1, etc.). No official "organ of unity" was yet
called for ; the connective tissue which held this larger
Fellowship together was still ἀγάπη or Love.

And the Koinonia showed the power of analysis. It
recognised and rejoiced in that differentiation of functions
—"diversities of operations," Paul calls it—which also
was the work of the Spirit. "Apostles," "evangelists,"
"prophets," "pastors and teachers," "workers of
miracles," "healers," "helpers," "administrators,"
"speakers in tongues," "discerners of spirits," "inter-
preters of tongues"—even that list does not exhaust
the varieties of talents, with corresponding varieties of
service, which were recognised within the primitive
community. These highly differentiated powers are
described as "set in the Church" by God, or as "given"
to the Church by the ascended Lord, or as grace-
workings of the Spirit. It will not be supposed, however, that in the case of any of these powers the gift
was an entirely new thing in the individual who received
it, a pure addition to faculties which were otherwise
without it. It was the doing and gift of God ; but,
looked at from another standpoint, it was in fact the
quickening, at the touch of the Spirit, of powers that
were already there, but dormant, the sudden release
of faculties that had lain below the "threshold" of
consciousness.

The purpose and function of all these gifts and
powers was "the upbuilding of the Body of Christ."
Devotion to Him, in which the whole experience started,
was translated into devotion to the highest interests,
whether intensive or extensive, of the Koinonia. And

in the impulse of self-communication, the realisation of the life, and service of the needs, of others, was found the secret of the intensification of individual life.[1] The nascent Church discovered the truth of its Master's teaching : " He that hateth his life in this world shall keep it unto life eternal."

Organisation followed. The question has been raised and copiously discussed whether the organisation was "from above" or "from below." It was neither ; it was from within. It arose within the sacred Body through the operation of powers belonging to it as the Body of Christ. "The body secreted the skeleton." The Fellowship displayed powers of selection and co-ordination. Tested by the one criterion, to what degree does it edify? the various gifts and powers were arranged in order of value. Sane judgement of spiritual values was one of the functions of the Fellowship. Some of those at the lower end of the scale, such as speaking with tongues, dropped out. They "failed," or "ceased," because they were of little value to the community.

This is illuminative not only of the power of the Spirit to enable men to discern proportionate values, but also of the true "end" or purpose of the gifts. That was not immediately, at any rate, the salvation, sanctification, or perfection of the individual, but the growth, purification of the community, and intensification of its life. The Apostle's language in Eph. iv. 12 is no illustration of the contrary. The "perfecting of the saints" (A.V.) means the knitting together of God's people, the continuous repairing of the fabric of the Body. Saintliness, according to the New Testament conception of it, is a social phenomenon. An isolated or individual "saint" would have appeared to its writers as little less than a contradiction in terms. And as personality has been well defined as " capacity for fellowship," so the society which educes and educates that capacity is at the same time the strongest force in

---

[1] Cf. A. S. Pringle-Pattison, *The Idea of God*, p. 308.

the development of personality. So far is it from being true that the New Testament, or any of the voices which speak to us through it, urges us to "save our own souls," that it preaches consistently and insistently that the way to self-realisation is found in that denial of self which is implied in and consecrated by the Fellowship.

By the use of these gifts, and in the exercise of these powers of selection and co-ordination, the Fellowship proceeded to develop an organisation, "in its growth taking to itself such outward form as it needed for its inward life." [1] There is no evidence in the New Testament that any particular form, Congregational, Presbyterian, or Episcopal, had been prescribed for it, or that any single form is necessary either for its existence or its well-being. In the earliest stage or stages which we can detect the organisation was fluid or flexible. Some of the factors in it which at the first were most highly esteemed either disappeared (like the Apostles) or even fell into disrepute (like the Prophets). The shaping of the nascent organisation was guided from the first by analogies which were already familiar —analogies of the family, the village community, the voluntary association ; at a subsequent period by the ancient institutions of Judaism (as in the threefold ministry), and then by the administrative forms of the Empire (as in the diocesan organisation).

But during "the high tides of the Spirit" it is evident that the community was conscious of the abiding possibility that new forms of service and of capacity for it might at any time emerge ; and further, that it was conscious of its own inherent right to recognise, adjust, or, if need be, dispense with any such form. For was it not the "Fellowship of the Spirit"? And "where the Spirit of the Lord is, there is liberty."

[1] J. L. Paton in *Cambridge Essays on Education*, p. 9.

What a close Examination shows to have been the Situation : a Modern Pentecost

What happened at Pentecost provides the classical illustration of what happens at the "coming" of the Holy Spirit. Christendom has not been without experience of such coming in a striking measure at different periods and in many parts of the world. But the Church has never ceased to pray that the Spirit of Christ may be given to it with a fulness hitherto unknown, that His presence may be realised on a scale such as the world has never yet seen. It may be worth while to consider what, in the light of the classical instance, we might expect to happen if these prayers were answered.

(1) The manner and the effect of His coming would certainly be stated in different terms from those familiar to us from the New Testament. There, as we have found, the experience is described, as is only natural, in terms of that conception of spirit which prevailed at the time. If that conception was akin to that of physical, though invisible, forces, such as air, wind, breath, carrying the suggestion of fluid or infinitely divided matter, it was inevitable that the experience should clothe itself in such language as we find. The Spirit "came upon them," was "poured out," "shed forth"; it "entered" into men as though from without; and its influence was regarded as impelling men as though by an external force (Rom. viii. 14; cf. 1 Cor. xii. 2). But it would make no difference to the reality of the experience if it proved natural to us to describe it in quite other terms, in terms derived not from the physical, but from the psychical nature of man.

For us spirit represents the subtlest element in personality, that which alone, and then only in favourable circumstances, can open communication between one personality and another. We ascribe to it in general "that indefinitely penetrative and penetrable quality, that power of embracing and stimulating other minds, which we know, from daily experience, constitutes the very character, actuation, and worth of our own spirit." [1] The Spirit " searches the depths of human personality " ; by it God penetrates all the outer envelopes of our individual being, and touches our spirit. And they are kin one to another, so that in what follows it is hard to distinguish what arrives from God from what arises from the subconscious self of man. And the experience would be not less truly due to the action (or arrival) of the Divine Spirit although what the New Testament describes as " the gifts " or " the power " of the Spirit were to be recognised as what had been dormant capabilities or unemployed determinations of the human self. Michael Angelo in his " Creation of Adam " has shown us the complete man vitalised into possession of all his powers by the touch of " the finger of God."

(2) The coming of the Spirit is to be looked for rather by a group than by an individual, unless it be at the moment when the individual merges himself in the group. It would be a group, or a community gathered round Jesus Christ as a centre, to whom they give the absolute value that belongs only to the Divine. For then all other values would be a part of this, or else subordinate to it. Stated in Scripture language they would " sanctify Christ in their hearts as Lord," and be seeking His Kingdom before all else. That is to say, the personal object of their devotion would be felt to include all social values which make for the true happiness of mankind ; and for the sake of these they would be prepared to sacrifice all other values. So that to this devotion, simple in its direction, yet complex in its grasp, would be subordinated every other interest, whether personal or corporate, ecclesiastical or social. Christ would be " all in all," because He is all that has eternal value.

[1] Von Hügel, *Eternal Life*, p. 229.

(3) The first result of the coming of the Spirit would be seen in the removal of diffinities. Christ being the centre, the centripetal forces would be found to exceed the centrifugal. The group, whether small or large, would discover its power to assimilate individuals or other groups which, while spiritually akin to it, were separated from it by differences of taste, social standing, or intellectual outlook. The common relation to a universal would outweigh all divisive relations to particulars.

A further result would be "life, more life," manifesting itself in a great enhancement of powers already operative, but also in the uprush of others which had been dormant below the threshold. We should see an overmastering sense of brotherhood (ἀγαπή), a serenity of mind and temper (εἰρήνη), and a restoration of religious joy such as Paul noted as the fruit of the Spirit ; and accompanying these a marked increase of qualities whose social value we have been inclined to under-estimate—long-temperedness, kindness, goodness, as well as of others the world has always valued —honour, considerateness, self-control.

But, judging by the analogy of Pentecost, we should have to be prepared also for consequences that might be described as revolutionary, whether in thought or in organisation. The Spirit is sovereign where He dwells, though His witness to the individual has always to be checked by His witness to the community. Even the doctrine of private property went up in that flame. Even the Temple and the system it stood for became an irrelevance. To pray for the coming of the Spirit with understanding of what His coming would mean, and "with faith nothing wavering," is indeed a great achievement. But the answer to such a prayer is prompt and decisive of all the supreme issues of life.

ADDITIONAL NOTE

The possibility of stages or of phases in the significance attached to the " Eucharist " within the New Testament itself is suggested by a careful comparison of the passages in 1 Cor. x. and xi. To the former belong the description of the rite as " breaking the loaf" (Acts, Didaché), the emphasis on breaking or blessing apart from partaking, and absence of allusion to the death of Christ. Of this stage we find the pure type in the very significant scene at Emmaus (Luke xxiv. 30), " He took the loaf and pronounced the blessing and brake and gave to them." And, as they afterwards related, " He was known to them in the breaking of the loaf."

This surely points to the fact that the disciples had been accustomed to see their Master act indeed as a Jewish house-father, and yet in some striking and memorable way peculiar to Himself, and probably to the fact that in His teaching He had explained the symbolism of the loaf. If they had been led to regard it as a symbol at once of their unity and of their dependence for spiritual nourishment (John vi. 33) on Him who made and kept them one, the subsequent history of the rite would be clear.

Meaning was given to the wine as well as to the loaf when (? through the teaching of Paul) emphasis came to be placed on the Lord's sacrificial death and the shedding of His blood. The same motive affecting the significance of the loaf would account for the successive stages τὸ ὑπὲρ ὑμῶν (Paul, according to best MSS.)—τὸ ὑπὲρ ὑμῶν διδόμενον (Luke)—τὸ ὑπὲρ ὑμῶν κλώμενον (Paul, T.R.).

In any case it seems clear that no interpretation of the rite can be true to its origin which fails to do justice to its social implication as a Sacrament of the spiritual oneness of those who are " one Body " in Christ.

V

THE PSYCHOLOGY OF GRACE:
HOW GOD HELPS

BY

C. W. EMMET, B.D.

VICAR OF WEST HENDRED
EXAMINING CHAPLAIN TO THE BISHOP OF OXFORD
AUTHOR OF "THE ESCHATOLOGICAL QUESTION IN THE GOSPELS," "THE EPISTLE TO THE
GALATIANS" (READER'S COMMENTARY), "CONSCIENCE, CREEDS, AND CRITICS," ETC.

ANALYSIS

INTRODUCTION.—The relation of personalities as seen in the conductor and his orchestra, the teacher and his pupils. The influence of the Spirit of God on man is of the same nature ; this influence is grace, which is not a semi-physical force, *sui generis.*

THE EUCHARIST AS A MEANS OF GRACE.—This point of view applied to the Eucharist. The "special" presence of Christ psychologically considered ; the words, the acts, the elements. True and false symbolism. The corporate aspect of the Eucharist. The minister ; his "unworthiness." The place of ritual.

NATURE AND GRACE.—The New Testament usage. The contrast not equivalent (*a*) to that between evil and good ; (*b*) to that between a lower and a higher type of goodness. All goodness due to the grace of God ; His constant action on man. Man's recognition of what is always there. The difference which comes with conscious fellowship with God (the catastrophic element in conversion). But grace not to be confined to its highest manifestations.

GRACE AND FREE-WILL.—Disputes as to various kinds of grace ; based on false assumptions as to its nature. The psychological parallel in human experience of the "I" and the "not I."

GRACE AS GOD'S UNDESERVED FAVOUR.—The legalistic method of approach. Is there a "contract" between God and man, and does He go beyond it ? The relation of love, as known in actual life, transcends such conceptions.

CONCLUSION.—Summary. Reality of communion not dependent on emotional thrill. The test and result in life.

THE PSYCHOLOGY OF GRACE:
HOW GOD HELPS

ALL who have any appreciation of music, even though they may be without technical knowledge of the subject, realise something of the work and function of a great conductor. It is not his business simply to correct false notes and secure uniformity of time and rhythm. He impresses on the performers his own conception of the music, an insight into the depths of its meaning which they would never have had if left to themselves. He also gives to them a power of expressing this meaning in a way they could not have done without him. He does this partly by word and gesture, but also by a more subtle influence which it is not easy to analyse or explain. We sometimes call it vaguely personal magnetism, but no one knows precisely what it is or how it works. It is a kind of telepathy, a direct influence of mind upon mind, bringing with it a real communion or intermingling of spirits.

It is to be noted that, though we may speak rightly of the spirit of the conductor entering into the members of the orchestra, though that spirit is absorbed by them so that their own ideas become subordinate to his, yet in the end it is they, each one individually, who execute the several parts. By the contact of his own richer personality with theirs he calls into being hidden potentialities which would otherwise have remained unrealised. They must have the necessary musical knowledge and power of execution, though he may raise these to heights of which they were quite unconscious. They must have also the artistic sense which enables them to penetrate into the subtlest meaning of the symphony, once contact with him has evoked this sense and discovered to them that meaning which had been beyond the range of their former understanding. It is the richer personality which by its influence elicits the latent or subconscious powers of the self; the result is an enhancement of the personality. It is "I, yet not I," but also it is "I myself through that which is not I." The violinist plays his part himself; he uses his own skill and powers, but these would never have reached so high a pitch without the influence from outside; this influence is a real and necessary factor.

The same law may be observed in other fields. It is seen in the general relation of teacher and pupil. You have the pupil plodding along doggedly and conscientiously, but making no startling progress and showing no unusual powers, and once more there comes the teacher with the mysterious gift of personality. A new thing happens; under the fresh influence the learner develops unsuspected powers of understanding and expression. He can do things when in touch with the new master which he could not do before; inspired achievement takes the place of mediocrity. Once more we may say that the spirit of the teacher enters into the spirit of the pupil, but still it is his own self which works, the old self raised to a higher plane.[1]

When we pass to the sphere of moral goodness we find exactly the same principle at work. It is a commonplace, confirmed by all experience, that the chief factor in moral achievement is personal influence. It works by way of word and example, and it is for

[1] We might illustrate further from the relation of the psychotherapist to his patient; see pp. 71 ff.

this reason that we insist on the value of reading the exploits and the life-story of good men and women. But it works most powerfully through personal contact. The presence of a good man or woman with the gift of a sympathetic personality is admittedly the greatest human force in developing character. This gift is found in very varying degrees. There are some whose lives seem to be lived on a high level, yet they do not attract or influence. On the contrary, their presence by a kind of instinctive reaction fills us with an unreasoning desire to be as wicked as possible. Certain teachers notoriously have this effect upon many of their children ; they have neither the charm of goodness nor the spell of personality. Others, whose lives may sometimes be more open to obvious criticism, have it to a marked degree. To be with them is the safeguard against sin and the inducement to goodness.[1] Once more there is a blending of spirit with spirit, but the self of the one who is influenced remains his own self, discovering unrealised capacities of moral greatness and hidden depths of character.

It will be generally agreed that this gift of evoking such latent capacities is seen at its highest in Christ. It meets us on every page of the Gospels. Men absorbed in their business, like Levi or Zacchæus, the outcast and abandoned, of whom all despaired and who had come to despair of themselves, the very convict at the point of death, find in personal contact with Him a new love of goodness and a new power of realising it. But the experience of Christianity has been that the possibility of such personal contact, with all that it implies, did not cease with the death of Jesus. The conviction of the reality of intercourse with Him and of the incalculable results of that intercourse runs through the whole of the New Testament. It is the centre of what

---

[1] It need hardly be added that an evil personality is equally the greatest force in the opposite direction. In the career of a Rasputin we have such a personality influencing in the most extraordinary way many of those who come within its orbit and degrading them to its own level.

is called the "mysticism" of St. Paul and St. John. Under varying forms of expression Christians of all ages have found that they can come into personal touch with God and with Christ. His Spirit dwells in them ; they are "in Him" and "He in them"; their own personality is purified and enhanced. They can do new things ; it is they who do them through God who worketh in them.

The whole process is personal, resting on the contact between the human spirit and the divine, and the argument of this paper is that this is always and solely what we mean, or ought to mean, by grace. Grace is simply the result of contact of man's personality, or spirit, with God's.[1] Personality has been defined as "capacity for fellowship,"[2] and it only discovers its full capacities in that fellowship which is the knowledge of God and of Jesus Christ whom He has sent.

It is not suggested that this is a novel conception. It has, indeed, always been the underlying experience of Christianity, and very often an important element in its teaching. But it has been confused and overlaid by artificial ideas of grace.[3] Grace has been conceived of as an external, semi-physical "something" which comes into some souls at certain times and under certain conditions, much like an electric current.[4] It is a force infused, a drug prescribed to counteract the microbe of sin, something which can be taken in quantities and at regular intervals, and which has its special channels and means.

Further, it is regarded as something *sui generis*.

[1] For our present purpose it is not very important whether we think of this as contact with God, Christ, or the Holy Spirit.

[2] J. L. Paton in *Cambridge Essays on Education*, p. 8.

[3] See detached note A on "The New Testament Conception of Grace."

[4] "Disregard of the fact of moral personality, as though religion could be passed into the soul like a stream of electricity, is invariably caused by or causes the thought of grace as a secret Divine energy, due solely to omnipotence, and acting on the human will with irresistible pressure—a quasi-physical force, stored within the Church, and applied to the soul-substance in its subconscious depths" (H. R. Mackintosh, *Enc. of Religion and Ethics, s.v.* "Grace"). The companion article, "Grace, Doctrine of (Roman Catholic)," affords abundant illustrations of this way of regarding grace.

The divine grace is not in line with ordinary human
experience. The illustrations we have been considering
would be admitted only as distant analogies of the way
in which grace may come. But our contention is that
they are more than analogies ; they are examples on a
lower scale of what actually happens when we come
into touch with the Divine Spirit. Grace is nothing
but the result of such contact ; it comes from the intercourse of person with person. " The means of grace "
are simply ways of getting into personal relation with
God. We have been almost afraid of this immediate
relation between ourselves and Him, and have substituted for the idea of the direct action of the Spirit,
which we find in the New Testament, the idea of grace
as a separate force, much as later Judaism interposed its
intermediaries between man and God. The substitution
has been helped by the external and legal analogies,
dear to the Latin mind, which attached themselves to
the word *gratia*.[1] It would no doubt be pedantic to
refuse ever to speak of grace as a force, or to banish the
familiar metaphors of the heavenly reservoir, and of pipes
and channels, which suggest that grace is conveyed to
the soul like a supernatural water.[2] But it is important
that such ways of speaking should not be central, and
that we should not press them too far. The fundamental idea is that grace is God Himself (or Christ, or
the Spirit) working in and influencing the soul, just as

[1] See detached note B.
[2] It is worth noting that these metaphors generally go back to the obscure, probably textually corrupt, apocalyptic picture of the candlestick, the pipes, and the
olive trees in Zech. iv. ; see Driver's notes on the passage in the *Century Bible*. As
is shown in note A (p. 193) phrases such as "means of grace" are not found in the
New Testament. It may be remarked that in the early days of mesmerism and
hypnotism, magnetism was also thought of as a mysterious invisible fluid, passing
from one body or mind to another, and all kinds of experiments were made to
discover the most effective means of conveying it. See, *e.g.*, the description of
Mesmer's famous *baquet*, a large trough filled with glass and iron filings and bottles
immersed in water, round which the patients to be influenced sat connected with
cords and holding one another's hands (quoted in G. B. Cutten's *Three Thousand
Years of Mental Healing*, p. 255). This false conception led to all kinds of
mistakes, and it is now realised that all the phenomena of hypnotism and suggestion
depend on the direct influence of mind upon mind (see above, p. 77).

one great personality influences another, though far more effectively and consistently.

This view must not, of course, be interpreted as implying that God is thought of as merely one personality among many, greater, but essentially on the same level. He is rather the all-pervading, the sole possessor of full and complete personality, the underlying reality of every human personality : from His all others are derived ; apart from His they are imperfect. But none the less we are justified in arguing from what we know of the relation of human personalities to one another to the relation of this Personality to ourselves, just because personality, incomplete though it is, is the greatest thing we know, that of which we have the highest and most direct experience. The mechanical conception of grace is based on something lower than personal influence as seen at its best between man and man ; much less can it do justice to what happens between man and God.

The Eucharist as a Means of Grace

It is fairly obvious that these principles apply to such " means of grace " as prayer, meditation, and the reading of the Bible ; they are all methods by which the soul can come into direct contact with God. But it may be useful to consider at some length what light they throw on our conception of the Holy Communion. It will be agreed by different schools of thought that, in spite of differences of theory, the essence of the Eucharist lies in its power of bringing us into touch with a personal Christ. This is, in fact, the underlying idea of the " real presence," apart from theories as to the effect of consecration on the elements, and so forth. The belief is in its way as strong in Nonconformist celebrations of the rite as it is in circles which hold the doctrine of transubstantiation, or something like it. In such celebrations the favourite passages for reading

are just those which speak of this " real presence " of
the Lord, the appearances in the Upper Room, the walk
to Emmaus, or the promise " where two or three are
gathered together in my name, there am I in the midst
of them."   Now there are, of course, obvious difficulties
directly we come to speak of the special presence of an
immanent Spirit, present everywhere.   It is best to
approach the question from the point of view of man's
realisation of that presence, a realisation which, as
a matter of experience, does admit of degree and
difference.   In the words of Dr. Illingworth,[1] " wherever an omnipresent God is specially realised, He
specially is."   " A Being who is omnipresent is,
vi termini, present at all times and in all places.
When, therefore, He is recognised at a particular time
or place, the recognition is not imaginary but real.
He is there and causes His own recognition, or reveals
Himself."   Such recognition must depend on man's
expectancy and receptivity, his faith.   Why, then, is
there a special presence of Christ, or a special
recognition of His universal presence, in the Holy
Communion ?   Simply because the whole rite is
charged with the associations of His personality.
The words, the elements, the acts, carry us back
directly to the supreme crisis of His life.   No one can
be present at the rite with a serious purpose without
thinking vividly of Him.   And, putting aside the
question as to how the case may stand with departed
friends, we are concerned here, not with one who is
dead and gone, but with One who is alive and spiritually
present.   To think earnestly and lovingly of Him is to
realise His presence, to be with Him, to open the heart
to all the influence which comes from contact with His
Spirit, to be in Him and He in us.   All this is not
metaphor, but experience, widespread and in direct line
with similar, though lower, experiences which come from
intercourse with human personalities.   Let it not be

[1] *Divine Immanence*, pp. xv, 132.

supposed that such a view is purely "subjective," that it is a case of faith creating its object. The whole point is that there is something, or rather Someone, really there. Faith, or the receptive mind, under the influence of the associations of the rite, realises and appropriates to itself the Presence which is there independently, which is striving to reveal itself.

We can see at once from this point of view why the words of institution, the bread and the wine, and the special acts of consecration, are "necessary" to the Eucharist. It is not because the gift is a mysterious force, which by a special divine *fiat* can only come through certain *media*, much as electricity must have its proper conductor, wire and not glass. Nor is it that it has been decreed that "something happens" if the proper words are used by the proper man. It is because these words, these elements, these acts, and no others, are instinct and alive with the personality of Jesus. Rice and milk in themselves might be the symbols of a meal of communion with the Deity, and of the worshippers with one another ; in some countries they would be the most natural symbols. But they would be arbitrary and artificial, and therefore psychologically ineffective, symbols of communion with Christ ; they are not charged with the associations of His personality, and therefore they would not be, to the same extent as the bread and wine, effective signs or means of fellowship with Him.

We notice further that, even before they attached to themselves these particular associations, bread and wine had a natural symbolism of their own, whether they were chosen by Christ for this reason or not. Not only are they the simplest, the most universal, types of food and drink, and therefore of spiritual nourishment and growth, these latter being themselves natural descriptions of the enriching of the soul which comes from personal intercourse with a greater personality ; but they also speak directly of the crushing of the separate grains and grapes, of their gathering together into one, so that they become through death the means of life. The very colour of the wine suggests the blood poured out. And so they are charged with the associations of the death and new life of Christ ; they " are " His broken Body and poured-out Blood, and the means by which, according to psychological law, His Spirit of sacrifice and service enters into us and calls out the same hidden qualities in our own spirits.

It may also be added that wine which maketh glad the heart of man suggests the joy of fellowship. It is not thought of as the indulgence of the isolated and selfish individual, but is associated with the joyful festivals of reunion and of gathering of friends. Christ, at the institution of the Eucharist, looked forward to drinking it with those He loved at the Messianic Feast in the Kingdom of God. This symbolism has its bearing on the corporate aspect of the rite, on which something will be said later on.

If, then, symbols are a means of grace, it is necessary to draw a distinction between true and false symbolism, between the kind of associations which are rational and psychologically valuable, and those which are merely magical and superstitious. In a true symbolism the connection between the symbol and the thing symbolised is natural and appropriate, not arbitrary and artificial, as in the crude analogies often drawn by primitive religions. Associations which are to be psychologically sound must go back to fact, not to fancy. If then, as we hold, the Eucharist does mediate a real communion with a present Christ, on account of its symbolism and associations, why should not a relic, or a fragment of the true cross, do the same ? Here there are two things to be said. (1) In fact relics have not as a rule been valued simply from their associations, as means of opening the heart of the worshipper to the divine presence. They have been regarded as themselves possessing a quasi-magical virtue, property, or *mana*, working their cure or imparting merit in themselves, through their inherent sanctity. Hence there has often been a readiness to venerate relics which are trivial, ludicrous, and even disgusting. No normally - minded mother would treasure the thigh-bone of her son or the parings of his toe-nails as a means of inducing loving thoughts of him. Saintly relics of this type can only be valued as wonder-working charms ; and a relic regarded as a charm can only lead the mind away from the true grace of God. (2) If a fragment of the Cross or a visit to Calvary is treated simply as a means of bringing vividly before the mind the love of Christ through its associations, it is, to some at least, psychologically effective and legitimate ; it does really help to communion with Him. But there must be reasonable ground for believing that the association rests on fact—that the site is the true site of the event commemorated, that the treasured piece of wood did actually form part of the Cross. A mother will not find consolation in visiting the supposed grave of her soldier-son in France if she learns that there is no evidence that he was in fact buried there. It may be argued that in all such cases it is better to leave people undisturbed in their happy belief. So long as the simple peasant *thinks* the relic genuine, it will have the same effect on him psychologically as if it were so. There may no doubt be special cases in private life, and perhaps also in religion, where it would be cruel to disabuse the trusting mind of some valued fancied association, but in the long run any such method of pious fraud brings its own nemesis. In the first place people do, and must in the end, find out, and indignation against those responsible for deceiving them sometimes has very far-reaching consequences. Secondly, we are looking at these things as means of coming into personal touch with God. Truth, which implies reverence for fact, and even for what may seem

trivial fact, is part of the very being of God, and therefore any cynical or easy-going indifference to truth is
itself an obstacle to real fellowship with Him, an obstacle
which will far outweigh any temporary gain brought by
associations believed in in spite of evidence. Neither
deceiver nor those who willingly allow themselves to
be deceived can under such conditions enter into full
communion with the God of truth. When, then, we
are told that, if we approach the Sacraments and methods
of worship from the side of psychology, we must leave
ignorance and superstition untouched on the ground
that they too work well, our reply must be that in the
long run they do not work well, nor can they ever do
so in a universe in which reverence for truth is a fundamental principle.

To return to the Eucharist, we may, from the point
of view we are testing, understand something of its
corporate aspect. We recall the parallel of the conductor and his orchestra. Just because, and in so far
as, the players are a group of men actuated by the
same purpose, the influence of his personality on theirs
is intensified. There is a common telepathic pull
which increases the responsiveness of each ; they are
knit not only to him but to one another by sharing
the same spirit. So it is in the Holy Communion and
in all common worship. While, as with the single pupil
and his teacher, there is a true contact between the
individual soul and God, *solus cum solo*, the response of
the human spirit to the divine, the intermingling of
the two, reaches its highest point when two or three,
or, better still, a great multitude, are gathered together
under the inspiration of a single purpose. Grace is
indeed no private privilege, nor is salvation ever purely
individual. Neither they without us, nor we without
them, can be made perfect. In the actual thought and
practice of the Church this conception of the fellowship
of grace and salvation has often been forgotten, and
nowhere more so than in the Eucharist. We have

been satisfied with the multiplication of a number of
separate celebrations, attended by mere fractions of the
faithful, in which each one " makes his communion."
We shall never realise the full possibilities of the rite
till we somehow make it the " fellowship meal " at
least of the whole parish.[1]   Such a fellowship is in no
sense a merely " human " brotherhood ; it is essentially
mediated by the common sharing of the spirit of Christ.
It is both a fact of psychology and also one of the
deepest truths of Christian ethics that our own joy in
receiving that Spirit is intensified by the knowledge
that others are receiving it too, and that our very power
of response is increased by their response.   Even
though the command " Drink ye *all* of this " is only
recorded in the First Gospel,[2] it undoubtedly expresses
the mind of Christ.

Here we may find the solution to a problem on
which our psychological method may seem at first sight
to throw little light.   Why, on these lines, should not
the Eucharist be celebrated by any private individual
who cares to do so ?   Why, by fairly general consent
of the Christian instinct, even outside circles which hold
the doctrine of Apostolic Succession, is the chief part in
the celebration confined to duly ordained ministers ?
It is not because in any quasi-magical sense this is the
condition of something coming into the elements or
the soul, but because in the rite the minister stands
both for Christ and the Church.   It is his function to
bring to the worshippers the sense of the present personality of Christ.   And, as we have seen, the Holy
Communion is essentially corporate.   Each Eucharist
expresses ideally the desire of the whole Church *as a
society*, as the Body of Christ, to come into communion
with its Head.   From both points of view the honour
of acting as the leader in such a rite cannot normally

---

[1] A fuller discussion of this point will be found in my paper " Mattins and Holy
Communion " in *Ideals of Common Prayer* (No. 1 of *Tracts on Common Prayer*, edited
by Dr. Sanday).

[2] St. Mark has " they *all* drank of it."

be taken to himself by any man ; he must be duly
authorised as the representative of the Church.[1]   If we
may adapt our initial illustration, not only do the
members of the orchestra enter into the spirit of the
conductor ; he also mediates to them the mind, the
personality, of the composer.   So all priesthood,
whether exercised in rite or in teaching, is a link
between the soul and God.   The true priest will have
the spirit of Christ, as the conductor must have the
spirit of Beethoven.

There have been long debates as to whether the
unworthiness of the minister "invalidates" the Sacraments, and the Church, faced with the appalling
consequences of an affirmative answer, has realised that
their objective validity cannot be regarded as depending
on so uncertain a factor as the moral condition and
sincerity of the officiant.   And just because, as we insist,
Christ is always there, ready to enter into any heart
which opens itself to the Presence, we shall certainly
agree that His coming is not made impossible by the
sin of the priest or of any part of the congregation.
But we have been too readily satisfied with a technical
answer which is largely based on the idea of grace,
and especially sacramental grace, as a special force
generated under certain conditions.   For though the
coming is not made impossible by any sin except the
sin of the worshipper himself, it is made more difficult.
Psychologically the worshipper cannot respond so
readily if he is conscious that the rite which should be
instinct with the personality of Christ is performed by
one whose whole life is un-Christlike, or with a careless
indifference which gives the lie to its spiritual meaning.
If by a correct ritual we understand simply the exact
repetition of a ceremony according to certain traditional

[1] We need not here enter into the question whether in fact only episcopally
ordained ministers can be regarded as such representatives, but it may be noted that
in recent discussions as to the validity of orders more and more stress has come to
be laid, not on the minister as possessing a special power to do certain things, but on
his being the representative of the Church, whatever the conception of the Church,
or the view taken of the proper method of his appointment.

and more or less mechanical rules, we shall not attach much importance to it.   But every public action, whether religious or civil, must gather round itself some ritual ; the purpose of such ritual should be to bring out the underlying meaning in whatever way is found to be most effective psychologically, that is to say in the impression conveyed to the mind of those present.   In such a ritual, while due weight is given to the inherited traditions and experience of the past, there should be room for variations according to the genuine and spontaneous mood of the moment ; it must be alive.   But a fixed outline is valuable just because we can none of us depend on always being at our best. Every minister in every denomination must sometimes find himself conducting a service when from physical or other causes he is not completely " in the mood." If his general method, whether of prayer or celebrating, is deliberately formed on principles of recollectedness and reverence, this disciplined habit will not altogether fail, even at seasons of deadness.   The habitual aware- ness of the presence of God will persist in the sub- consciousness even when the actual consciousness is faint for the moment.   And both the minister and the worshipper will at such times be safeguarded by a ritual which is not simply an unthinking and mechanical imitation of the past, but represents the predominant instinct of a genuine reverence.   There can be little doubt that clergy of all denominations need to pay far more attention than they sometimes do to the psycho- logical effect of their method of conducting divine service.   Revision of the text of the Prayer Book is urgently needed, but the constant complaint of the laity that the clergy do not from the point of view we are considering make the best of the Prayer Book as it stands is not without good ground.   There is food for thought in the remark of a working man after a certain rapid rendering of Mattins that he supposed " the parson was paid by piece-work " ; speed is not

the primary condition of helping the congregation to
feel the presence of God.   In the last resort the minister
will only succeed in doing this in proportion as he trains
himself to feel that presence.   According to the highest
conception of true priesthood the unworthiness of the
minister is by no means irrelevant ; there is a sense in
which he is the mediator between God and man.

The significance of Baptism may be treated very
briefly.[1]   To the adult it both symbolises and, according
to the principles already suggested, it does in fact
psychologically mediate a personal union with Christ.
In the Pauline phrase the convert is baptized into Christ,
or puts on Christ.   In the case of Infant Baptism,
while it is impossible to speak of conscious fellowship,
it does stand for incorporation into the community, or
spiritual atmosphere, in which that fellowship may
subsequently be best realised.   It marks the initial stage
of that personal union which, if the rite is more than
a form, later training and religious experience will
make actual.

NATURE AND GRACE

A familiar phrase in the Anglican Church Catechism
states that we are " by nature born in sin and the
children of wrath " and are in baptism " made the
children of grace."   It rests on a misapplication of
Eph. ii. 3, " we also all once lived in the lusts of our
flesh, doing the desires of the flesh and of the mind,
and were by nature children of wrath."   The last phrase
is a Hebraism, like " sons of disobedience " ; there is
no reference to infancy or to original sin ; St. Paul
" is speaking of actual transgressions," and " by nature
means simply ' in ourselves,' as apart from the divine
purpose of mercy." [2]   In fact the New Testament
writers use the words " nature," " natural," only

[1] It is discussed more fully on pp. 257 ff.
[2] J. A. Robinson, *Epistle to the Ephesians, ad loc.*

occasionally, and when they do, it is in a good, or at least a neutral, sense (Rom. i. 26 f., xi. 21 ff., 1 Cor xi. 14 ; 2 Pet. ii. 12 comes the nearest to a bad sense). In some passages, such as 1 Cor. ii. 14 (" the natural man receiveth not the things of the Spirit of God ") or xv. 44 ff., a different word (" psychic ") is used ; and we do in fact find in St. Paul a sharp contrast between *psyche* and spirit, or between the " flesh " (very nearly equivalent to man as he is) and the spirit, between the unregenerate and the regenerate man. Grace is confined to the latter. It is true that pre-Christian Abraham is the type of faith, but the principle of the working of grace before or outside the Christian Church is not carried further, as it is in the list of heroes of faith in Heb. xi. There is little idea of the presence of grace or faith below the surface even in Judaism, which controversial requirements lead St. Paul to contrast sharply with the Christian dispensation ; such a conception as " that rock was Christ " is quite exceptional. Much less is there any hint of it in the Gentile world ; redemption and the work of grace are confined to the Christian community, understood strictly. It is true that in Rom. ii. we hear of Gentiles doing by nature the works of the law, a conception which it is not easy to harmonise with the standpoint of the rest of the Epistle. For the moment St. Paul is arguing from the point of view of ordinary morality. His object is to establish the responsibility of all before God and the indifference of the law, not to suggest that Gentiles could be " justified " by their good deeds. The whole passage is exceptional and out of keeping with the strict Pauline theory of salvation. In general, though the exact terms are not used, we do find in the technical theology of St. Paul something which corresponds to the sharp opposition between the realms of nature and of grace which, since the time of Augustine, has been part of the common Christian tradition.

In itself this conception is not an easy one, but we

must not make it harder by interpreting the distinction
between nature and grace as equivalent to the distinction between evil and goodness, as though nature were
in itself bad. As we have seen, this is not the teaching
of the New Testament ; it is in fact Manichean rather
than Christian. Nor is it the teaching of Augustine.
" All nature," he says, " in so far as it is nature, is
good ; in so far as it corrupted, it is evil." " The
nature of the devil himself, in so far as it is nature, is
not bad, but perversity makes it bad." [1] According to
his view, sin alone is against nature ; even in our fallen
state all human actions are good in so far as they are
natural. The rebellion of the flesh is due to the
weakness we have earned by sinning, and this does
become a kind of second nature. He also sometimes
treats the natural as the fixed and necessary, opposed
to free-will, *e.g.* natural movements in contrast to
voluntary.

We may, then, reject without qualification the view
that the distinction between nature and grace corresponds to that between evil and good. According to
another view, which is at first sight more reasonable and
has behind it the authority of Augustine, the difference
between the two is the difference between a lower and a
higher kind of goodness, more or less corresponding to
the distinction between natural and revealed religion.
There are, it is held, natural virtues which go a certain
way and are independent of grace. Ordinary temptations can, it is suggested, be resisted by man's natural
strength, but others, and especially sensual temptations,
require the grace of God. " God does not command
impossibilities, but bids you do what you can and ask
for what is beyond your power." [2] Number XIII. of
the Thirty-nine Articles speaks of works—clearly what
the ordinary man would call good works—done before
the grace of God and having the nature of sin. In the

[1] I owe these quotations to T. A. Lacey, *Nature, Miracle, and Sin*, pp. 92, 115.
See Aug. *De Nat. Boni*, 1 ; *De Civ. Dei*, xix. 13.
[2] *De Nat. et Grat.* 43 (quoted by Lacey, *op. cit.* p. 127).

N

phrase wrongly attributed to Augustine, but true to hi s thought, they are *splendida vitia.*[1]

The underlying conception here is that grace is super-natural, in the sense that it does not come to man as man ; it is given to some, not to all. To Augustine grace is expressly not the general providence and benevolence of God ; it is " that by which we are Christians." " It is not nature, but that by which nature is saved."[2] The accepted view since his time has been that supernatural grace was withdrawn at the Fall and restored by Christ.

We ask what bearing our psychological conception of grace as the result of the direct impact of the Divine Personality on the human has on all such distinctions between nature and grace. We cannot believe that God has ever left man alone ; He has been always seeking and drawing him to Himself, establishing that contact between His Spirit and the human spirit which is the essence of religion. Or, looking at it from the other side, man, everywhere and always, is made in the image of God, and has within him something of the divine nature which yearns for fellowship with God, like seeking like by the law of its being. What happened when Christianity came into the world was that the new religion manifested this eternal seeking on God's part in a new way ; it opened to man new possibilities of satisfying his yearning for fellowship.

In the fresh enthusiasm engendered by it, when its experiences were novel and vivid, and when the need of distinguishing it sharply from Judaism and its other competitors in the mystery religions was widely felt, it was natural to emphasise, and even to over-emphasise, the uniqueness of its gift. Christianity, it seemed, had brought into the world and man's life a new power with which the non - Christian had nothing to do. Both St. Paul, and subsequently Augustine and Luther, who have been the main in-fluences in moulding Christian language and thought

[1] See Lacey, *Nature, Miracle, and Sin*, p. 141.   [2] Lacey, *ib.* pp. 128 ff.

on the subjects of redemption and grace, had specially
potent personal experiences of a conversion bringing
with it an entire breach with the past.   But it was
also very soon realised that it was impossible to deny
the existence of goodness or of fellowship with the
Divine outside Christianity.   St. John states, though
he does not develop, the doctrine of the Word, or
Logos, lighting every man who comes into the world.
This aspect is emphasised by Justin and the Apologists.
Accepting the position that salvation, fellowship with
the Father, and real goodness could only come through
Christ, there were two alternatives.   It was possible,
though not reasonable, to deny the reality of such things
outside Christianity, and to ascribe them to demonic
imitation of their only genuine manifestations ; or, on
the other hand, to say boldly that, wherever they
were found, there was Christ, the immanent *Logos*—in
Socrates and Plato, as well as in the Christian convert.
This second alternative was boldly developed by the great
Alexandrians, Clement and Origen.   Though Christian
theology has sometimes ignored it, it has never cast
it aside, however much it may have hesitated to draw
out its full implications.   To us to-day no other view
is possible.   The corollary of the truth "no man
cometh unto the Father but by Me" is that wherever any man in fact finds God there Christ has been
present.   The historic Christ and historical Christianity
become the supreme manifestations of a principle and
power at work in men always ; the Spirit cannot
in the end and in the strict sense be confined to the
Christian dispensation.   The doctrine of uncovenanted
mercies is only the epicycle introduced when the facts
refuse to be squared with the circles postulated by
theory.

It is, however, clear that the distinction between
nature and grace is in some sense central to a good deal
of Christian thought, and we may be sure that there
must be a vital spiritual truth behind it.   We return to

our illustration. We saw how the teacher with the gift of influence and personality does make such a difference to the work of the pupil that the result is, in a true sense, a new thing. He rises from mediocrity, from an uninspired accuracy, to a new stage of achievement. He does so precisely in proportion as he opens himself without reserve to the inspiration of his master. If there is on the side of the pupil any antagonism, conscious or unconscious, if there is any clash of ideals and values, the flow of the new influence is blocked and ineffective. The spirit of the conductor cannot work in a player who insists on his own reading of the music, who refuses to meet him with a complete self-surrender of his own preconceived notions. So with the soul and God. There comes a point where the soul definitely realises the Divine presence and deliberately opens itself to His influence, where it surrenders its own lower and opposing will, and makes its own the higher ideals and values. Here too the result is a new stage of achievement. In place of the dull level of respectable, plodding, average morality, we find a fresh type of character, heroic, self-forgetting, full of charm and attractiveness, bringing to others a sense of the Divine. It is not the imitation of an external code, the painful attempt to live up to a standard of duty imposed from without ; it becomes the spontaneous expression of a life and personality identified with and penetrated by the Divine Personality.

Here then, it might be said, we have after all the old sharp dividing line between nature and grace. Yet still there is a difference, in so far as the old view rests on the assumption that God influences some men and not others. For though, as we are arguing, the way in which God influences man is not essentially different from the way in which we influence one another, there is one important distinction between the two cases. The influence of the great teacher or conductor is a

new thing introduced into the life at a particular stage ;
but the influence of the Spirit of God is not a new factor;
it has been there all the time.   The new thing is that
the soul realises and responds to it in a way it had not
done before.   The main obstacle to such response is
always sin in some form, a self-centredness which shuts
out the divine influence.   This is the underlying truth
of the doctrine that supernatural grace was withdrawn
at the Fall.   Without entering upon the question
whether in fact there has been a breach in man's
spiritual evolution, it is at least clear that sin is the
barrier which blocks the way to a free communion
between man and God.   We see why repentance is
the first stage in opening the way to a high degree
of such communion, and why conversion, the complete
surrender of the self (perhaps better regarded as the
complete dedication of the self), sometimes coming at
a definite crisis, does mark a new relationship to God.
Even from the strictly psychological point of view, sin
needs to be taken very seriously ; it is not an easy
thing to open the soul completely to the divine
influence and indwelling.   At the same time we must
remember that after all God has been there all along,
even in a sense within the soul, unrealised, His influence to a great extent thwarted.   Whatever there has
been of goodness and achievement, however imperfect,
has, so far as it is good, come from Him, from His
grace and presence in the heart.   "Every virtue we
possess and every thought of holiness are His alone."
The Collect, "O God, from whom all holy desires, all
good counsels, and all just works do proceed," cannot
in the last resort be taken as referring only to the
"converted" Christian.   We cannot maintain that
there is a natural goodness which takes man up to a
certain point, and that then supernatural grace comes
in as a new factor.   The difference is in the degree of
man's response to the same divine influence which is
always there.

It is, then, in the degree of this response that we must find the difference between the converted and unconverted, the regenerate and unregenerate man. Facts do not allow us to hold that it corresponds closely to any external distinction between the baptized and unbaptized, the communicant and the non-communicant, or even the Christian and the non-Christian. It is simply that, speaking roughly, each one of us has opened his heart to God or he has not ; he is, or he is not, recognising and striving to live by higher values ; he does, or he does not, bring his will into harmony with God's. But of course in actual experience the distinction is confused and ambiguous. Men are not entirely in the flesh or in the Spirit ; salvation is a process which implies continual struggle, and an ever-increasing identification of the self with God. " Even the man most centred in himself responds to the prompting of some affection and some loyalty every day of his life." [1] Such language is used constantly, even by the strictest of theologians when writing from the ordinary standpoint ; it implies not only that every man has the grace of God, but that, to however small an extent, he uses it.

Our problem, then, is to do justice to the double truth. There is in the coming of the grace of God both the catastrophic element and also the fact of its continuity. On the one hand we need to recognise the startling, sometimes the abrupt, change which marks the breaking down of opposition and the deliberate identification of the human will and purpose with the divine. In this change there may be stages. The soul may have come to range itself on the side of goodness and the grace of God, without recognising it for what it is. There may be a real fellowship with the Spirit which is an unconscious fellowship. On the road to Emmaus the two travellers find themselves in intercourse with a stranger which becomes more and

---

[1] *Competition : a Study in Human Motive*, by John Harvey and others, p. 169.

more intimate as the barriers of despair and reserve are broken down. Even then their hearts burn within them and fresh powers of insight and hope are called into being. Had nothing more happened the experience would have been genuine and fruitful. But it is a greater experience still when their eyes are opened and they know Who is the friend who has been with them all the time. The recognition colours and interprets the earlier experience. Unconscious fellowship with God is neither to be denied nor despised, but conscious fellowship is something more. "To recognise the grace of God, to affirm it, is to be aware of the very scent of God and to be drawn by it the more power-fully because it is known for what it is. The scent of bluebells is stronger and sweeter to us if we know what it is than if we think it comes from a soap factory or is produced in us by some digestive process of our own."[1] It is not always true psychologically that "a rose by any other name will smell as sweet." Even in our sense perceptions we are not passive. What we receive effectively depends on attention, on the deliberate response of our powers of appreciation. The delicate bouquet of the wine will often be missed unless the expectation is sharpened by the knowledge of what is offered to us. Still more in personal intercourse we can only reach the complete intermingling of spirit with spirit when we know the friend or the great personality for what he is. Life becomes a new thing when this awareness of the companion God, known as such, bursts on the soul for the first time, as it may in a hundred different ways. And it is an experience which may be often repeated.

> So even I athirst for His inspiring,
>   I who have talked with Him forget again ;
> Yes, many days with sobs and with desiring
>   Offer to God a patience and a pain ;

---

[1] A. Clutton-Brock, *Studies in Christianity*, p. 105.

Then thro' the mid complaint of my confession,
Then thro' the pang and passion of my prayer,
Leaps with a start the shock of His possession,
Thrills me and touches, and the Lord is there.[1]

" The shock of His possession," the knowledge that
" the Lord is there," the dweller in the innermost of
our being, the source of all our good, is grace at its
highest. It might indeed be argued that we should
keep the term "grace" for what happens when the
touch between the human and the Divine reaches this
stage of conscious awareness, but this would be to
ignore the other side. The phraseology which confines
grace to its supreme manifestations inevitably suggests
that what has gone before is not grace, that whatever of
goodness the soul has reached in the past has come
from some other source. It implies that God has
given or done something which He had not done
previously ; it is not the natural way of saying that
man has opened his heart more completely to that
which has always been there. Side by side with the
catastrophic element we need to insist on the continuity
of God's influence on the soul, on the fact that this
influence is universal, and that it is the one source of
all goodness and achievement, moral, intellectual, and
aesthetic, always and everywhere. Though it is true
that certain kinds of virtues do grow more readily on
Christian soil, they are not altogether peculiar to it,
nor are they generically different in kind to others.
Moral goodness is homogeneous ; we cannot divide it
up into that due to nature and that due to grace,[2] nor
can we hold that there are essentially different types of
divine help and influence, as though humanity outside
the range of Christianity were a vessel propelled by

[1] Myers, *St. Paul.*

[2] In fact much of the goodness which is held to be supernatural and due
specifically to grace is conventional and negative, having little of the heroism, self-
forgetfulness, and charm which are the real marks of the close fellowship of the
human spirit with the Divine. On the other hand, some non-Christian, or Stoic,
virtues lack much which is found in Christianity. But this is not to say that so
far as they are virtues, they come from any other source than the grace of God.

steam, while within its borders the new driving power
of electricity had suddenly come into play.

It is worth quoting some words of Dr. Hort[1] on
the Article "Of Works before Justification," to
which we referred earlier in this section : "The
principle underlying Article XIII. seems to me to be
this, that there are not two totally different modes of
access to God for men, faith for Christians, meritorious
performance for non-Christians. . . . Faith itself . . .
is present in a more or less rudimentary state in every
upward effort and aspiration of men. . . . Practically
the principle of the Article teaches us to regard all the
good there is in the world as what one may call *imperfect
Christianity*, not as something essentially different,
requiring, so to speak, to be dealt with by God in a
wholly different manner." We may doubt whether
this is really what the Article means to say, but it will
certainly be our own position. From our point of view,
indeed, the discussion as to good " works done before the
grace of God " is meaningless. The test of the presence
of grace, *i.e.* of some contact with God, is found in the
fruits. In so far as these are present, we conclude that
grace has been at work and that there has been some
response. We shall really reverse the way of putting
the question. We do not ask whether certain people
are within the range of grace (*e.g.* in the Church), and
if the answer is in the negative, conclude that their
" works," though apparently good, are not so in fact ;
we look at the character, and say that, in so far as this
is good, there must have been some response to grace.[2]

[1] *Life and Letters*, ii. 337 (quoted in full by Gibson, *Thirty-nine Articles*,
p. 422).

[2] An emphatic recognition of this truth is given by Lord Halifax : " ' Without me
ye can do nothing.' Now, what follows from this ? Surely that in whatever
degree we see this Christian life being lived there we may be certain God's grace
has been given, and that as long as any soul faithfully corresponds with the grace
given to it, that soul is living in God's favour, and that as such we have no need to
be disquieted about its spiritual condition." The reference is specifically to members
of different Christian bodies (*The Church Times*, June 21, 1918).

Grace and Free-Will

The pages of Christian theology are full of somewhat repellent technicalities and hoary controversies as to the kinds of grace and its relation to free-will. Echoes of all this are to be heard in the Articles of the Anglican Church and in the Confessions of other Churches. The candidate for Orders still spends much time in attempting to grasp the precise difference between *gratia preveniens* and *cooperans*, *gratia de congruo* and *de condigno*, or between sufficient and efficacious grace. Two quotations will suffice. "Starting from the view that the Fall only involved the loss of the *donum supernaturale* [the supernatural gift], and left man with moral and religious faculties belonging to him by nature, [the schoolmen] taught that the exercise of these faculties was the natural transition to grace, and that a good use of them was the medium of grace, or, in their phraseology, merited it of congruity (*de congruo*). God, they said, was not bound to reward such actions, but it was congruous or fitting that he should. But after grace was received, the work done in dependence on the aid of the Holy Spirit was really good, and this God was bound to reward, crowning His own gifts in man. Such actions deserved grace *de condigno*, and for them God was a debtor." [1]

A Roman Catholic theologian [2] sums up the teaching of Augustine and the Church in this way : "God provided for the fulfilment of His decree of predestination and for the preservation of the freedom of the will, by granting to the unpredestined only sufficient grace, which they were sure always freely to disobey by their own fault, and by providing for the predestined efficacious grace, which they were sure always freely to follow." And then he goes on to explain how it is that a grace which is "really and truly sufficient"

---

[1] Gibson, *Thirty-nine Articles*, p. 419.
[2] E. L. van Becelaere in *Enc. Rel. and Ethics*, s.v. "Grace (Roman Catholic)."

should always be disobeyed, while a grace "infallibly efficacious" yet does not infringe upon the freedom of the will. Readers of Pascal will recall some of the irony of *Les Provinciales* with regard to such conceptions.

It is obvious that all such subtleties presuppose the idea of grace as a force *sui generis*, something sent by God at special times and under special conditions. No doubt the questions they raise are sometimes of real importance, but they will be stated very differently when grace is interpreted in terms of personal influence. This is especially the case with the problem of grace and free-will. In our parallels from human experience we found a blending of personalities, of the pupil with the teacher, the violinist with the conductor. The learner has the sense of being in the grip of a power higher and other than himself, yet it is he who acts, his own personality transformed and enabled by that which has become part of his very self. So it is with man and God : "work out your own salvation, for it is God that worketh in you." But there is no substitution of the divine nature for the human, no depersonalising of man. In the last resort each must save himself, but the self which saves is a different self, a self delivered from the bondage of corruption and transformed by the renewing of the mind through the indwelling Spirit of Christ. No doubt the ultimate philosophical problem remains as to free-will, predestination, God's power and foreknowledge, but it loses much of its sting, and is in fact solved in experience, so soon as we cease to regard grace as a force introduced into the soul *ab extra*, and approach it from the point of view of the relation of personalities to one another.

Grace as God's undeserved Favour

Grace is often defined as the undeserved, the unexpected, favour of God, and the idea of His free love and undeserved mercies is a fundamental element in the religious instinct. But the conception has often been stated in a way which is artificial and repellent. It is held that God as creator is bound to give His creatures a certain degree of help and a certain possibility of happiness hereafter, such a vision and possession of Himself as the natural man can desire and appropriate. But " by a munificent and gratuitous decision "[1] He has gone beyond His bond in sending His Son, in restoring the gift of supernatural grace, and in fitting some men for the supernatural reward of the beatific vision itself. Or, as it would be put by the older Protestant theology, man by the sin which is common to the race deserves hell, but some are saved from this by God's special and unlooked-for grace. It is as though hell and death were the ruling principles of the universe, and other principles of life and salvation had been introduced as an unexpected afterthought. Such statements of the case simply provoke objections in the spirit of Omar's cry, which is not blasphemous but ethical :

> Oh Thou, who didst with pitfall and with gin
> Beset the road I was to wander in,
>   Thou wilt not with Predestined Evil round
> Enmesh, and then impute my fall to Sin !
>
> Oh Thou, who Man of baser Earth didst make,
> And ev'n with Paradise devise the Snake,
>   For all the Sin wherewith the Face of Man
> Is blackened—Man's forgiveness give—and take !

If God has put His children into a world in which as a matter of experience they all inevitably fall, is He not bound to save them ? The fact is that in all such ways of putting the case we are in the grip of cramping and mechanical legal analogies. The conception is of a father who is bound by law to provide a certain minimum of support and protection for his children, but is not bound to risk his life to save them from

---

[1] See *Enc. of Rel. and Ethics, s.v.* " Grace (Roman Catholic)," where this point of view is stated quite clearly.

a burning house. And yet if he is a true father he cannot do otherwise. His act is not an unexpected extra ; it is the necessary manifestation of his character, the inevitable result of the relationship between him and his children. This is not to say that they will take it as a matter of course that they have been saved by their father's devotion and suffering, or that their gratitude will be any the less, but the point is that where the essence of the relationship is love we cannot argue on the basis of strict and limited legal requirements.

We must not, then, split up God's gifts and dealings with men into two classes, saying that some are required by an implied contract between the Father and His children, while others go beyond the minimum and are something added. All He does and gives is the expression of His love, though that love may be more clearly seen in some things than in others. We could not have said *a priori* that this love would go so far as the sharing of man's sufferings, but once this has been shown it is understood to be the inevitable outcome of His essential nature ; He too could do no other. This way of looking at the matter really heightens our adoring love and gratitude first for what He is, and then for what He does. It removes it from the sphere of hard legal analogies to one where the only bond, the only compulsion, is that of mutual love. The Cross and the offer of eternal life are the supreme manifestations of that love, and they reflect back on all the divine dealings with us.

This is the real principle which underlies the great Pauline opposition between faith and works, and the insistence on salvation as the free gift of God. Anything of the nature of a debit and credit account between man and God is as much out of place as it is between father and child, or husband and wife. At our best, and in our noblest relationships, we do not deal with one another on any such basis, nor does God so deal with us, or we with God. "By grace are ye saved," by the unstinted sacrifice and self-giving flowing inevitably from the love which is the essence of the divine nature, just as the devotion of the mother, even unto death, is the inevitable expression of true mother-hood. The child who is saved does not ask in such a case whether he deserved it or not, or whether she could reasonably have omitted the sacrifice. He meets it with a responsive love and a humility which resolves to make himself worthy of it and of her.

Indeed, the best safeguard against the external and legalistic point of view is to realise that grace is not something which God gives; it is God Himself knocking at the door of the soul and admitted into its inmost sanctuary. Think of it as a " gift " which is something other than God, and there is always the danger of self-seeking ; we stumble against that which is the most subtle obstacle to true religion, the tempta-tion to use God for our own purpose, even if the purpose be the salvation of our soul. We must learn to allow God to use us ; it is a greater thing to seek Him for His own sake than to seek the highest of His gifts for our own. When we know that grace is this intimate relation between the soul and Him, the heart is flooded with the self-abandonment and devotion of the lover ; it can no longer think in terms of the market-place or law-court, claiming this as desert, welcoming that as unmerited favour.

Conclusion

We have tried then to look at grace, not as a special force imparted by God to some men, under certain conditions, and at certain times and for certain purposes, but as the enhancement of personality which is the constant result of the proper relation between the divine and the human spirit. We believe that there is in all men, at least unless they have quenched the Spirit, some degree of personal contact with Him, even if it be but partial and unconscious. Every effort after goodness, however faint, implies this and can be ascribed to no other source. The differences in degree are indeed impressive and far-reaching, just as the differences in the standard of character and attainment vary almost beyond measure. These differences depend on the extent to which we let God in, on the closeness of the intercourse between our Spirit and God. Let it be repeated that such a view is not, as is sometimes supposed, a purely "subjective" view of religion, reducing it to a matter of what we think or feel. There seems to be a widespread impression that to offer a psychological explanation of anything is equivalent to treating it as pure imagination; in particular that it reduces the religious experience to auto-suggestion from our "better self." But the psychologist is free to hold that there is Someone there whom we may come to know, a power not ourselves on which we may and must depend. In the last resort the difference between one man and another must turn upon the extent to which he opens himself to the divine influence which is always there, available in its completeness for every child of God. This is indeed true on any view of the nature of grace; even if we think of it under the old picture of the inexhaustible reservoir on which we are to draw, it depends on ourselves how much we draw and how often. Few, if any, will deny that the divine love is all-embracing, and that it is for us to respond to it. "According to your faith so be it done unto you" is the law which Christ lays down as governing the relation of man to God and Himself, and no one will call Christ's doctrine of faith, or St. Paul's, purely subjective.

It is further important to remind ourselves that the reality and closeness of our contact with the Divine Personality does not depend on, or always vary very closely with, our emotional sense of this contact. Where it is at its highest there is indeed, as we have seen, always some deliberate recognition of God, something which may be called a sense of His presence. But this is not dependent on any emotional thrill; it is rather the deliberate orientation of the will Godward. And His influence may be very real, even where there is but little consciousness of it. It sometimes happens that we are profoundly affected by scenery, pictures, or books, while hardly conscious at the time of the influence they are exerting on us. In our psychological parallels the supreme influence of the great teacher or the good friend, stealing into the inmost depths of our being, is not always recognised till years after. And so the reality of our communion with God —and this is especially to be remembered in connection with the Eucharist—does not stand or fall with the extent to which we can honestly say that we realise or feel His presence. The final test of such communion is to be found in its effects on the life and character. "No man hath beheld God at any time : if we love one another, God abideth in us, and his love is perfected in us : hereby know we that we abide in him and he in us, because he hath given us of his Spirit." If a man is growing like God and Christ, it can only be because he is in a vital relation with the Divine Spirit. This relation will at its highest bring with it at times a real awareness of God, yet it may also be completely independent of anything of the nature of emotional thrills. And if it be asked what may be the full results of such relation, we can only reply that they are, in the moral sphere as in others, limitless. It draws out the hidden capacities of human nature at its best, and that nature is in its essence divine. It is when St. Paul thinks of his converts as strengthened with power through the Spirit of God in the inner man, of Christ as dwelling in their hearts through faith, that he bursts out into his cry of praise "to him who is able to do exceeding abundantly above all that we ask or think, according to the power that worketh in us." For this power is not an effluence or an influence, not a force or a gift from God ; it is Christ Himself, present in us through His Spirit.

DETACHED NOTE A

The Meaning of Grace in the New Testament

"Grace" has come to mean, both in technical and in popular theology, a specific power or help granted by God to man, usually in order to resist temptation and to do what is right. But this is not the ordinary meaning of χάρις, the Greek term which is translated "grace," either in the Septuagint or in the New Testament. In the former it is usually the translation of the Hebrew ḥēn, or favour, and the same idea is primary in the New Testament usage. Grace is a characteristic of God, something He feels or shows to man ; the nearest equivalents are *loving-kindness* or *mercy*. It will be found that in most of the New Testament passages some such word can always be substituted for the English "grace." It is noteworthy that the *Twentieth Century New Testament*, in fact, uses these or similar translations and avoids grace altogether. "By grace ye are saved" becomes "By God's loving-kindness you have been saved."

The term χάρις is not found in Matthew or Mark ; it is rare in the Johannine writings, and is most frequent in Luke and Paul ; in other words, it belongs, especially in its theological use, to the specifically Pauline vocabulary. God's loving-kindness has been shown pre-eminently by the gift of forgiveness and salvation through Christ, and in St. Paul χάρις is specially connected with the extension of these to the Gentiles.[1] Hence, besides denoting the loving-kindness of God, it sometimes denotes the gifts which come from

[1] See on this point J. A. Robinson, *St. Paul's Epistle to the Ephesians*, pp. 221 ff.

O

that loving-kindness (1 Cor. iii. 10 ; 2 Cor. vi. 1). In such a passage as Acts viii. 8 (Stephen " full of grace "), it is doubtful whether the meaning is to be looked for in this direction or rather in the classical sense of charm or attractiveness. But for our purpose it is not necessary to discuss the details and shades of the actual use ; the point is that with all its varieties it does not include the modern technical sense. " The later technical use [of grace], esp. of the Latin *gratia*, for the divine prompting and help which precedes and accompanies right action does not correspond exactly to the usage of N.T." [1] And in particular we never find in its pages phrases such as " means " or " channels " of grace, or any conception of different kinds of grace, *e.g.* sacramental and other.

We may note one or two passages which come nearest to the modern usage.

1 Cor. xv. 10, " By the grace of God I am what I am " ; *i.e.* by His loving mercy.

2 Cor. xii. 9, " My grace is sufficient for thee " ; *i.e.* he can trust in God's love and mercy. But note " strength " in the parallel clause, which easily paves the way for the later usage.

Heb. iv. 16, " Come with boldness to the throne of grace " ; cf. " throne of glory " ; the throne where grace or mercy sits enthroned, not where " grace " is dispensed. The meaning in this clause determines the following words, " find grace."

James iv. 6, " Giveth greater grace," *i.e.* greater acceptance than the world or its friendship ; cf. the quotation from Prov. iii. 34 which follows ; see Hort, *Epistle of St. James, ad loc.*

1 Peter iv. 10, " As good stewards of the manifold grace of God " ; this is nearest to the modern use, suggesting a store which is to be dispensed, though the reference in the context is to specific endowments.

Such passages are transitional ; taken alone they

---

[1] Sanday and Headlam, *Romans*, p. 11.

might be interpreted in the modern sense, but it is clear that their strict exegesis must be determined by the general use of χάρις in the New Testament.

DETACHED NOTE B

THE CONCRETE MEANING OF "GRATIA"

The change of meaning in the Latin *gratia*, from an abstract quality to the concrete expression of that quality, may be paralleled from the history of the word *liberalitas*. Imperial coins bear the inscription *Liberalitas Augusti*, celebrating the generosity of the Emperor as a quality, just as they celebrate his piety or clemency. The usual type is a female figure with a cornucopia. But other types are found with an elaborate composition representing the Emperor distributing a *congiarium*, or largess. And successive *congiaria* are enumerated on coins with the inscription *Liberalitas Augusti II, III*, etc., for which *Congiarium Augusti II*, etc., is sometimes found. That is to say, *liberalitas* has come to have the concrete meaning of "the gift bestowed," equivalent to *congiarium*. See also Tacitus, *Hist.* i. 20, "decuma parte liberalitatis apud quemque eorum relicta."

For the substance of this note I am indebted to the kindness of the Rev. C. H. Dodd of Mansfield College, Oxford.

VI

THE PSYCHOLOGY OF INSPIRATION: HOW GOD TEACHES

BY

C. W. EMMET, B.D.

ANALYSIS

INSPIRATION AND GRACE.—The question with Inspiration, as with Grace, is of the influence of the Divine Personality on the human. The parallel between the two cases.

THE DESIRE FOR A SPECIAL METHOD OF REVELATION.—The primitive identification of inspiration with the psychically abnormal; the modern identification with what is psychologically inexplicable. Dr. Hamilton's view of the origin of the Hebrew belief in monotheism. The distinction between "Revelation" and "revelation" untenable. God revealed in nature. The belief in immortality due to a diffused popular inspiration.

THE FLASH OF DISCOVERY.—Boy calculators. The conscious and subconscious preparation for what seems the spontaneous intuition; examples. The principle applied to the prophets.

THE SENSE OF OTHERNESS.—Examples. The conviction not in itself a guarantee of truth; Nietzsche; H. G. Wells. The parallel with grace; intermingling of the divine and human.

THE TEST OF INSPIRATION.—The criterion the truth of the message, not the method of revelation. The responsibility of judging for ourselves. The instinct of selection to which we owe the Bible.

THE UNEXPLAINED RESIDUUM.—Discovery, or revelation, dependent on man's response. Why does one respond, while another does not? The unexplained personal factor always present. God not to be sought in the gaps.

INSPIRATION AND COMMUNION WITH GOD.—The underlying condition always contact with the Divine, though this cannot be used as the primary criterion of truth. The supreme inspiration of Christ.

THE INSPIRATION OF THE ORDINARY MAN.—Inspiration in the last resort not peculiar to a few or confined to the sphere of religion. The danger and the value of individual intuitions.

VI

THE PSYCHOLOGY OF INSPIRATION :
HOW GOD TEACHES

Inspiration and Grace

We have been discussing the question how God helps
us, and have tried to find the key in the relation of the
Divine Personality to the human, interpreted on the
lines, though not within the limits, of the relation
of human personalities to one another. We may now
apply the same key to the problem of how God teaches
us. Our illustration of what happens as between master
and pupil has obvious bearings on the question of
inspiration. We have found that the secret is the
action of mind upon mind, not only by the direct
methods of speech and instruction, but most of all
through the more subtle gift of personal influence.
The result is the inspiration of the pupil, whether for
conduct or for creative thought, the enhancement
of his personality to a degree which could not have
come otherwise. This inspiration often comes suddenly
and mysteriously, sometimes in ways hard to account
for ; it brings with it in a true sense the embodiment
of the teacher's idea and spirit. But this spirit has
been blended with the pupil's spirit ; it has not dislodged
it or taken its place. It does not in any way supersede
the need for study and personal effort. The idea has
become the pupil's, and in the expression of it there

is always something individual, whether for better or for worse.

If we keep this point of view clearly before our minds we shall be saved from the fundamental misconceptions which have often vitiated the popular ideas of inspiration in the past. It is persons who are inspired, not books. No doubt it is perfectly legitimate to transfer the epithet and to speak of an "inspired" poem or piece of music; but we must never allow ourselves to forget that such a use of the term is secondary. Inspiration is the quickening of vision, the enhancement of the personality, which can only come to a person. The distinction is not merely verbal; it excludes at once any notion of a message or book of which the words have simply been miraculously dictated. We shall therefore approach the problem of inspiration from the side of psychology and personality. However it comes and however it works, it is the result of the influence of the Divine Spirit upon the human.

Speaking generally, we shall find that the principles which we have discussed in our treatment of grace will hold good here too. On the one hand we insist on the universality and the continuity of the creative working of the Divine Spirit. If He is always and everywhere helping and raising man, He is also always teaching him. Any discovery of the good, the true, the beautiful, can only come as the result of God's revelation of Himself and His works to the mind of man. The inventor, the thinker, the artist, in whatever medium, is inspired in so far as his thoughts and the expression of them correspond to the divine thought. But on the other hand, while we refuse to draw a sharp line between divine inspiration and human discovery, just as we refused to draw it between natural and supernatural goodness, we must not ignore the supreme importance of the difference of the degree in which men, whether in science, or in art, or in religion, do succeed in entering into the mind of God. As with goodness, so with beauty and truth, the appropriation and expression of that mind may be unconscious, commonplace, partial, or it may rise to heights of genius. The barriers of sin and self-will, of blindness and ignorance, are abiding facts which need to be taken very seriously in this context as in the other.

The Desire for a Special Method of Revelation

The question, however, at once arises, Can we discover any criterion as to the degree of inspiration—in other words, of the closeness of communion with the Divine Spirit—in any given case, and the amount of truth in the result as expressed in word or art ? The purpose of this essay is to suggest that this criterion is in no way dependent on any one particular mode of discovery or revelation. In quite primitive times inspiration was connected with what is psychically abnormal, the dream or trance, ecstasy or frenzy, where the human reason is at its lowest. Such a position has long been abandoned. The time has passed when men could agree with Tertullian in holding that "the majority of men learn God from visions," or when an ignorant peasant could be made patriarch of an important see in obedience to a dream of his dying predecessor.[1] Studies of psychical phenomena, whether in trance or in automatic speech and writing, prove conclusively that, even if such methods may sometimes be a channel of truth, they are in no possible sense a guarantee of truth, or the necessary accompaniments of the highest types of revelation. But old delusions die hard. There are still those who would make the extent of the revelation depend on the degree to which it is psychologically unintelligible. Is the message unexpected ? Has it come by a sudden intuition ?

[1] See Inge, *Christian Mysticism*, p. 16.

Is it apparently inexplicable as the result of previous study and reflection ? If so, it is suggested, we have at last evidence of a direct self-revelation of God. The idea of the verbal infallibility of Scripture is dead, not so its chief presupposition, that somehow revelation must be the imparting of correct information, and inspiration the power of receiving it. And so attempts are still made, even by those who claim to accept the modern view of inspiration, to vindicate a special position and authority for the Bible, based not on its inherent truth and intrinsic appeal, but on something which can be regarded as unique in the manner of its composition. It must at all costs be given a special status in a class by itself, different in kind, not only in degree, from all other books.

A typical example of such an attempt may be found in a comparatively recent book, Dr. Hamilton's *The People of God*. He argues that the monotheism of the Hebrew prophets (*i.e.* their belief that Jehovah is the sole God of the world, opposed to the older idea that He was the God of the Hebrews) was due to a special self-revelation of God. It cannot, he urges, be explained as the result of environment, or reflection on the facts of life and history, or intellectual dialectic. Its origin is quite different to that of the Greek philosophical monotheism, and can only be accounted for by an inner spiritual experience in which God manifested Himself directly and immediately *by a mode confined to one race*. In the same way A. Sabatier has maintained that the new and critical ideas in the history of religion—the unity of God, His Fatherhood, and the Brotherhood of man—cannot be explained as due to inference or reflection ; they must be regarded as due to an immediate revelation.[1] Dr. Hamilton therefore draws a sharp distinction between discovery and Revelation, or between revelation with a small and Revelation with a large " R " : " ' revelation ' means the knowledge about

[1] See Rashdall, *Philosophy and Religion*, p. 115.

God which man derives from reflection on the facts of existence, and would perhaps be better called ' human discovery.' ' Revelation' stands for a knowledge of God given directly to man by God Himself, and not mediated through reflection on the nature of existence. . . . In the one case man arrives at a knowledge of God's existence and character by a slow and painful process of endeavouring to solve the riddle of existence ; in the other case this knowledge comes directly without being mediated through such a process of reflection." [1]

Not for a moment would we quarrel with the position that the prophetic insistence on Jehovah as the one God is an outstanding example of inspiration, or revelation, at its highest, though Dr. Hamilton's view of the uniqueness of the Hebrew monotheism is open to some question. What we have to ask is whether there is a special channel and type of Revelation in an ex- clusive sense, confined to one race and religion. How far is it true that certain truths are directly revealed by God, while others are discovered by man through the exercise of his own reason?

In the first place, let us consider the suggested distinction between " Revelation " and " revelation." Dr. Hamilton himself seems to have some difficulty in drawing the line as sharply as he suggests. For between the two sentences just quoted comes another which, carefully considered, endangers his whole posi- tion. "The dividing line between Revelation and revelation is not that the former is God's effort to seek after man and the latter man's effort to seek after God ; for we do not know that the Eternal Spirit is not seeking to disclose Himself to man through his own powers of observation and reflection." Here precisely is the crux. As we have already suggested, all dis- covery is in the end revelation. Man is seeking, God is revealing, always and by many channels. In all

[1] *Op. cit.* i. 165.

progress of thought, in all approach to the fuller knowledge of the good, the true, and the beautiful, there is
some contact between the divine and human personalities.   To the Christian there can be no other source
of truth.   The difference between one man and
another is a difference of insight and of nearness; in
some the divine is clogged, in others it flows freely.
We have tended to treat discovery as active at the
human end and passive at the divine, while with
revelation we have reversed the rôles.   Discovery is
regarded as a process in which man looks through
the telescope and the divine is simply seen.   In Revelation God is thought of as speaking through the
telephone, while man has only to listen.   The reality
is always a blending of the two : man both hears and
sees ; God both speaks and makes Himself seen.   No
doubt there are differences of method, diversities of
operation, but one and the self-same Spirit is at work
in all.   There is the desire to discover truth, beauty,
and moral goodness, and to express them in word, art,
or conduct ; there is the seeking for the divine fellowship
in prayer and meditation; there are immediate intuitions
bringing with them a direct sense of His presence.   But
can we ultimately separate sharply between them, label-
ling some discovery and others Revelation ?   Are not
most of them found in varying proportions in the same
persons, and in all their activities ?

Again, it cannot be denied that there comes to many
a sense of direct contact with God through nature.
Dr. Hamilton would regard this as " revelation " or
discovery, a means of getting to know about God by
our own efforts, but such a position is simply untrue to
the experience of nature-mystics and poets of all ages,
as well as to that of many plain men and women who
claim to find here a personal communion with the
Divine.[1]   While we reserve the right to analyse such

---

[1] See Illingworth, *Divine Immanence*, chap. ii., and Inge, *Christian Mysticism*,
chaps. vii., viii. ; also the essay in this volume on " Spiritual Experience."

experiences, and to distinguish between the psycho-logical fact and its supposed content and expression, we must accept them as valid so far as they go, precisely as we accept the fact of religious experiences in the narrower sense. And it is worth adding that this experience of God through nature is of two kinds. There is the case of those who have already found God through the more usual religious channels, and then go on to find Him in the world without. But there are also others to whom nature is the primary, and even to the end the predominant, means of communion with Him. One result of such communion, here as else-where, is inspiration or vision. We need not discuss whether Wordsworth is more or less inspired than some of the Biblical writers, but we are concerned to maintain that God does reveal Himself through nature, and that so far as He does so the result is a knowledge of divine truth and beauty.

Let it be repeated that we do not wish in any way to deny or undervalue the reality or the significance of the personal experience of the prophets. What we are asking is whether that experience is peculiar to them and is the unique method by which God reveals new truths about Himself. Even in the field of religion itself we may find important truths which have not come through the special channel which is regarded as the peculiar vehicle of Revelation. At least as wonderful as the original discovery of monotheism by a few chosen spirits (the prophets) is what happened after the exile in regard to the belief in Immortality —the emergence of which is, equally with mono-theism, a crucial stage in the history of revelation. In the later books of the Old Testament, in the Apocrypha and the Apocalyptic literature, we can trace the stages of its growth, here a little and there a little. It cannot be claimed as the outcome of some outstanding revelation to one or two favoured seers. Those to whom we owe it do not seem to have been men of any conspicuous religious or literary genius. Their very names are unknown, and in most cases their writings have only survived by accident and in translations. Yet under the pressure of experience the belief gradually emerged till it became so strong that Christ and His Apostles could take it for granted. And up to a point we can see why this happened. The old view that earthly happiness corresponded to desert was increasingly contradicted by facts ; there was a growing sense of personality which both looked for the permanence of that communion with God which had been felt to be the highest thing in life, and also refused to be satisfied with some glorious future for the nation, receding ever further and further, in which generation after generation of faithful souls was to have no personal share. There was also a closer contact with other religions, especially Zoroastrianism, in which the belief in a life after death played a large part. The growth of the belief among the Jews thus becomes psychologically intelligible ; none the less it marks an epoch in religious history. It is due not to any unique self-revelation of God but to a diffused popular inspiration, shared by more than one race.

The Flash of Discovery

To the Hebrew prophet the "word of the Lord" seems often to have come as suddenly and inexplicably as lightning from a clear sky. But, we must ask, is the mere fact of suddenness or psychological unintelligibility *in itself* a criterion of a special revelation of the highest truth, or even of truth at all ? The most startling examples of knowledge flashed into the mind by a process which is at present inexplicable are to be found in the boy calculators, who solve the most complicated arithmetical problems in a moment by a kind of intuition.[1] Or we may instance the perfectly

[1] Examples may be seen in Myers's *Human Personality*, pp. 64 ff. ; or we may instance the following account of the powers of a Tamil boy : " Representatives of

authenticated faculty of water-finding, whereby certain persons can discover water at some depth by the twitching of a twig in the hands as they walk over the ground. In such cases the results have not been prepared for by previous study ; they are immediate and inexplicable, and not due to conscious reflection. No doubt these faculties are valuable, and do give us something which is true and therefore in its measure divine, but they are concerned with comparatively low grades of truth, and no one would argue that they are due to a special self-revelation of God.

When, however, we examine their experiences we see good reason to doubt whether the direct revelation which is claimed for the prophets is either so inexplicable or so independent of the ordinary human means of discovery as at first sight appears. Modern psychology by its analysis both of the phenomenon of religious conversion and of the processes of discovery and artistic production has thrown much light on the whole subject. What seems the spontaneous, unexpected, and inexplicable flash is shown to be in fact the outcome, emerging into consciousness, of a long period of subconscious reflection on material which the conscious mind has supplied. A good illustration is afforded by the dreams of Professor Hilprecht.[1] He went to bed on one occasion after a hard spell of work on the translation of an Assyrian stone, of which he had assumed a false interpretation, and awoke in the morning with a new

---

the Ceylon Department of Education had prepared a series of complicated sums. Each of these he answered within a few seconds. One sum was : 'A chetty gave as a treat to 173 persons a bushel of rice each. Each bushel contained 3,431,272 grains, and the chetty stipulated that 17 per cent should be given to the temple. How many grains did the temple get?' Within three seconds came the answer (which had to be translated) : 100,913,709, with 52 as the fraction over. The boy was told that the answer should be 100,913,719. He shook his head, and though the sum was several times repeated to him maintained he was right. The Education Department representative the next day had to admit that he had miscopied the answer, and had also omitted the fractional part in the copy he had made.

"In some cases hardly had the last word of the interpretation of the sum been uttered before the correct reply was begun" (*The Times*, October 1, 1912).

[1] See Myers, *Human Personality*, pp. 365 ff. (one vol. edition).

translation in his mind which turned out to be correct. He had a dim consciousness of having continued his work in a dream.   Much more remarkable is his account of a dream in which a priest of Nippur leads him to the treasure-chamber of a temple and explains to him the history of two fragments of agate which he had been studying from a sketch, telling him how they may be fitted together and the inscription deciphered.   He had had no idea that the two fragments were in fact connected, since they were described as being of different colours, but the " revelation " was found to be absolutely accurate in all verifiable particulars, and entirely probable in the parts where proof was no longer possible.   The point to note is " that not one of these items of information was beyond the reach of the processes of associative reasoning which Professor Hilprecht daily employs."   In each case the final solution of the problem, coming in this dramatic and unexpected way, appears to have been the crystallising, or precipitate, of weeks of apparently fruitless study. In particular he uses in his second dream a piece of information given to him some years previously by a friend and entirely forgotten by his waking mind.

Numerous illustrations of such subconscious menta-tion, following hard and sometimes apparently fruitless thinking, may be found in the realms of literature and art.[1]   A contemporary instance is Donald Hankey's description of his writing of *The Lord of All Good Life* : " I would have you realise that it was written spon-taneously, in a burst, in six weeks. . . . I had tried and tried, but without success.   Then suddenly every-thing cleared up.   To myself the writing of it was an

[1] See, *e.g.*, Myers, *Human Personality*, p. 71 (one vol. edition).   F. B. Bond (*The Gate of Remembrance*, p. 48) gives a remarkable example of a reconstruction of a lost piece of architecture, which was afterwards discovered to be quite correct. He holds that such mental pictures of the past become spontaneously apparent to the artist " when in a state of mental passivity after intellectual exertion in the particular direction needed."   This instance is independent of the discoveries he describes as made at Glastonbury through automatic writing, which indeed may be explained on the same principle.

illumination."[1]   Most quite ordinary workers will in
fact be able to illustrate from their own knowledge this
experience of the sudden solution of a difficulty long
pondered over in vain, of the apparently spontaneous
arrangement of a complicated train of thought, often
after the problem has been laid aside for some time, or
of the flashing into the mind of the artistic or literary
inspiration.   They will understand how these things
come with a sense of mysterious authority, as though
from some source outside themselves.   But they will
also know that the result is always the outcome of the
work and effort which have gone before; it is not a gift
dropped mysteriously and spontaneously from heaven.
It is only a half-truth to say that "art happens."
Genius is no doubt more than "an unlimited capacity
for taking pains," but this is almost invariably one of
its conditions.   A classical description of the process
is given in Myers's *St. Paul* :

> Lo as some bard on isles of the Aegean,
>   Lovely and eager when the earth was young,
> Burning to hurl his heart into a paean,
>   Praise of the hero from whose loins he sprung ;—
>
> He, I suppose, with such a care to carry,
>   Wandered disconsolate and waited long,
> Smiting his breast, wherein the notes would tarry,
>   Chiding the slumber of the seed of song :
>
> Then in the sudden glory of a minute,
>   Airy and excellent the proëm came,
> Rending his bosom, for a god was in it,
>   Waking the seed, for it had burst in flame.

In view of these considerations we shall not have
much doubt what answer to give to the question asked
by Dr. Davidson[2] with regard to Biblical inspiration :
"When truth suddenly dawned on the prophet's mind,
which formerly he strove unsuccessfully to reach by
means of reflection, did the feeling he had at such a

---

[1] *The Student in Arms* (2nd series), p. 31.
[2] *Old Testament Prophecy*, p. 111.

moment differ from the feeling men still have, when oftentimes, in peculiarly spontaneous frames of mind, difficulties are broken up and problems solved which before resisted all conscious and direct efforts of the mind ? "   We may take as an example Isaiah's account of his call.[1]   Here we have a religious experience which seems at first sight to be entirely spontaneous.   Yet we may find the key in the opening words of the chapter : " In the year that king Uzziah died."   The king had been the hero of the young prophet ; the shock of his tragic end led him up from hero-worship and imperialism to religion and God.   The subsequent vision and revelation become psychologically intelligible as the outcome of a spiritual crisis, due to historical events and reflection on them.[2]   But they do not therefore cease to be true and epoch-making.   We cannot indeed always trace the psychological antecedents which condition the experiences of the Biblical writers.   They were not interested in psychology or in the process by which they arrived at their conclusions ; in many cases they were probably unconscious of any such process.   But there is no evidence that their minds did not work in the same way as the minds of other men ; what seemed spontaneous had really been prepared for.

Once more, while what seems to be the intuitive flash of genius is often of supreme significance, whether in religion or in art, we must not make it the special criterion of discovery or of communion with the Divine.   " ' What constitutes the true artist,' says a master of style, ' is not the slowness or quickness of the process, but the absolute success of the result.' . . . Beauty and truth may come together and find the exactly right words in the flash of a moment, or after many attempts." [3]   A piece of music such as the last movement of the Ninth Symphony, hammered out

---

[1] Isaiah vi.

[2] Cf. G. A. Smith's discussion of the passage in *The Book of Isaiah* (" The Expositor's Bible "), pp. 58 ff.

[3] E. T. Cook, *Literary Recreations*, p. 316.

after many experiments and rejected themes, may be as inspired as Schubert's Songs, flashing into the mind unexpectedly and almost ready formed. St. Luke's Gospel, the result of the comparison and blending of earlier documents and materials, or the considered argument of the Epistle to the Romans, are no less inspired than the vision of the Apocalypse. The highest examples of revelation are not necessarily to be found where the process is obscure, or where the outcome seems to be spontaneous ; still less should this obscurity or spontaneity be regarded as the tests of revelation.

The Sense of Otherness

It is, indeed, not surprising that in such cases of apparently spontaneous emergence the feeling of "otherness" and of external inspiration is especially strong. The popular use of the phrase "it came as an inspiration" is of an idea flashing unexpectedly into the mind, as though from some outside source, and welcomed at once as valuable and correct. Stevenson, not altogether playfully,[1] attributes his stories to his "Brownies," both when he is asleep and even to some extent during his waking hours. Blake attributes his poems to spiritual helpers. As he walked along the seashore he was haunted by the forms of Moses and the prophets, of Homer and Milton, who seemed to communicate to him directly what he was to write. "I may praise it," he says, "since I dare not pretend to be other than the secretary ; the authors are in eternity." "I have written this poem from immediate dictation, twelve, or sometimes twenty or thirty lines at a time without premeditation, and even against my will."[2] So Böhme,[3] speaking of his visions, says : "Whatever I could bring into outwardness, that I wrote down. The work is none of mine ; I am but

[1] *Across the Plains*, "A Chapter on Dreams."
[2] See F. Granger, *The Soul of a Christian*, pp. 215 ff.
[3] Quoted in Inge, *Christian Mysticism*, p. 277.

the Lord's instrument, wherewith He doeth what He will." The account which the prophetic writers of the Bible give of themselves is often in line with this conception. No doubt it is difficult to be quite sure how far "The Lord said unto me," or the language of visions, whether in the prophets or the Apocalyptic writers, represents in all cases a real psychological experience, or whether it is sometimes merely an accepted literary and religious mode of expression. But in either case it unquestionably stands for a conviction that the message is not only true but in some sense is not the prophet's own, coming from a higher source outside himself.

But this sense of otherness is not in itself the hallmark of a divine revelation. We find, for example, in the realm of art works which have been produced by this intuitive process, by what Myers would regard as specifically the method of genius, without being in themselves works of genius.[1] He instances Haydon's *Raising of Lazarus*, which, as his *Autobiography* shows, flashed upon him with an overmastering sense of direct inspiration, or Voltaire's "unreadable tragedy *Catilina*," written in a week and ascribed by him to a flash of genius, the gift of God. Where Blake insists most on his "inspiration," as in the prophetic books, the result is on a lower level than in the lyrics produced in a more normal way. In the same way immediacy, or the overmastering sense of certainty and "given-ness," is no guarantee of superior excellence or truth in philosophy or religion. Here is Nietzsche's account of his own experience of "inspiration" :

If one had the smallest vestige of superstition left in one, it would hardly be possible completely to set aside the idea that one is the mere incarnation, mouthpiece, or medium of an almighty power. The idea of revelation in the sense that something which profoundly convulses and upsets one becomes

---

[1] *Human Personality* (one vol. edition), p. 60.

suddenly visible and audible with indescribable certainty and accuracy describes the simple fact. One hears—one does not seek—one takes—one does not ask who gives : a thought suddenly flashes up like lightning, it comes with necessity, without faltering. I have never had any choice in the matter.[1]

The account is combined with an extravagant insistence on the absolute truth and pre-eminence of the result : "If all the spirit and goodness of every great soul were collated together, the whole could not create a single one of Zarathustra's discourses."[2] As Dr. Figgis points out, Nietzsche's philosophy is not in fact so original as he supposed, and we certainly shall not accept it as divinely inspired, but here we have a sincere conviction of inspiration in the prophetic sense. Of course Nietzsche himself rejects the *prima facie* impression that he is in communion with a higher power, but even in the case of those who insist, and no doubt insist rightly, that they are in such communion, we cannot consent to accept their message as true on this ground alone.

Claims to such communion are found in many religions ; we cannot reject as delusions all which are not associated with our own creed, nor on the other hand are we compelled to accept the teaching based on them as "revelations." Such considerations are a commonplace with regard to the experiences and the writings of the mystics, as well as of the prophets, true and false, of the Old Testament. Again, let us listen to the testimony of Mr. Wells :

Then suddenly, in a little while, in His own time, God comes. This cardinal experience is an undoubting immediate sense of God. It is as if one were touched at every point by a being akin to oneself, sympathetic beyond measure. . . . It is like standing side by side with and touching someone we love very dearly and trust completely. "Closer is he than

---

[1] Quoted from *Ecce Homo*, p. 101, by J. N. Figgis, *The Will to Freedom*, pp. 160 ff.
[2] Figgis, *op. cit.* p. 163.

breathing, nearer than hands and feet." The moment may
come while we are alone in the darkness, under the stars, or
while walking by ourselves, or in a crowd, or while we sit and
muse. It may come in the sinking ship or in the tumult
of battle. But after it has come our lives are changed. God
is with us, and there is no more doubt of God.[1]

These words undoubtedly represent a first - hand
religious experience, but they do not compel us to
accept the theology of *God the Invisible King* as the
outcome of a special revelation. Are we then justified
in arguing in the case of the Bible that the unquestioned
genuineness of the religious experience of its writers is
in itself the proof of the truth of everything in their
teaching ? In the Psalms we find the sense of personal
fellowship with God at its highest, but this does not,
as has sometimes been suggested, carry with it any
guarantee that the attitude towards enemies adopted in
some of them corresponds to the Divine Mind.

We may remind ourselves of the parallel problem
which we found in connection with grace. There too
there was the sense of " otherness." It is a conviction
of all deep religious experience that it is " a power not
ourselves" which raises and saves, and which also reveals
and teaches. But in the moral sphere this " otherness "
did not justify us in drawing a sharp line between
natural and supernatural virtues, or imply a class of
actions which could be called perfect. Both with grace
and with inspiration the Divine influence works by
entering into the personality so as to co-operate with
it ; it does not supersede it by way of possession.

It follows that it is impossible to find in anything
which comes through the medium of a human mind an
absolute " Revelation." There is always some dross
with the gold, something individual and peculiar,
temporary and inadequate. " No man hath seen God
at any time," nor is His voice heard speaking from
heaven. We insist on the absolute reality of com-

------

[1] *God the Invisible King*, p. 27.

munion with Him, but we cannot take certain forms of this communion and say, " This is seeing God face to face, as a man sees and talks with his friend in the body, while at other times we only know *about* God as we may read a letter from a friend, hear or talk or think about him." We cannot say, " Here God comes personally to the prophets and reveals Himself, while in all other cases He merely leads men to discover something about Him." The outside element, the divine entering into the human spirit, is indeed a reality and does make a difference ; but it is not confined to any one type of communion, nor is it ever found in isolation from the human contribution. The prophet, whether in religion, art, or science, is justified in his claim " Thus saith the Lord," but it cannot be held to carry with it the elimination of the human element or to place the content of his message beyond criticism. Nor again does it imply an access to a mode of inspiration wholly denied to the ordinary man.

The Test of Inspiration

What, then, is the final test of inspiration? We can only reply that there is no special criterion peculiar to the realm of religion, or applicable to one particular type of literature such as the Bible. The test whether a writer is inspired is simply whether his message is true. The criterion of truth is indeed a much vexed question of philosophy, but no system makes truth, or the highest truth, dependent on the special channel through which it comes. The test may be congruity with experience, or with the whole correlated body of truth ; it may be a certain self-evidencing power, or even the fact that it " works " in the broadest sense. But in any case the appeal must be to the reason, to the whole personality at its highest and best. All revelation must be judged by its inherent truth, by its power of finding us and appealing to our conscience, by the degree in which it calls out the best in us and awakens the response of the highest part of our being. It cannot rest ultimately on any external authority because we ourselves can be the only judges of the claims of such authority. In particular we have found reason to believe that it is not bound up with any one psychological process, or peculiar to any one age or set of people. We cannot escape the responsibility of judging for ourselves by throwing ourselves in blind faith upon the method of revelation and finding in that a guarantee of divine truth.

To many religious minds it will seem to be no light thing to abandon this hope of some external infallible authority. In our weakness we crave something definite on which to lean, something which may tell us without possibility of error what we are to do, what we are to believe. And yet here too the message of Christianity is that by losing our life we find it. It tells us to live dangerously and take risks. It never allows us merely to play for safety ; in thought no less than in action we must be ready for adventure, to set forth into the unknown, each one for himself, in reliance on the Spirit of God.

But though it is true that each of us must take the responsibility of forming his own judgement, yet it is equally important to insist that ultimately the individual does not stand alone. The organ which decides on truth is in the last resort the community of which he is a member, the *communis sensus fidelium*, by which we mean agreement of the highest and best trained minds in any field, working over the generations. A decision so reached is slow, and it is not at any given moment, or in respect to any given point, infallible, but, in the long run, *securus judicat orbis terrarum*. And it is to this general instinct of the religious community that we owe the Bible. By a gradual and unconscious process of selection this instinct picked out the best books from their competitors—the best Psalms, for instance, from the Jewish sacred poetry of many centuries, the best Gospels from the various Lives of Christ. When we are able to compare, as we can to some extent in this latter case, or in the case of the Jewish literature which arose subsequently to the Old Testament, we see clearly that this instinct, though not beyond mistake or question, did on the whole work out right. The official stamping of books as canonical was simply the formal endorsement of this instinctive selection. And it is worth noting that the process still goes on, as the Bible is used. The pages of St. John or the Epistle to the Philippians are thumbed, while Chronicles or Esther remain untouched. Whatever be the official rules as to the use of the Psalms, those who are free to choose unconsciously select their favourites, and, within limits, the selection is much the same in all ages and in all classes. It is further of the highest significance that the verdict of the simple devotional reader of the Bible agrees on the whole with the verdict of the professed student, and even of the advanced critic, as to the books and the passages which stand on the highest level of inspiration. The more we abandon external tests of inspiration, the more impressive becomes the fact of the universal appeal of the noblest parts of the Bible to the religious instinct of mankind. It is the same general method that we see at work in the selection of the highest achievements of art or literature, no less than in the sifting of truth from error. As the mills of judgement grind slowly, so does this process of testing and sifting. The Spirit of God gives us no clear-cut information as to what we are to approve or value most highly. He places no external hall-mark of authenticity on His revelation, yet gradually, but surely, He trains the divine faculty in man by which he may respond to the true and the beautiful, and sift the gold from the dross.

THE UNEXPLAINED RESIDUUM

Neither in religion nor in philosophy, art, or science can we in the last resort say why a particular discovery or revelation comes to one man or one age rather than to another. Men living at the same time have the same raw material to work upon ; some of them may be engaged on the same line of thought or artistic effort with apparently equal sincerity and devotion ; the same fellowship with the Spirit is open to all. Yet the flash of discovery, or the special gift of expression, comes to one and not to another. Sometimes we can in a measure explain the reason ; sometimes we are baffled. But in general we may surely conclude that, whereas God is always and everywhere seeking to reveal Himself to the mind of man in the perfection of His goodness, truth, and beauty, how much man can receive depends on his power of response and vision. Even when inspiration was regarded as direct dictation, this fact was dimly recognised. There is a Jewish legend that when the children of Israel sinned with the Golden Calf the divine writing vanished from the Tables.[1] The measure of apprehension depends partly on the spiritual atmosphere of the whole community, partly on the preparedness of particular individuals within the community. The genius can never be independent of this atmosphere, nor can he be indefinitely in advance of it. He focusses in himself all that is best in the thought or the artistic instincts of the many, and so progress comes. Up to a certain point we can explain psychologically the conditions and the method of such progress, but there is always the unexplained residuum, and this depends on the personal factor. We cannot completely account for the fact that the highest insight into the character and being of God came to the Jew and not to the Babylonian or the Greek. Why, in the last resort, does one generation, race, or individual open itself to

[1] *The Biblical Antiquities of Philo*, xii. 7 (edited by M. R. James).

the all-pervading divine influence, while others absorb but little of it? But the problem is not in any way peculiar to the region of the revelation of religious truth. Precisely the same problem faces us in considering any great advance in moral goodness, scientific discovery, philosophic insight, or artistic achievement. It is the same question why, in the ultimate nature of things, one man is worse or more stupid than another ; why one responds to the grace of God while his neighbour does not. From this point of view it is no easier to explain why one is a dunce, unable to master the *pons asinorum*, than it is to account for Shakespeare and his plays, or the religious insight of Isaiah.

The problem, then, is really parallel to the biological problem of explaining the origin of valuable variations in the species, a problem to which no complete answer has been given. But because there is always this unexplained factor, the personal x, in goodness and badness, in success and failure alike, this does not justify us in arguing that the degree to which God is present depends on the amount which seems to be left unexplained in any given case. The only test of the presence of God, of the extent to which we have entered into His mind, is the result : how far is it good, beautiful, or true ? The method or the degree of unexpectedness is, as we have seen, irrelevant. The fact that we may be able to trace the working of cause and effect does not banish God, nor is He specially present where we have so far failed to unravel the sequence. We do not look for the peculiar evidence of the Divine in that which we cannot explain by hitherto deciphered laws, whether of nature or psychology, in supposed breaches of the process of evolution, in discoveries of which the genesis is obscure. God is in the order of nature as a whole, not specifically in what seem to be its gaps.

Inspiration and Communion with God

But though there is no external criterion of inspiration, though there is no one method or process of its working, none the less it has one fixed condition. It is that from which we started, the contact of the human spirit with the divine, the right experience of God. Without this there can be no revelation of God, and where it exists there is always some measure of revelation. Such contact may come through dream or vision, through trance or ecstasy, or it may come in the sober light of common day, when the faculties are fully awake and the reason stretched to its point of highest tension. The revelation of the truth may seem to flash into the mind as a sudden intuition, apparently unprepared for and inexplicable by ordinary psychological law ; it may be arrived at slowly, here a little and there a little, by what seems to be the natural result of hard study and thought. It may be mediated by prayer and meditation, or by the search for truth, beauty, and goodness, pursued unselfishly as absolute values. But in proportion to the extent and reality of the contact will be the measure of the inspiration, and therefore we shall not be surprised to find it at its highest when the communion is deliberate and conscious. And this is precisely the case with the Bible as a whole. Many, though not indeed all, of its writers do manifest quite clearly the sense of personal contact with a personal God. He is to them not the personification of an abstract principle, but a vividly realised friend, teacher, and leader. They make it their deliberate purpose to enter into direct communion with Him, spirit meeting with spirit. We do not indeed accept their inspiration or the truth of their message primarily on account of such a claim. But once their teaching has commended itself to the conscience and reason by its inherent appeal, we can then go back to that claim and accept it fully and without reserve ; we can see that it has indeed been the condition and the explanation of their high inspiration.

The same holds good with regard to other seers. The truth, the beauty, the moral grandeur prove their inspiration ; it is not the inspiration which proves that their message is true. But especially where religious values, such as the innermost being and character of God, are concerned, we do find in general that where the highest truth has been discovered there has been some form or other of conscious communion with Him ; the Divine Spirit has entered into the human.

We shall agree in finding the supreme example of inspiration in Christ. And here to a pre-eminent degree the condition of personal communion with the Father, constant and unbroken, is fulfilled. In a special sense He claims to know the Father, *i.e.* to be in touch with Him. His message is not His own, but His Father's ; the sense of "otherness" is very strong, and with it the conviction of authority and certainty. But, once more, the ground on which we accept His teaching, the revelation which comes through Him, is the appeal which it makes to the highest instincts of mankind, an appeal confirmed by, though it does not logically start from, the impression left by our records that Jesus was in a unique sense in touch with God. The proof to others of the reality of such intercourse can in each case only be found in the effects on the character and insight of him who claims to experience it. There are indeed several features to be noted with regard to the inspiration of Christ which confirm the line of thought we have been following here. (1) There is a striking absence of any claim to peculiar or abnormal modes of intercourse ; we hear but little of ecstatic vision or mystic absorption. What Christ experienced was a close and unsullied union with His Father through the normal means which are open to every child of God. (2) It is now generally agreed that this personal inspiration did not bring with it any externally revealed knowledge of historical or scientific fact ; what He knew of these matters came through the ordinary channels ; His originality lay in the insight which He brought to bear on the interpretation of life. (3) He left no written record of His own to stereotype the revelation of which He was the bearer. More and more do we realise the profound significance of the fact that the highest example of inspiration which mankind has known works primarily as a living Spirit in the hearts of those in touch with Him. There is the written record of the Gospels which allows us to know the character and outlines of His teaching, but this teaching comes to us in a diluted form ; it is not fixed in a series of *ipsissima verba* which might be regarded as final, infallible, absolute truth. Thus even in the case of the record of the sayings of the Master Himself the principle holds good that nowhere can we put our finger on a direct undiluted word from heaven ; always there is the human medium which lends its own colour to the revelation.

The Inspiration of the Ordinary Man

We have been speaking of the supreme examples of inspiration, and in general usage we confine the term to these, though the line may be drawn at very different points. And it is important to remember that in all fields it needs the genius to originate or discover, while the ordinary man can but assimilate and understand, at best improve and develop. At the same time, while recognising this general usage, based on a real difference of degrees of insight, we are concerned to maintain that in the last resort it is a question of degree. Inspiration is not a rare thing, peculiar to a small class ; in its measure it is open to, and does often actually come to, the ordinary man. The limitation is parallel to a similar limitation often made in connection with conduct. Holiness, or sainthood, is spoken of as the mark of a few select spirits who have climbed the heights, and yet all God's children, and particularly those who are in fellowship with Christ, may, and often do, attain to their measure of holiness. Even so, as all are called to be saints, they may all be taught of God. Further, while we think specially of inspiration as concerned with religion and spiritual values, in the wider sense it covers all life. It is open to the artist and the man of science, to the historian and the statesman, to the merchant and the labourer. Only from God can each get the right judgement in whatever his hands find to do, and this right judgement is in the last resort of the same nature and comes from the same source, with the same variety of method and process, as inspiration in the narrower sense. We are sometimes suspicious of such inspiration because it has often been associated with illogical, detached intuitions, received as special divine leadings without serious examination, shifting the responsibility of thought and decision from the shoulders of the individual, and acted on with disastrous results to himself and those around him. There is the constant desire to be able to cry "Lo here or Lo there is the finger of God directing me in my way and determining my future." Few, indeed, who have had their eyes open to see the working of God's providence in their life, and have tried to train their ears to hear the voice which says "This is the way, walk ye in it," will deny that at times such leadings do come with a real authority and certainty. But the point which emerges from our investigation is that such supposed intuitions cannot be accepted blindly and without thought as the direct and unquestioned voice of God. They must be approved of by the conscience and reason ; inspiration implies not the disintegration of personality but its enhancement, not the overriding of the faculties of insight and decision, the God-given powers by which each one of us must direct his way on his own ultimate responsibility, but their purging and quickening. If this be remembered, we may, and should, look in joyful confidence and without reserve for the inspiration of the Spirit in our daily life. Not for one moment would we underestimate the supreme value of the inspiration of the seer or the saint, the poet or the thinker, but it is crucial to realise that God has not one method of speaking to and teaching the prophet and something quite different for us ordinary folk. We, too, may find the same personal guidance and illumination, just in so far as by prayer and meditation, by study and thought, by experiment and honest work, on the particular material with which we have to deal, we succeed in opening our hearts to the Presence which is always there.

VII

THE LANGUAGE OF THE SOUL : SOME REFLECTIONS ON THE CHRISTIAN SACRAMENTS

BY

L. DOUGALL

ANALYSIS

Language is developed by fellowship.

But spoken language is never a perfect vehicle of thought.

Conversation is necessary to the development of the soul.

Action is needed to express thought when words fail.

The language of action, like speech, is traditional, but also mutable.

Religion needs its language of action—ritual.

A symbol is something that manifests to human sense a non-sensuous reality.

Much of the action of daily life is symbolic.

The Christian language of action.

The two main ideas of early Christianity—the joy of fellowship with Christ in God's family, and the getting rid of habits of ill-will in order to enjoy it—are symbolised in the Eucharist and Baptism.

Two points necessary for vital Christian ceremonial :

(1) It must express definitely the differentia of the Christian religion.

(2) It must both embody tradition and also register the progressive understanding of truth.

Psychological explanation of the power of the Sacraments :

They act through the psychic law of suggestion.

The potency of a suggestion is in proportion to (1) the arrest of attention in the receiving mind ; (2) the suitability of the suggestion to the prevailing mental attitude.

Objections, and an illustration.

The significance of infant baptism.

Confession and Absolution.

The rites associated with the Eucharist, and their suggestive significance.

Need of appropriate ceremonial.

VII

THE LANGUAGE OF THE SOUL: SOME REFLECTIONS ON THE CHRISTIAN SACRAMENTS

The Evolution of Language

In its simplest form language must be the attempt of one living being to communicate with another living being. In this sense the yap of the hound to attract the pack would be language, even if it were the first yap that the first hound ever gave. But by language we ordinarily mean something more developed—the use of signs agreed upon by the communicators. In so far as a man is solitary, language is impossible, although, having first learnt language by fellowship, he may make of himself an imaginary fellow, and in solitude take great delight in discoursing with himself.

Any system of words which we call a human language has been produced by centuries of psychical development through fellowship; and any language that can be written, however simple and elementary, carries with it the story of a civilisation which is a fellowship systematised. There is a real mystery, and one which ought to evoke our reverence and wonder, in the growth of a highly organised language. Where has its grammar come from? Grammarians discover; they do not create. If the language in which any great literature is written were a production of conscious art or ingenuity, we should honour its creator as in the first rank of human genius. But no man made it, although every

227

man who ever used it aided in its construction. So
when we commonly say that a written language is produced by the genius of a people, we do not mean that
any individual or any number of individuals consciously
set to work to construct it. Language is not a thing
of conscious construction ; it is the unconscious product
of many minds, and reflects deep resemblances of
character of which no one of them may be aware. I
see no reason to suppose that the corporate soul of a
tribe or nation has any one centre of initiation. A
language is the result of the interaction of souls in a
fellowship, and it becomes flexible and highly developed
only when fellowship is intimate and prolonged.

LIMITATIONS OF VERBAL LANGUAGE

What, however, we need more particularly to consider here is the limitation of even the most highly
developed verbal language. The failure of words to
express what is most essential in life is so constantly
with us that, like the ticking of a clock, we do not
even notice it. It is not alone the deep things, but
also the shallow things that we cannot say to one
another except when the subject is matter of common
and familiar experience. I remember once being in
the company of some educated people when a new
fruit had been exposed for sale in the market of a
midland town. Half of my companions had eaten the
fruit, while half had not seen it. Those who knew
it were unable to explain its nature to those who did
not know it. Those who had not seen it agreed with
one voice that they were only confused by the different
descriptions. When an object is quite novel, words
fail to express what an instant's experience of sense-
perception will fully convey. What words can possibly
convey the idea of a new sound or scent or smell or
texture ? Old words fail ; new words must come into
being to describe the new experience.

If this be true of the attempt to describe mere sense-perceptions, it is much more true of the attempt to describe new ideas. To do this the race is constantly using old words in a new sense.

Thus wherever there is development of mind or experience, language is developing to produce new words and new meanings for old ones ; but it always lags behind experience — new words are always being coined and new meanings given to old ones. Language is never static, but its advance is never adequate to express the whole advance of thought or experience. There must always be a fringe, not only of novel discoveries, but of novel thought in any community which its words fail as yet to convey. The original thinker on this account always finds a large part of his exposition must consist in carefully defining his terms.

There is, however, another failure of verbal language with which we are all familiar. There are in every man stirrings of emotion and volition, and half-seen glimpses of complex thoughts, which he cannot put into words even to himself. It is not only that he cannot, or does not wish to, reveal them to others ; his own comprehension of himself fails in that he cannot say at such times what he experiences ; he cannot resolve into its constituent parts an experience confused, blurred, fleeting, elusive.

Beneath the level of our conscious and therefore acquired habits of thought lies the conflux of our primary and secondary instincts. Impulses prompted by any of these provoke in developed minds half-linked associations of thought with other instinctive emotions. In this region appetites and aspirations are blurred, and emotions and desires are like a tangled web. One feeling touches the sympathetic psychic associations of many diverse feelings. It is quite impossible to express what is felt, or what is thought, or what is willed, because when we say it is this, we know that it is also that, and that other, that we feel and desire.

Of course a great deal of human experience that must once have been confused and inexplicable has become clear, because it has been analysed. The pleasures of eating and drinking, for example, are very real emotions, and there is very little in this common experience that an intelligent man cannot analyse, comprehend, and talk about if he wishes to ; but it is quite probable that to a dog the emotion roused by hunger may be a half-comprehended and sacred fervour, associated inextricably with affection for the usual donor of food, and with the deeper and blind instinct of self-preservation and the appetite of sex, and with dim memories of hours of ecstasy in the hunt and the fight. If this be so, whatever means the dog has of communicating with his fellows and with men, such language could only express the main fact of immediate hunger ; but beyond that he would be experiencing things unutterable and inexpressible. The whole attitude of a hungry dog asking for food suggests a quivering intensity of experience which seems to find no adequate vent in the various yaps and attitudes by which he expresses the immediate fact.

In man the emotion of vague longing roused by objects of surpassing beauty or sublimity may produce a fervour of desire incommunicable because it touches the deep spring of other associated instincts. The best verbal utterance we can find for those half-formed thoughts and unanalysed emotions and desires which transcend common speech is poetry ; and poetry usually satisfies us as the expression of such experience by what it suggests rather than by what it says. There is, however, still much that is unexpressed in words, and as the soul can only develop as it finds some means of self-expression, some language of action must supplement the language of words. But before considering the language of action let us pause to realise how true it is that the soul can only develop as it finds means of expression.

CONVERSATION NECESSARY TO THE DEVELOPMENT OF THE SOUL

If we would understand the Christian ideal of fellowship we must fully realise that communication is necessary for the growth of the living soul. We so hug to ourselves the idea that we are deep and great beyond the powers of speech that we are apt to value ourselves mainly by what we do not even try to say ; but the inference we superficially draw from this valuation—that expression is comparatively unimportant to the growth of the soul—will not bear a moment's reflection.

Everywhere we see that as animals rise in the scale of life they rise also in the power of making themselves understood by their kind, and by man when they come into contact with man. Human intelligence is seen to rise above animal intelligence when it is able to use one sound for a whole class of sensations or ideas. A little child begins by gesticulation, and then by words, to say "I want that flower," "I want that ball"; but it goes on to generalise as to the attributes of all balls, all flowers ; and then to classify things accordingly, and to give to the class a common name. Thus it is only by learning to speak that it learns to think. Without distinguishing individuals and classes, subjects and pre-dicates, it is impossible to think. When the child or the savage acquires a language by which these things can be expressed, it has for the first time a means by which to compare its sensations with the sensations of others, and to argue about them, and thus increase its experience. History shows that men grow in power over circumstances and in mutual usefulness at a pace exactly proportionate to their power of thought, which again depends upon their power of exact expression. They can learn only a very little more than they can express, and everywhere the soul is filled with a passionate desire to express that little more, so man is a talking animal. At his highest, as at his lowest, he must talk.

There are three things that move the human soul supremely to desire and admiration—truth and beauty and generosity. A man's conception of truth may be debased or exalted. His pursuit of truth may be that of a Newton or a Darwin, or merely that of a pastry-cook seeking the best way of making pastry. His idea of beauty may be that of one of the world's greatest artists or poets, or it may be the ecstasy of a factory girl over the show in a draper's window, or it may be the ploughman's love of an even furrow. A man's idea of generosity may be expressed in the casual dole out of an abundance, or in dying to save the world. The sum of all that a soul desires or admires may be merely its own comfort, or it may be the God of the most exalted prophet; but whatever it is, that it will pursue unremittingly ; and to this pursuit understanding is essential, and to understanding language is essential.

Language is necessary both for what a man would learn from his fellow-men and for such dialectic as he must carry on within his own mind. Its necessity for progress is brought out by the fact that when anything is fully mastered by the race or the individual, the necessity for conversation in regard to it tends to pass away. On the other hand, wherever man in his pursuit of the good for which he lives begins to transcend what has become a commonplace, there speech of some sort becomes a vital necessity. The whole ferment of his mind is there on the fringe where the unknown enticingly glimmers just beyond the known : at that point he must talk or fail of his desire. He may be most conscious of the need to talk to himself, or to talk to other men, or to talk to God ; but talk he will, for talk he must, for talk is necessary to further understanding which must precede further acquirement. The working of this law is so constant and invariable that we hardly notice it.   How little talk there is in any village about the boiling of potatoes or the digging of the ground !   If a new industry is established, a new vegetable introduced, what an amount of talk is required before the corresponding necessary habit becomes established.

But what is it that happens when the acquirement upon which the soul has staked its all is something for which the race has coined no word ?   Language is still necessary ; nay, it is then most necessary of all.

But, lest we go too fast, let us, before considering further this need of self-expression, estimate the value of solitary self-culture.   Of course the speech common to any race fails to express the idiosyncrasies of individual experience.   Not only is the self of the friend or companion always something to be appre-hended by faith, but also every soul, when it comes to interrogate itself, finds that what is most its own, and therefore most precious, has no verbal expression. This fact gives colour to a conviction abroad in our civilisation, that the individual mind lives at its highest when it withdraws itself from all communication with others.   It is natural enough that this idea should have become prevalent, because in every civilisation there comes a stage when it is observed by those of superior education that many ideas which are in the true sense of the word vulgar, *i.e.* common to the multitude, are of a tawdry and artificial character. They do not represent the realities by which alone the noble mind can live ; and the first reaction to this discovery is, very naturally, an undue emphasis upon the comparative nobility of a state of solitude and the idea that the merely individual reaction on life is the highest truth attainable.   Such proverbs as "God made the country but man made the town," "Speech is silvern, silence is golden," testified to the cult of solitude by the votaries both of sensibility and of religion, and also by

that scholarly class of men who have thought kindly of
the Stoic conception of the self-contained life. It is the
first and most obvious reaction of the mind that finds
itself making some progress beyond the ideas and sentiments which have become the common property of its
generation. " Mob " and " crowd " psychology, the
so-called " psychology of the herd," are new phrases
often used to cover the premature generalisations and
conclusions which psychology, like every infant science,
makes ; but in all ages of the world there has been
instinctive recognition of certain truths of crowd
psychology by reasonable men. The inference they
usually drew from them was the desirability of being in
some things a law to oneself and living an inward life
apart from men, either holding no communion whatever upon the deep things of the heart, or holding such
communion only with a God conceived as unrelated to
all those things which occupy natural human speech.
The self-sufficing idea of Stoic philosophy and ethics,
the self-and-God sufficiency of monastic religion and
of the mysticism of the Plotinus tradition, were in
each case an individualism bred of some distinctive
education which the ordinary man of the world did not
enjoy. When in the fifteenth and sixteenth centuries
education became a more common grace, this idea that
wisdom lay in aloofness naturally spread to a much
larger class in the community. In our last two decades
fellowship, rather than Stoicism, has been the fashion of
the hour, but to some it appears a mere fashion :
Wordsworth has not yet lost his influence when he
sings praise of solitude.[1]

---

[1] " In aloofness and loneliness of mind [Wordsworth] is exceeded by no mystic
of the cloister. . . . In his youth he confesses that human beings had only a
secondary interest for him ; and though he says that Nature soon led him to man,
it was to man as a ' unity,' as ' one spirit,' that he was drawn, not to men as individuals. See *Prelude*, viii. " (Inge, *Christian Mysticism*).
Compare the closing lines of *Prelude*, bk. viii. :

> Nature had led me on ;
> And oft amid the " busy hum " I seemed
> To travel independent of her help,

Before we can estimate fully the need which every soul has of a language that will express its whole mental life, we must satisfy ourselves adequately as to the truth and the untruth of that attitude of mind which regards retirement within itself—either for the purpose of discovering religious or philosophical or ethical truth, or for the enjoyment of beauty,—as a condition superior to any phase of communication with fellow-minds. We can see its partial truth in the case of the man who perceives that he has ideas and aspirations in advance of those current among others. It is evident that he is quite right in believing that solitude or inward retirement is more favourable to his progress than participation in the babble of the market-place or street. For example, the man who to-day wished to form a just estimate of the faults and virtues of his nation's enemies would certainly do well to retire often from the Stock Exchange, or the political gathering, or the fashionable club. To withdraw mind, if not body, from the common talk of these assemblies would be necessary to the formation of conclusions characterised by outstanding justice or nobility. Humility would not stand in the way of his knowing that he had within himself a higher guide ; if he did not know this he would be blinded by folly.

If, however, such a man hugs himself and is satisfied in such retirement, his mistake consists in his ignorance of the fact that in a fellowship of souls as eager or more eager than himself for justice and nobility of mental attitude, he would attain to still higher insight, and be able to form truer conclusions. Under the stimulus of this higher fellowship individual variation of thought would find constantly increasing power of

---

As if I had forgotten her ; but no,
The world of human-kind outweighed not hers
In my habitual thoughts ; the scale of love,
Though filling daily, still was light, compared
With that in which *her* mighty objects lay.

expression, and would thus become more, not less, distinctive. Thus we see that while the superiority of self-communion embodies a very important truth, taken by itself it forms a half-truth which amounts to pernicious falsehood; for communion with others is necessary to the soul.

Yet further, it is essential to the development of the soul that it should learn expression in all ways and on all aspects of life. That is why the small community of select souls, exceedingly valuable as it is, is not an end in itself. The truth learned in such a fellowship must be made explicable to the world. The outer world must constantly be being drawn into the fellowship, or else the members, having no universal aim, will be satisfied with only that partial expression necessary for their mutual understanding. The individual remains dwarfed except as a member of a "beloved community," and the loving community degenerates except when it seeks to save the world.

The Language of Action

Because the need of self-expression is so imperative it follows that action must be used when words fail. While power of expression and consequent understanding will always increase by communion between different minds, it will always lag behind power of insight. As we have seen, the suggestions of poetry carry us beyond the precise meaning of the words in which it is expressed, and the language of action comes in to aid when words fail utterly. Thus poetry lies upon the border line between the language of speech and the language of action. True poetry is not written about anything that can be fully said in words; it is the use of words to suggest what lies just beyond their power to express. It gives us pictures of things that are like other things for which there is no picture; and when these things are the great and deep realities of life, and the pictures that poetry presents create an adequate suggestion of what cannot be pictured, it is great poetry. But just beyond the language of poetry there is the language of look and of gesture and of the action that "speaks louder than words." We understand our own laughter and tears as a language expressing amusement or sorrow when words for these fail us. Not very long ago human laughter was used to express happiness when that transcended words, but at present in our civilisation we only use laughter for the particular kind of joy we call amusement ; other and deeper joy has neither word nor sound. The language of tears is also inadequate. When Wordsworth says :

> To me the meanest flower that blows can give
> Thoughts that do often lie too deep for tears,

he is expressing the inadequacy that we all recognise of even the language of tears.

And the mind as well as the body has its gestures inexpressible in words ; indeed, as men develop more self-control they express themselves less and less in the glance and in bodily gesture, but the mind retains its downward and its upward look, its inquiring look, its look of love. We speak of aspiration, of pessimism, of curiosity, or adoration, and perhaps we do not always realise that these are merely words for the way in which the eyes of the soul act toward what is just beyond the soul's power of verbal expression. We speak of the feeling of being baffled, the feeling of being on the verge of illumination, the feeling of impulsion toward we know not what, and many other phrases we use to describe what are really gestures of the mind, inarticulate gestures like the dropping of the arms when effort is useless, like the stretching out of the arms to denote a yearning to receive, like the attitude of alertness assumed by a messenger when waiting for the word of command.

Every man has within himself unappeasable desires for beauty, for truth, for generosity, and in his attitude toward these he seeks to express in action what he cannot express in words. All art is, in a sense, the language of action ; by music and painting we express our unspoken conceptions of the best. Art must be individual or it is nothing—" Le style c'est l'homme." What is not original genius is valueless as art, and every man and woman is in some aspect of life an artist.

Now if the soul in regard to its deepest inward individual experience and aspirations cannot do without the language of action, it is quite certain that it cannot do without this form of language in any phase of communal life. It is for the topics men have in common that such language is most in use. In corporate life the meaning of actions must be agreed upon. Caresses such as mothers give to children are understood the world over, except in a few savage tribes. The shaking of the fist, the menace of the eye, the toss of the head in scorn, the bowing of the head in shame or shyness, the handclasp of friendship—all these are signs of a language which is common to Western nations. If by some process of rigorous training a clique in society reaches the point where such signs are in abeyance, we know that vitality in that class is waning, and that what was artificial and cold has taken the place of the natural and warm-hearted. On the other hand, where such language of action is violent it is also crude, and as it becomes subtle, with more various gradations expressing more, it is, for that very reason, more restrained. For whatever purpose men are associated together, some common language of action is necessary to them. What would public life be without cheers and hand-clapping and groans ? What would social life be without the dance of festivity and the slow procession that follows the bier ?

It is most important to observe that all this necessary language of action is expressive and wholesome only so far as it is both natural in its mode and spontaneous at the time of action ; and in so far as it is both these it will always be both traditional and ready to break with tradition—that is to say, it will be handed down, like the language of words, from one generation to another, and at the same time, like the language of words, it will be undergoing ceaseless modifications. It goes without saying that a language will remain fundamentally the same from generation to generation. The English language has been the same language through all its developments, although Beowulf could not be read easily in the fifteenth century, or Chaucer in the eighteenth.   Nor did its changes come by mere individual pleasure ; variations had to be approved by the corporate sense of the community before they became part of the national language.

On the other hand, it is to be noted that whenever naturalness and popular variation in the use of words is not tolerated, and some classic standard is rigidly adhered to by the educated, the art of speech becomes the artificial practice of a few.   It moves stiffly, like a man walking on stilts.   One who talks and writes in that way may be admired for singular dexterity, but he can company only with the few who also walk on stilts.   Great literature is not produced in periods when men seek to conform their whole diction to rules of speech bequeathed by a former age, but when popular language is virile and growing.

So is it with the language of action.   It is, of course, traditional, handed down from father to son, and yet it is mutable.   There are at different periods, in different classes of society, mannerisms which remain fixed till they are lifeless and become the symptoms of social decadence.   Certain Oriental habits of obeisance and compliment, which are senselessly repeated generation after generation at great expense of time and energy, could not be tolerated by a nation in a vital, alert, and progressive state.   In the West we have had our social rituals, both in courts and cottages. At the time they arise such rituals express truly the taste, dignity, and sense of order of those who use them, but as rigid survivals they express nothing, and are thrown off when there is a revival of vitality.

All this applies equally to the rituals of religion. We have seen that the deeper and more instinctive our outgoing impulse toward any object of desire, the more it becomes mixed up in our thought with all else desirable. Hence the most inexpressible outflow of the heart is toward the source of all good things, *i.e.* toward what constitutes God to each soul. It is thus most of all in religion, whatever a man's religion may be, that the language of action is most necessary. Accordingly we find that wherever religion has emerged as something which requires separate associations and separate treatment from the rest of life, it has had its separate phraseology, its separate poetry, and its separate language of action.

All evidence, both historic and psychological, goes to show that personal or corporate religion must find expression not only in words but in rites. He who believes that for all men religion would be better or purer if it ceased to find expression in the language of action is surely mistaken. He is doubtless right in his disapproval of a merely conventional language of action or rigid ritual, but wrong in supposing that men do not require to give their religion the fullest expression of which they are capable. Religion needs to employ the language of reason, as precise and as full as it can be made, the language of art, which carries into different regions of the depth and height, and the language of action, which is like a hand pointing to the distance where clear vision fails, like a hand held behind the ear in the consciousness of a music whose vibrations are barely audible. Looking upon the past, we see that wherever religion has, by the clearer vision of some great prophet, received a new start and a new

VII   THE LANGUAGE OF THE SOUL   241

impulse, it has begun at once to form a certain language of its own, using the common speech to express as well as may be its new ideas, giving old words new meanings and coining words by new combinations of syllables. It has also produced a new poetry and a new art ; but even before these have come into being it has had new ceremonies and rites.   Psychologically it is not possible that it should be otherwise ; historically we see that it has always been so.

WHAT IS A SYMBOL ?

There is an idea prevalent that a symbol is something that pretends to be some other thing which it is not, or, to speak more accurately, that it is something which is set up or used as a pretence for something else.   Just as a child, for example, who wraps a kerchief round a poker and nurses it, pretends that the poker is a doll, or as a child may nurse a doll pretending it is a baby. We are told that in the rites of initiation practised by nations in a certain stage of development, men use the heads of fierce animals as masks, and, pretending to be the animal personated, get carried away by the excitement of the ceremonies into the belief that, for the time being, they really are the animal they pretend to be.

Now, in these three instances, the poker, the doll, and the head of the lion or bull are properly not symbols at all ; they are toys which a child-like imagination, always ready with its make-believe, determines for the time to regard as something which they are not.

A symbol, on the other hand, is something which manifests to human sense a non-sensuous reality ; and the truest symbols are those things in human life which are the most natural manifestations of the unseen reality.

A national flag is a symbol of the national ideal so long as the great majority of the nation can unite in an ideal for which one symbol may stand.   When there is civil

R

war the same flag cannot be the symbol of opposing ideas, and two will be necessary, *e.g.* the red flag of Socialism has often opposed a national banner. A flag, however, is in essence a military symbol ; in its beginning it was a banner held aloft in order that the followers of chieftain or king might rally round him. Although it has long been used in time of peace to rally the forces of national sentiment, as in primitive times it was used to rally the force of their spears, it is still an anti-foreign sentiment to which it usually and naturally appeals. It is quite possible that when all swords are beaten into ploughshares flags will become as much relics of the past as are the emblems of heraldry to-day, and nations will evolve new symbols more consonant with their ideals. The point to be noted, however, is that there is no pretence that a flag is what it is not. The British flag is not, and does not pretend to be, British justice or British honesty or British kindliness or British honour or power ; but these realities, tremendous though they are, are unseen ; they are spiritual realities which, by reason of their nature, can only be made actual to our senses by a visible and material symbol. The crew of a wrecked ship, drifting without compass and without star upon the sea, if it came in sight of shore or ship on which our flag was waving, would have no doubt whatever as to the invisible realities for which it stands and of which it is the accepted manifestation.

The other point about the flag is that, although it may now seem a purely arbitrary symbol, it was at first chosen as the most natural and convenient expression of tribal unity. It was as natural for a chieftain in war to wave some particular colour to rally his particular men as it is for a rabbit to display the white lining of her tail when she runs before her little ones to guide them into safety. Further, as no cumbrous object could be carried into battle, it was necessary to use cloth that could be unfurled and furled. In so far as our symbol of nationality needs to be carried about and waved aloft to-day, a flag is for the same reason necessary ; nothing else would practically do as well.

If we want to understand further the true nature of a symbol we may examine some symbols which seem to us still more natural than the flag.   Take a mother caressing her child.   She kisses the little one : the kiss is not her affection, it is only a symbol.   If the mother knew herself to be the prey of some infectious disease, she would love the child just as much, but she would not kiss it.   If a cold-hearted nurse found it to her interest to pretend to love the child, she would caress it although she did not love it.   Caresses are not love ; they are its natural symbol, and, like all symbols, when honestly used they make manifest a great reality.

Again, let us take any of those things acknowledged to be the customary signs of a certain relation between people.   Friends clasp each others' hands ; domestic servants stand in the presence of their employers.   The hand-grasp is not friendship, though it can be made to symbolise every varying degree of friendship.   If a man's hands are otherwise occupied, or if he have lost the use of them, no one would suspect the absence of the hand-shake to indicate any necessary alteration in his friendship.   An English servant stands before his employer because that is his way of symbolising his loyalty to the engagement he has entered into to be alert to carry out the other's wishes : in some parts of America a man with another training, who had entered into a similar engagement and with the same loyalty at heart, would remain seated in a lounging attitude.

Symbols, then, of necessity enter largely into the daily life of any community that has a past in common. Certain actions have come to stand as the expression of certain inner realities.   The expression is in no sense a pretence ; it is the only way, or at least the commonly accepted way, of manifesting forth a reality which otherwise could not be seen or heard or touched.

Christian Language of Action

Not long ago two girls sat by my fireside talking of sacramental religion. The elder ended the conversation by saying, " Our Lord commanded us to do these things ; that is why we do them." She spoke with shining face and serene faith ; but when she had left the room the other spoke with passionate disagreement in words like these. " Every educated person knows that we do not know precisely what words our Lord used, and His meaning needs interpretation. As to St. Paul, when he could make so big a mistake about the Second Coming he may easily have made mistakes about the Sacraments. I cannot honestly do what seems meaningless to me upon mere ecclesiastical authority." I think we must admit that the first of these girls represents a dwindling minority, the second a growing majority of earnest-minded young people, for a very small proportion of the young now frequent our churches. Can we face this fact without fear ? Have we any need for fear if we appeal to truth rather than to mere tradition ?

All religions have a language of action. Christianity is no exception to the rule, and it will be worth while to consider how far its rites are natural and appropriate.

If we had no record of its early days, if there were no written command that we could even suppose to be the authentic fiat of its founder, if all that we knew about it was the main emphasis of its idealism, we might yet make a shrewd guess at what its peculiar language of action would at first be. The privilege of companionship with God, the duty and privilege of fellowship with men, one dependent on the other, and the joy of both, is certainly the main theme of the earliest Christian teaching. This is commonly expressed as the Fatherhood of God and the brotherhood of man ; and thus expressed the two elements are seen to be one theme, one idea—that of God's family on earth.

But to love God and to love man is an art ; it is the very art of living ; it is the art at which all religions and all civilisations have been aiming ; for by love we mean, not only a certain personal liking, but such goodwill that kindness must govern all the changeful moods and developments of life.   The common life of men who love displays harmony, not only in chords here and there, but throughout all the movement of the symphony of public and private life.   All laws, all morals, all rituals have been efforts to get rid of discord, to set the movement and development of the individual life or the community life free from the clash and anguish of the antagonistic elements that hamper life.   When primitive man realised the fear of the unseen he had to invent modes of propitiating the supposed anger of spirits.   When the individual quarrel or family feud weakened the tribe, some court of justice was set up, so that within the tribe there might be peace.   The effort to get agreement in greater and greater areas of common life was not only the beginning but the method of each successive stage in all religion and all civilisation.

The world into which Christianity came was civilised and religious ; a world also in which communities of people, not satisfied with the general conception of civilisation and religion, were on all sides setting up brotherhoods—the so-called Mystery Religions—with elaborate secret ways of getting into harmony with God and with each other.   The joy and simplicity of the main Christian idea was the recognition that the art of living harmoniously with God and man was not recondite, was not a secret shut off from the common man by mysterious initiations or by long and severe disciplines, but was very near to all men, something that would spring up spontaneously in the lives of men who sought it, the very reign of God within the heart, which would be expressed in all the simple and common things of life.   Yet in the very hour in which the inspiration and technique of this fine art of living joyfully and freely with God and man was seen to be possible to the common man, the one reason of his failure so to live was seen also. When it was realised that the Spirit of God was the love that attracted but did not compel, it was realised that man's failure to be its instrument was due to those habits of ill-will and repulsive antagonisms in forming which he had forged his own chains. Jesus taught that goodwill to men was a necessary condition of divine inspiration.[1] His followers came to see that aspiration and desire were in antagonism to habits which the Jew naturally called "sin" and the Greek called "ignorance." So that the second main idea of Christianity became the need of getting rid of these habits of ill-will. Intense desire was naturally felt for some way of leaving sin behind, as one would leave the soil of dirty work in the water of a bath before joining the family meal.

These two main ideas—the joy of life in God's family, and the getting rid of habits of ill-will in order to enjoy it—had a very natural language of action in the feast of the Eucharist, and in washing as a rite of initiation into the community.

In thinking of early Christianity as instinct with these two ideas, we realise that the early sense of joy in them would not only necessarily imply, but in reality be, an outgoing of affection and loyalty to the Master who had so pushed back the veil of confused human thinking, so dissipated the murk arising from deified ill-will, as to bring their sunlight to earth. No language of action could grow up in such a community that was not centred in His memory, so that the natural expression of the truth that He had revealed might easily come to be spoken of as memorials of this, or as acts done in obedience to His verbal commands, even if no proof of such commands survived.

So far we can see how the Christian Sacraments

---

[1] Mark xi. 25.

would come into being, and therefore we can the more easily believe that they were given by the Master. His insight into the heart of man and the ways of God was too deep to find expression in arbitrary commands.   Can the various phases of Church teaching concerning these Sacraments be shown to be psychologically natural ?

We are familiar with the human habit of calling two ideas when closely associated by the name of one, or using the picture of something that can be pictured to stand more especially for something that cannot be pictured.   Thus we speak of "the State," meaning the liberties and securities and the unifying of many into one for which the State stands, and also its political machinery and material defences ; but most of our language concerning it presents to the mind's eye, not the great ideas which make the State of value, but the machinery which has been created—the mere instrument of ideas.   In periods of national deadness the ideas are more and more lost sight of, and the machinery becomes an end in itself.

In all personal affection the body and soul and thoughts of the object of our affection are welded into a unity not to be dissociated in thought : we love—not the body, nor the soul, nor the thoughts of a friend—but we love him or her.

But most of our language referring to the soul presents to " our mind's eye " only the body :

> Now my soul hath elbow-room.
> *King John*, Act v. Sc. 7.

> I'll wear my heart upon my sleeve for daws to peck at.
> *Othello*, Act i. Sc. 1.

> Friends, Romans, countrymen, lend me your ears.
> *Julius Caesar*.

> I saw Othello's visage in his mind.
> *Othello*, Act i. Sc. 3.

> Drink to me only with thine eyes.
> *To Celia*.

Such language understood figuratively when life beats high becomes pernicious when life is flat and uninspired. It helps us to lose sight of all that in the reality of things not only ought to make, but does make, the body dear. Thus in uninspired times of the Church we naturally find an exaltation of the body of Jesus in the interpretation of the Sacrament of the Eucharist without submission to His spirit.

Again, we see the same with regard to truth and personality. We closely associate our heroes with that truth for which they stood, not only by virtue of the law of association, but because a man is the truth that he takes his stand upon. It is something inherent in his soul which causes that ray of light to burst through him to the world, something inherent in his character that causes him to be the living exponent of the truth he reveals. Just as the body is the expression and instrument of the soul and is therefore rightly reverenced as the vehicle of a soul worthy of reverence and adoration, so, in a closer sense, a man's character revealed in his action and teaching is the expression of such part of God's eternal truth as the prism of his soul lets through. But here again the language we use naturally pictures for us, not the invisible truth, but the man speaking and acting ; and wherever hero-worship degenerates, the truth which was an inseparable part of the man himself is lost sight of, and the name and perhaps one or two dramatic actions of the hero become objects of reverence in themselves to thousands who are not actuated by the truth that he made his own. This is proved by the fact that nearly all proverbs in which great men are remembered leave out their true greatness—" A Daniel come to judgement " ; " Alexander weeping for fresh worlds to conquer " ; " As meek as Moses." Thus in many Catholic countries we get genuine enthusiasm for the name of Christ as honoured in the Eucharist among populations rife with cheating and adultery and quarrels of every kind. It is found on inquiry that in such communities little is known of Jesus except the dramatic stories of His birth and death.

What is curious in this whole process of substituting the seen for the unseen is that those who lose sight of the spirit and adore the visible expression as something sacred in itself, proceed to impugn, as a violation of this sanctity, any teaching that body can only be an evanescent expression of the soul; and when they come to worship merely the name and the dramatic actions of their heroes, they regard those heroes as in some way profaned if the truth in which they lived and which they disseminated be greatly magnified. In our own Church to-day we find many who deprecate insistence upon the fatherhood of God and the brother-hood of man, because they imagine that the Cross and Atonement and Sacramental Grace will be belittled thereby.

In our Lord Jesus Christ we see a character able to perceive and assimilate, not some one particular ray of the eternal light, but the light itself. Truth, as far as it concerned the relation of God and man, formed His soul and thus became one with Himself. What He seems to have seen in constant vision was the whole concrete harmony which would be effected by the Spirit's unfettered activity, and which He called "the kingdom of heaven." His truth-seeing, truth-assimi-lating soul was manifested naturally in a body symbolic of ideal humanity, whose presence brought joy and peace, whose touch was health. If, then, we do not lose sight of the truth of the kingdom, or forget that body must always be a transient vehicle of spirit, we are right in seeing in Jesus Christ the way, the truth, the life. But to find, amid the various vicissitudes of the society He founded, discrepant phases of devotion to Him is only what we should expect. We should expect to find times when the body of the beloved would stand for the spirit and would veil any adequate perception of that spirit. And, again, we are not surprised to find that some picturesque expression of certain phases of the action and passion of our Lord have at times been allowed to eclipse the eternal truth of which He was the manifestation. These vicissitudes, patent in the history of Christian doctrine, are all chronicled also in the various phases of the Christian ceremonial which grew up around the rites of Baptism and the Eucharist ; and because the interpretation of that language, and the consequent usages that have grown up in connection with it, have passed through these various phases of partiality and succeeding falsity, it is not surprising that many of the most earnest lovers of the Master should begin to feel that the language of action is so likely to become misleading as to be in itself undesirable, or at least unnecessary. But such an attitude, though natural as a reaction against crude and mechanical conceptions, goes too far. Sacramental language is in itself of surpassing value, and it cannot mislead so long as Jesus Christ, His outward manifestation, and the great truths for which He stood, are all recognised as *one* object of devotion, and so long as it is not stereotyped by a rigid, unalterable tradition.

Christian Ceremonial

In all religions the language of action is complex, and Christianity is no exception. Ordinarily Christians observe a somewhat long ceremony of mingled words and acts. We have just discovered two points necessary to ceremonial vitality : (1) its words must express such thoughts and feelings as are common to the worshippers ; and (2) there must be constant modification of its words and actions which must display both the traditional and the revolutionary character of language.

(1) The Christian ceremonial must be Christian—

i.e. it must definitely express that which differentiates the Christian religion from other religions, even where other religions express truth.   Truth when vital is not patient of abstraction ; no part of it can be dissociated from the rest ; so that we cannot with accuracy say that minds differing really and vitally from one another have common ground, or that religions differing in one basal part are the same in other parts, although this way of speaking is often sufficiently accurate for convenience.   Two fields may be green with the same green corn, lying in the same sunshine ; but if one field contains a splash of red poppies and the other has a grey ruin within its circumference, the green of the two fields will be seen to reflect the light differently because of the different colours with which it is contrasted. Two men may be equally honest, but if one is honest because of loyalty to his neighbour and the other because he wishes to be respectable, it cannot be said that their honesty is in reality common ground.   Men who express the same truths differently may, in reality, have far more in common than would appear from their expression, but if they do really apprehend any part of truth differently, the whole of truth that they apprehend will be modified accordingly.   So, while it remains true that many who sit at meat in the kingdom may be found to come from the East of a nominal agnosticism or the West of some other religion, and many of the children of the profession may be cast out, it still must also remain true that a Christian has a special way of apprehending all truth which comes to him in the light of the revelation of God in Christ, and which makes a permanent difference in his apprehension of all truth.   It is just this difference which ought to be expressed in the Christian's language of action. That action must have definite relation to the historic Jesus.

(2) The details of the ceremony are an effort to interpret the central rite.   A form must never crystallise ;

when it does so it ceases to be spontaneous speech and becomes rehearsal. The twofold value of language is that while it registers the knowledge attained in the past it is also an aid to progressive understanding, and it is not in mere rehearsal or recitation that we obtain further light and new experiences. It is of the very essence of life that every day must bring the casting off of something old, the acquirement of something new. We see this process going on even in the hills which are called eternal, and in all organic nature. In nature, or in human history, there is no real repetition, but the incessant and permanent use of the same simple elements and methods to produce an ever-increasing variety, with the constant change toward what is more worthy or towards degeneration. In the same way ritual, to be vital, must, while making permanent use of the same elements and methods, be always passing into some new phase, always leaving some older phase behind. It is no valid objection to the ceremonial of the Latin Mass to point out how far it is removed from the usage of the second century. It *is* a valid criticism to urge that in an ever-expanding civilisation it has been practically at a standstill for a thousand years.

The Psychological Explanation of the Power of the Sacraments

In an earlier generation the scientific discoveries concerning common sequences of cause and effect in the visible world—what are popularly called "laws of nature"—gravely disturbed the religious mind, before the new knowledge could be assimilated to what was indestructible in the old. A similar disturbance is being caused to-day by the application of the same methods of science to sequences in the unseen world of thought and feeling, especially by their application to Christian religious experience ; and in some quarters we have a repetition of the old mistake—the desire to deny the new knowledge or to insist that it does not apply to some particular sphere of fact. It is unfortunate that so many of those who are ardent for the old religious truth should be ardent also for that old religious error— the error of refusing to learn from experience.

But whether those who are religious desire it or not, the psychologists will bring forward what they call their "explanation" of the power generated by Christian usages. Attempts to consider religious practices in the light of the newly discovered laws of Mental Suggestion are constantly being made. We are told that preaching produces its effects, not only by its appeal to reason, but by the power of quasi-hypnotic suggestion ; that hymn-singing has the effect of rendering the mind peculiarly open to suggestion ; that the power of prayer is the power of auto-suggestion ; and that the power of suggestion is an explanation peculiarly applicable to the results of rites and ceremonies. The law of suggestion appears to be this—*The potency of a suggestion upon an individual mind at any given time corresponds with the quiescence of that mind's initiative energy at the time of receiving the suggestion.* That is to say, the more the energy of the mind is being expended upon what it of itself wills to think or to do, the less it is open to suggestion ; the more its initiative energy is suspended, the more it experiences the force of suggestion. All traditional forms of religious ceremony are calculated to produce both quiescence and forceful suggestion in greater or less degree. Religious ceremonies grow as the grammar of any language grows, and their form is the result of their effectiveness. They survive because they are fitted to survive. When the potency of a ceremony, or the effectiveness of any portion of it, ceases, men neglect it. Ceremonies are potent just in the degree in which they lead the mind up to a moment of supreme receptiveness, and lull it or persuade it into yielding to present suggestion offered from without or to past teaching arising within the soul at the receptive moment.

We may be over-suggestible by nature, *i.e.* we may be inclined to follow every suggestion that comes to us, as is a happy child, without exercising rational criticism on our own inclination, or exerting a due power of self-initiation. We may be contra-suggestible by nature, *i.e.* we may be inclined to oppose whatever any other human being suggests to us, as a peevish child does, without rational criticism of our own disinclination or attempting to exert our power of self-initiation. Or we may be well-balanced, and use all suggestion merely as grist for the mill of instinctive or reasoned judgement. But in any case we are constantly subject to suggestion ; without suggestion from outside we lose individuality, our faculties atrophy. But suggestion coming upon a distracted mind, over-busy or anxious, has no force ; and just as hunger previous to eating is necessary for the proper assimilation of food by the body, so quiescence before receiving suggestion is necessary for the full force of the suggestion to be realised. Experience will always teach religious leaders, by degrees, how to produce that condition of mind in a congregation without which any ceremonial is ineffective. The modern psychologist merely discovers and explains the law by which the Church has instinctively worked in thus formalising the garnered fruit of religious experience.

It may be well to observe that this whole matter is confused in the minds of many by the trivial and more or less accidental fact that the word "suggestion," used in this scientific sense, first became popularised in connection with some fact—and much exaggerated fiction—concerning the control exercised by certain charlatan hypnotists over hypnotic subjects. Such instances of the tyrannical power wielded over innocent subjects by hypnotists bear the same relation to the ordinary laws of mental receptiveness and the usefulness of suggestion that sensational instances of the cruelty of parents to

children bear to the common order and discipline of
every nursery and schoolroom. We do not argue that
all school discipline is wrong because we have read of
Mr. Squeers, or that all education for little boys is wrong
because Paul Dombey and others in the same case are
killed by mental overwork; but this is the sort of argument which lies behind the popular prejudice against
the idea.

There is, however, a better reason why a number of
well-informed people are afraid to admit that mental
quiescence and mental suggestion are the method by
which the Spirit uses religious ceremonial. The constant effort of pietists in religion and pietists in politics,
of the demagogue and newspaper writer, to govern the
world, or what little part of the world is in their power,
by abuse of the law of suggestion—making appeal to
the emotions of the masses while the facts on which
they might form a rational judgement are withheld—has
always been a serious evil in human society, and is
perhaps the worst evil of our modern life. It is the
spirit of pseudo- or anti-democracy in Church and State,
which, feigning to be true democracy, deceives the very
elect. In the Christian Church this abuse of the power
of suggestion to arouse party spirit might indeed be
called Antichrist. But such abuse of psychical law
only proves the universality of the law, which, working
as it does in religious ceremonial, may by participants
be abused or rightly used, just as the power of public
speaking or writing may be. The misuse of all these
is a great anti-social sin, and lies in some degree on the
souls of the people who are willing to be misled, as
well as in a greater degree on the souls of those who are
still more aware of what they are doing in misleading
them. But if we analyse this sin we shall find it consists *first* and *mainly* in asking people to form opinions
while withholding or slurring over facts the knowledge
of which is necessary before the average mind can form a
right judgement; or *secondly*, in suggesting to them that

people better able to judge than themselves have discovered the truth, so that they will be justified, or are
even to be commended, in saving themselves the trouble
of using their reason and taking the proffered decision
on authority ; or *thirdly*, in making appeal to the
emotions of people when their minds are insufficiently
informed upon the matter to be decided or they have
been persuaded not to use them. Any appeal to human
beings which has any or all of these three elements is an
act of great wickedness, wickedness in which people
who allow themselves to be thus led participate. But
we cannot argue from this that any appeal to the
emotions of a crowd is wrong, or that bringing the
crowd into a quiescent state of receptiveness and
expectancy before that appeal is made is wrong. An
appeal to the emotions of men when their minds are
hushed by the gravity of the hour is a perfectly
legitimate way of dealing with them, provided that the
people thus dealt with have been given no *ex parte*
statements but have the fullest information and knowledge that can be given concerning the matter in hand,
and provided their reasoning powers are stimulated
and encouraged at all other times.

Professor McDougall defines suggestion as "a process
of communication resulting in the acceptance with conviction of the communicated proposition in the absence
of logically adequate grounds for its acceptance." [1] But
to this must be added that it is also a method of convincing the subconscious mind of propositions which
the reason has accepted, but which the will cannot act
on. *E.g.* a drunkard reasonably believes that he ought
to refrain from drink and can, yet, like St. Paul,[2]
what he wills he cannot do. When suggestion drives
his conscious conviction into his subconscious mind he
can reform. Such suggestion may be forcibly conveyed
by a sacrament.

---

[1] *Social Psychology*, p. 97.   [2] Romans vii.

Baptism

I remember once seeing a baptism on the shore of the Atlantic in the State of Maine. Two mission preachers—one a Presbyterian, the other a Canadian Anglican—had joined in an open-air mission, and that evening, when the sun was setting, they baptized their converts, dipping them in the surf of the ocean. A curious and solemn silence fell upon the little crowd of spectators who gathered between a fragrant pine-wood and the incoming tide. Baptism by immersion is the traditional use of the American camp-meeting. The missioners, their black Geneva gowns floating behind them on the water, looked intrepid and serene in the rolling waves. The candidates went through the high surf and returned with a swinging, elastic step, enthusiasm upon their faces. Of one or two cases I happened later to get personal details, and learnt that this baptism had marked a turning-point in the life. An hour after his baptism I walked with one of the men. Although trembling with cold and excitement, he told me that his ecstasy of inward joy was so great that he could hardly refrain from shouting aloud. He said that for many years he had been resisting the belief that he ought to be baptized by immersion, such baptism for him involving publicity, from which he shrank ; but that for some time he had been convinced that the Holy Spirit would not come into his soul till in this matter he conformed. He had been baptized in infancy, but had grown up a fretful and self-centred man ; he became radiant and self-forgetful. Those who believe that " all grace is the grace of God " will not deny that for this man this particular form of baptism became the natural channel of enhanced life, because when he at last ended the inner conflict there ensued a state of passivity in which the powerful suggestion of the dramatic ceremony moved, not only

s

his conscious, but his whole instinctive, life. He went forward in the power of that suggestion until a new habit of mind was established.

The baptizings of the Primitive Church were, no doubt, similarly dramatic; the preparation of the candidates would lead them to expect a corresponding dramatic change in their life, and the rite would be a channel of divine grace. The tradition of a supernatural power being received would naturally grow up; but if by "supernatural" is meant something differing both in kind and degree from that which may be obtained through non-sacramental forms of right mental suggestion, the word appears to imply a misreading of the ways of God. Christian adult baptism, or confirmation, is normally accompanied by the acceptance on the part of the candidate of those standards of value which are typical of traditional Christianity. In so far as these standards are truly Christian they are the highest that the world knows, and their acceptance, especially when worked into the inner consciousness by a suggestive rite, has transforming force. It is such transforming force that is the mark of the Spirit's working. To believe that salvation is magically conferred by the rite, where there is no change in the trend of life from downward to upward, is to believe something for which there is no evidence. Where there is such change in the life-current there is surely adequate proof of the endowment of God without the assertion of any further non-natural endowment.

Another way in which baptism in the early Church would be found in practice to conduce to new life in a convert was by his translation into the new environment of the Christian society, then sharply cut off from pagan laxity. Such a change would operate powerfully to make a new man. That complete change of environment was not possible when the world became nominally Christian, but the tradition of a complete change lingered and could not fail to be suggestive.

If, however, this point of view appears to some inadequate to express God's ways with those who seek His grace in holy rites, we would ask such whether, in view of what we know of " mental suggestion " and the law of its working, they can maintain that it is absent in the observance of religious rites.   I think all will admit that it forms the natural *modus operandi* of the power experienced at such times, that whether the grace of God as realised by the soul in such rites be natural or supernatural, it comes, at least partially, by suggestion.   It must also be admitted that the suggestibility of the mind can on occasion be used by preacher or orator to produce effects in the lives of men quite as notable, either for good or evil, as can be observed to follow from religious ceremonies.   Is it not, then, more honouring to God to believe that He respects the nature He has given to man in refusing to affect him in any non-natural way, than to suppose that at certain times He gives supernatural aid, when this particular aid, so far as the world can see, is no more potent than the aid which the heaven-sent preacher or teacher can give through verbal suggestion ?   It was quite natural and proper, while the psychological laws of suggestion and attention were not understood and the latent powers of the human mind largely unsuspected, that men should believe that all results beyond their comprehension were effected by supernatural power, either good or evil.   That they should doggedly hold to the same phraseology in accounting for certain religious facts and no others, when clearer knowledge of natural possibilities has come, appears to many only to make the religious truth thus tricked out in the fashion of a more ignorant age seem trivial.

Such a psychological explanation cannot, of course, be applied in the case of infant baptism ; nevertheless I would urge that the practice is one that can be justified psychologically, though in a somewhat different way. In infant baptism we have the ceremony of bringing a child within the doors of some church, if possible, of handing it to the priest to be sprinkled with water and formally received into the Christian Society, of offering prayer for its spiritual welfare and thanksgiving to God on its behalf.   People thus bringing children have various reasons for their action, various notions of the result effected by baptism ; but a common motive actuates the vast majority, and that is the desire to bring the child in some way within the focus of a Power greater than that of parent or guardian, which is recognised as making for good.

If we believe that God is always ready to reward those who seek Him, and that the reward He gives is not something arbitrary or in the future, but the impart-ing, here and now, of so much of His own life as the soul, often close shut, is able to assimilate, our question becomes, How can this special action of baptism, accomplished jointly by the priest and the friends of the child, bring about in the child any special assimilation of the divine goodness ?

In answering this question we have, first, fearlessly and frankly to face the undoubted fact that large populations in different parts of the world, which have been, and are, scrupulous in bringing all their children to receive Christian baptism, at the same time have lived, and live, in moral degradation.   The child by baptism is outwardly made a member of the Christian community in which he lives, and theoretically a member of the whole Christian church on earth and in the immortal life.   But unless the immediate community into which he is received be Christlike, there is no evidence whatever that baptism introduces the life of Christ into the infant soul.   Just to the extent to which the community is bringing forth the fruits of the Spirit will the average child manifest them.   I was once in a little company of seaside visitors, mostly Protestants, in a Roman Catholic province when a small schooner was driven upon the rocky shore in a storm.

It was night, but of course every one turned out.   A hardy man managed to swim out with a rope to the distressed vessel, and then the hope of her salvation lay in being pulled toward a sandy beach where the crew could save themselves.   A long string of visitors, who were soon hauling at the rope, included Red Indians, Agnostics, and a Quaker.   Even some women tourists were helping in the long and tough piece of work.   The Catholic residents, who alone made a living in the place, stood idle, demanding a price for their services.   Time and again the group of watching women thought they saw the gallant little vessel drift too near the rocks to escape, and then some flicker of lightning through the storm showed that there was still hope.   All the time the company of good Catholic mercenaries were standing out for a better bargain. They were not specially to blame.   That was the level of the local community into which they had been baptized.   They had no public spirit, and their money harvest was the short tourist season.   What had they received in Catholic baptism as infants ? A dogmatism centuries old assures us that they had received the grace of regeneration.   But our world has recently passed through flood and fire; we are born again into a new day of thought and social regeneration.   What value for us have these old assertions of ecclesiastical theory if no evidence can be found to give them support ?   When it is asserted to-day that the Pagan Indian, the unbaptized Agnostic, and the Quaker, who strained heart and limb at the rope on that remote shore, lacked the assurance of God's grace possessed by the others who stood aloof, we Christians think such a belief dishonouring to Christ as the captain of our salvation while the outer world gives one short whistle of ironic incredulity and goes on its way.

Is infant baptism, then, an empty form?   Surely not !   We cannot adequately express in words all that we hope for a little new-born life.   Our desires for its earthly life of joy and fellowship, and for the immortal grandeur to which it may develop, raise in us thoughts unutterable.   We may be only dimly conscious that the fears and hopes that cluster round an infant centre in God's saving grace ; but whatever religious notions a parent may have must be stirred by the responsibility of a new-born child.   If these notions be Christian they cannot find expression in action and symbol more truly than in a rite which enrols the child as a member of the larger family of God and touches him with the same water that in time past was used to symbolise the washing away of the pagan terrors and pagan atrocities of his remote forefathers.

In our ceremony of baptism there is, first, the element of intercessory prayer.   Parents and sponsors offer, not only their own faith, but the faith of the Church at large, on the child's behalf ; and if they are godly they thus bring to the delicate mind of the unconscious infant the telepathic force of love and hope.   In this atmosphere something is done once and for ever on the child's behalf ; there is a symbolic gesture of the Church toward the throne of God, and an action used to express the Church's faith that God understands the prayer and the gesture, and rewards it by looking on the child with acceptance.   It in no way contradicts the larger fact that unbaptized children are the subject of the Spirit's educative care, and that all such, sharing inevitably the Christian environment, may also share the Christian salvation.   Indeed, the acceptance of God's fatherhood for the one child constitutes him for the hour the representative of all children.

Meagre indeed must be the conception of God, of the ideal friendship, or of the issues of life bound up in a little child, existing in the mind of man or woman who could find words adequately to express what is involved in the dedication of an infant to God.   We appreciate the point of view of the Baptists, who postpone the rite, or the Quakers, who, adepts as they are in exploring the power of silence, eschew it altogether ; but we believe the more general instinct of Christendom is sound which finds in this common Christian symbol of infant baptism a meaning that overflows all verbal channels and will not be suppressed.

CONFESSION AND ABSOLUTION

The soul's need of expression has been not only proved, but much forced upon our attention of late by the astonishing success of the therapeutic method known as psycho-analysis. Briefly, the discovery of a certain medical school is that many mental and nervous diseases are caused by some emotional experience which has never found vent in open expression. Such an experience leaves a memory, conscious or subconscious, which causes a prolonged emotional strain, the suppression of which works mischief in the soul, with consequent ill effects upon physical and mental health. The original cause of this strain may be forgotten or ignored by the patient, but when it is brought to light, and the patient persuaded to converse freely on the subject, the result is great relief. The physician, by convincing the patient that he need no longer go in bondage to the past, completes the cure.

The parallel between this scientific discovery and the Catholic doctrine of sacramental confession and absolution is obvious. The following is quoted from the book by Dr. A. E. Davis, of the Liverpool Psycho-Therapeutic Clinic :

A frequent cause of obsession, or obsessive thoughts, is the feeling of shame or regret arising out of bad habits in early life. These obsessions are most intense, persistent, and painful in character. Of all classes of obsessions this is probably one of the most easily and permanently curable. If psycho-analytic treatment had no other justification than in this class of case it would have fully justified its inclusion in psycho-therapy. By its means, and the power of classification which its practice gives, one is enabled quickly to expose the painful complex. The rest is easy. The patient is encouraged to give a circumstantial account of his former habits, his struggles, regrets, and the literature which first planted the seeds of fear and remorse in his mind.

The unburdening of the mind, the discharge of the pent-up, painful emotions, the feeling that the secret burden under which he has toiled for years friendless and helpless, is no longer secret, but shared with a sympathetic listener ; the sum of all this relief is so great as to be almost incredible. This is no flight of fancy, it is a tragedy in real life. Only those who have suffered, or have heard the confessions of sufferers, can conceive the awful, ever-present remorse, fear and shame, haunting them day and night for years. It is probable that some cases of insanity and suicide are due to this cause alone.[1]

From this it is easy to see the power of the Catholic confessional in all cases where the burden of shame or remorse or fear has weighed upon the soul. The act of confession, the dramatic words of absolution, the advice of a kindly confessor, bring to the believing heart the recognition of God's forgiveness, and naturally produce in the penitent a new sense of power and freedom such as a prisoner feels whose chains have been broken. It is certain also that, in the case of penitents struggling against bad habits of body or mind, the practice of frequent confession would always be a comparatively simple method of conforming the character to the new ideal aimed at, because confession and penance inevitably impose on the subconscious mind a forceful suggestion as to the suppression of certain habits and the formation of others. Thus we see how a conviction would arise and become traditional, attributing to the confessor the power to dispense the grace of God ; and the ritual, not only of this rite of confession, but of the priestly ordination which conferred such power upon him, would be modified in accordance with the belief.

[1] *Hypnotism and Treatment by Suggestion*, pp. 46-47.

We find, then, that the Church has been guided by a sure instinct in accord with psychological law in instituting a practice by which burdened souls could find this relief, relying upon the absolute secrecy of the confessor. In Protestant congregations, where there is no official on whose secrecy a frightened soul can rely, there is a great lack.

While this is true, there appears to be no justification for much of the Catholic doctrine and practice of the confessional. The sooner a patient becomes independent of the psycho-therapist the better. No medical psycho-therapist would ask for the confessions of the healthy or would count his work for the diseased successful if the patient needed to come to him frequently all his lifetime. Such dependence would indicate and perpetuate mental and moral weakness, unless it became a mere form, in which case it would be worse than worthless. Unless psycho-therapy produce in morbid characters a new freedom in which they can develop a healthy initiative inspired from within, it must necessarily tend to weaken the moral fibre.

Likewise, from the mental and moral point of view, compulsory confession for the healthy, or frequent confession throughout a lifetime for any, has no justification. Can it be justified from the religious standpoint? Religiously all institutions must stand or fall by what they imply as to the character of God. The doctrine of sacramental confession and absolution grew up in an age when Christian theology was dominated by legal conceptions. In Semitic and in Roman law a criminal had only his misdeeds measured by legal requirements. No court of law has ever weighed the good deeds of a criminal and balanced them nicely against his transgressions, which is what the natural heart of man demands as justice. As far as law is concerned, any consideration of merit is gratuitous, and each infringement of the code must be penalised and the account settled before the criminal can live at

ease.   In the age of which we speak God was thought
of as the great giver of such law, the great Judge who
dispensed it.   The divine event toward which the whole
creation moved was thought of as a great legal assize.
It was under such a juristic conception of sin and
God that the doctrine of priestly absolution grew up.
Absolution is essentially the formal pronunciation, by a
properly qualified agent, of the divine forgiveness of
certain definite offences.   Do we to-day really feel that
God's attitude toward evil in the human heart is rightly
represented by such a conception?   Can a sentence of
absolution pronounced on a definite act of sin cleanse
the disposition of soul out of which the act sprang?
If God the Spirit dwells with the aspiring soul, always
changing it from day to day by His personal companionship, can the vicarious representation of an external juristic authority, pronouncing judgement upon particular
offences, bring home to us the reality of His constant
forgiving renewal and encouragement?   Does the
confessional cause us to understand the transcendent
Father who manifested His attitude to men in the
living service and dying love of Jesus Christ?   Do we
recognise in the ritual of confession and absolution the
outward and visible sign of a salvation which is in the
soul a perpetual well-spring of living water,[1] which flows
forth from every saved soul like a river of living water[2]
for the healing of the world?   If not, the practice of
sacramental absolution does not appear to have justification, though the occasional practice of private confession is often a necessary means of grace to souls
burdened by past sins or present infirmities.   Every
Christian minister ought to be carefully trained to be a
trustworthy "spiritual director," in order that he may
win confidence and convince the oppressed of God's
forgiveness and certain and practical help.

[1] John iv. 14.   [2] John vii. 38.

THE EUCHARIST

Let us turn now to examine the traditional ceremonies associated with the celebration of the Eucharist. We find that in all cases the unconscious instinct of the Church has produced forms likely to bring about in the soul that quiescent or receptive attitude in which the suggestion of the acts will have greatest power. The psychological instinct has worked with a sure touch in producing these forms. Thus in the service of the Roman Catholic Mass, words, music, silences, the sharp tinkling of the bell, are all admirably calculated to produce a state of mind quiescent to all else, concentrated upon one idea and expectant, a state in which the mind is ready for the most powerful working of any suggestion. The offering of the elements of life to God as symbols of the life of Christ carries the soul to the offering of self as a living sacrifice. The act of giving and receiving the holy food is, of course, in itself extraordinarily suggestive of some augmentation of inner strength which passes from the Source of all life to the individual life of the soul. The whole service prepares for and enhances the act of reception : first, whatever burden of sin may be upon the communicant's mind is laid aside by confession and absolution ; secondly, its anxieties are allayed by intercession and thanksgiving, and all acts of worship that pass between that and the act of reception tend to increase concentration and expectancy, so that the suggestion of the act pierces, as it were, like a two-edged sword underneath the disquiet and distraction of the upper levels of consciousness, into a region of calm psychic life where it can act with a compelling power. In more modern forms of the Communion service we find a similar touch of sure psychological instinct.[1]

[1] *E.g.* the Presbyterian service.

So far as the reception of Holy Communion goes to the building up of moral character, or—what is the same thing—to the bringing forth of the fruits of the Spirit, the Christian graces, we are again bound to face the evidence that, except in the case of rare souls, the characters of the devout conform to the standard of the local religious community. Whatever is current as the Christian ideal is formed—given time and normal conditions—in the character of the constant communicant. In different parts of the world these ideals are different—a fact which certainly harmonises with the hypothesis that the formative force is auto-suggestion combined with the suggestion of power as given in the holy food.

But why, it may be asked, do we need such periodic suggestion? When I was a child living in a Roman Catholic country I caught up some phrases of religious polemic and was repeating them to my father, when he said, "No intelligent person who believes that God is a Spirit questions the Real Presence in the Mass; it is the Special Presence they question." This is, of course, true; no one who realises the spiritual presence of the Christ can fail to feel the full import of the words, "Where two or three are gathered together in my name there am I in the midst of them." But what relation do time and space bear to such spiritual presence? Is there any point of space or time —even though that point centre in a material object— of which we would dare to assert that the divine presence was absent?

"If I take the wings of the morning and dwell in the uttermost parts of the sea, even there shall thy hand lead me and thy right hand shall hold me." [1]

"Lo, I am with you alway." [2]

Nor can we fail, unless we accept a materialist philosophy, to regard the material universe as instinct with God.

---

[1] Ps. cxxxix. 9-10.　　　　[2] Matt. xxviii. 26.

"Who layeth the beams of his chambers in the waters : who maketh the clouds his chariot." [1]

" He flew swiftly upon the wings of the wind.   He made darkness his hiding-place." [2]

" Raise the stone and thou shalt find me ; cleave the wood and there am I." [3]

" And every common bush afire with God." [4]

By the Special Presence, then, in any place or time we must mean a special awareness of the divine presence by human spirits.   But just because the consciousness or awareness of the divine presence is, in every individual, so dependent upon our subjective states, it appears necessary that the faith of the Church in the all-present Christ should be summed up and brought home to the individual in a recurring action.   Such action expresses not only our assurance too deep for words, but also our common relation to the all-present Christ and our fellowship with one another.   That is the reason not only why this special awareness of the divine presence can come to us with the supreme act of the Church's language of action, but why we have good ground for our belief that, however languid and oblivious we may feel, we may verily come into touch with the presence by our participation in that action.[5]

Such periodic acts of attention are necessary, or at least most helpful, to the soul's vitality.   The finite life of all things proceeds each by a certain rhythm peculiar to itself.   The living organism sleeps and wakes, acts and rests, feeds and assimilates.   The morning stars sing together, the waves of the ocean clap their hands, in rhythmic motion ; from the whole of creation there arises a music in which time is meted out in regular rhythm.   So it is with the soul of man, except that he has a certain power of controlling his own rhythm, and a bad jar and jangle he often makes of it.   But the more he yields to the experience of salvation—the more

---

[1] Ps. civ. 3.   [2] Ps. xviii. 10.   [3] Oxyrhynchus Logia.
[4] Mrs. Browning.   [5] Cf. Essay V. p. 167.

he responds to the comfort or comradeship of the Spirit—the more right will be the rhythm of his religious action ; and he finds that regular times for private worship and public worship, for learning what other men have discovered concerning God and for meditating upon this garnered knowledge, are the best response to God's constant presence, just as regular times for refreshing the body with the food that is always within reach are essential to that body's well-being.

If this be granted it is evident that we want, for such ceremonial, the most beautiful setting of edifice and furniture that we can give, and the actions of our ritual must be true, absolutely true, to our best instincts of prayer and praise. In the degree in which these things become ornate rather than beautiful the rite will be neglected by healthy souls. The issue has long been obscured by the confusion of moral and aesthetic values, and also by the party spirit which has entered into controversies on this subject. Whether any observance had its origin in Pagan or Christian Rome, or in the Byzantine Court, is unimportant. If it conformed to our ancestors' ideals of truth and beauty it was right for them. If we do not now hold it true to our sense of beauty and truth and our highest ideals of worship, it is wrong for us.

I have only seen one modern church building that appeared to embody the ideal of a living community. It was made of logs, and it stood in a little open space in the forest. They were the best logs that could be got, and they lay upon one another unhewn in all their natural beauty. It was a simple, oblong building of good proportions—something better than any dwelling-house around, and homely. From inside people looked up through large windows to see the arching branches of trees, and above them the kindly blue or the hurrying clouds. There was, for the Eucharist, one plain broad table—the best table that could be made—covered with the whitest of cloths. The little log church in the forest was perfect in its way because it was the best of its kind and homely. The most splendid Gothic cathedrals were also, for those who built them, the best they could give, and homely, for their homes were also Gothic—dark, cold, ill-aired, but of their type beautiful. But imitation Gothic in the midst of the ugly, box-like tenements of the poor is ugly and unhomely. What would be the best church edifice that modern wealth in centres of civilisation could produce ?   We cannot tell ; and we never shall be able to tell until we get the beauty of holiness in our homes, and return to simplicity and homeliness in our churches.

When young I was often taken to a service in a chapel on a steep hillside.   Its interior was very simple and austere ; but on one side the high windows were clear to a great expanse of sky, and on the other, up the steep slope of a hill, was a convent garden in which, at a regular hour, a long procession of nuns in their black and cumbrous mediaeval gowns walked, through the gracious summer, with heads bent, into a darkened church.   Above them was a screen of fluttering poplar leaves and the splendour of the summer sky ; but they never looked up.   I have never forgotten the sky as seen through those windows of clear, latticed glass in the chapel, nor the poetry of the Psalms and the simple drama of the Gospel story as they came to us with the changeful lights of sun and shade and the endless procession of the summer clouds.   The contrast between this and the picture on which we could look not far away—the black, draped figures entering a dark door, with, beyond, the twinkle of artificial altar lights— has always remained with me.

Here, I believe, were represented—not, as the shallow would say, two temperaments, but two different standards of aesthetic value, so different that they implied two different conceptions of God.

This judgement has nothing whatever to do with

controversies between Romanist and Protestant. It is
an aesthetic judgement, and implies that the love of
beauty is part of virtue, and that we ought to bring
of all our best to our religious ceremonial. As a child
I was sometimes taken into Roman Catholic churches.
In that part of the world, and at that time, the altars,
of which there were many in each large church, were
usually decked with paper flowers. Sometimes they
were dressed with white paper cut into marvellous
patterns, or with cheap muslin not over clean ; and
images of the Virgin were very often dolls dressed in
cheap white satin and lace, with glass jewellery. It was
bad taste, but I am sure that a dear old charwoman,
who often used to spend a day's wages on candles and
paper flowers, was as commendable as the widow who
threw her mites into the treasury of the temple. But
my point is that there is objective beauty, just as there
is objective truth and goodness. God alone knows
these in their perfection, but if we would keep our
ceremonial pure, we must be ever approximating as
nearly as we can to beauty in church edifice and ritual.
To keep what is tawdry, cumbrous, and artificial merely
because it is traditional is a sin.

It must be admitted that in our towns many people
do desire, on entering a church, to be transported into
a dream-world in which nothing reminds them of the
ugly, jarring world of home or factory. But what is
wrong is always the jar and ugliness of the slum or
suburb, and in that wrong God is suffering. To
emphasise the distinction between the house of God
and the homes of men is surely to build on sand. The
paraphernalia of a mystery-religion may be a necessary
relief from a hideous world, but at the best it can only
be a temporary expedient, suffered until Christianity
is vital enough to transform the work-a-day world.
Surely no soul that has access to nature fails to find
in the simplest things in life—in the depth of the
sky, or the sigh of the wind in the trees, or in the

homes of men—a depth of mystery which makes them fitting symbols of the mystery of godliness. If we want darkened windows and air foggy with incense in order to testify that the things of God are too great for us to understand, it is surely because we have never considered the lilies, never really seen one blade of grass.

It is small wonder that the plain man does not find our churches homelike, and that our rites and cere-monies usually express so little to him. The one strong, purely aesthetic passion which is evident in the masses of our people is the love of flowers, which suggests that they would respond to natural beauty in our churches if we could once get rid of all ugli-ness, as well as of such beauty as belongs only to a ritual which is like a dead language, no longer spoken spontaneously but as matter of scholastic attainment. If the workman's home were beautiful he could bring the very best of the same sort of beauty and make a church in which he and his fellows could find a cor-porate home. That must be for the future! At present we have the choice between entire simplicity and the best we can supply of gorgeous traditional reproductions in which, in an environment of Byzantine colouring, our celebrating priests are arrayed like Solomon in all his glory. What said our Lord? That one aesthetic judgement of His might have more weight than it has with us in our choice of church furniture and vestments.

Again, as to ritual, our language of action must represent the aspirations and deepest desires of our hearts. If in any cathedral we watch in particular the gestures of officiating priests, do we feel that to-day they express what we believe to be the truth concerning the relation of the human soul to God in its moments of adoration, contrition, and humble approach? We get the attitude of the celebrant in elevating the offering to God, and we get another

T

attitude, appropriate to real prayer, when, as a suppliant, he kneels, with head bowed and face covered, for some appreciable time. We get, also, constant passing genuflexions, and the bobbings and bowings of assistants and acolytes, stepping backwards and sideways to avoid turning the back to the altar.

If we can take away from the ceremonial of the Mass what comes to us from a lower and more primitive idea of God, the attitudes of the officiating priest are expressive. The bending of the knees is an attitude entirely suitable and expressive when the head is bowed and the face covered and time is given for prayer and meditation. It expresses the privacy of the soul, the withdrawal of the attention from all that is external, the humble deference of the mind of man when inwardly laying the burden of his own life or of the world before God. Given time and quiet, this attitude is as noble as hasty genuflexions are ignoble and absurd.

Further, when the priest, standing before the altar, elevates his offering toward heaven, every line of his attitude appears beautiful and expressive. To raise the arms, to look upward, is indicative of humble aspiration. Nothing could be finer than this attitude. There is perhaps no gesture so native to adoration and prayer as that of holding up empty hands while raising the face heavenward. It would be gracious for congregation as well as for celebrant ; but as yet we have no congregational observance so expressive.

We also get the frequent genuflexions which are intended to express humility and adoration, and imply a sense of reverence for a superior. If, however, we no longer believe that the God we adore is pleased with grovelling genuflexions, such attitudes no longer express for us either adoration or humility. The ideas of glory and power, founded upon compulsion and terror of the arbitrary caprice of Eastern potentates, made grovelling attitudes suitable in their courts. It

was in such courts, when they represented the world's
greatest wealth, that the etiquette of " falling down
before the footstool" of the sovereign culminated.
The idea which then gathered world-wide prestige has
since slowly waned, only lingering now in the tradition
of ancient courts and their conventional ceremonies ;
but it is a conception of reverence which no longer
exists in the open sunshine of work-a-day life.   It is
scarcely two centuries—if we may trust our novels of
manners—since men went down upon their knees to
their superiors if they wished to ask forgiveness for a
fault or to entreat a boon ; but we do not now feel
that a fellow-creature worthy of respect would be
pleased with such behaviour.   We no longer think
that true dignity in sovereign or father or bene-
factor can in any way be enhanced by anything that
belittles the personality of others ; and attitudes that
are undignified and ungainly express such belittle-
ment.   We think of God as a good father who can
only find his own dignity in the dignity of his sons
and daughters, or of a good king whose glory is in the
dignity and friendship of his subjects.

SUMMARY

We have found that language is necessary to the
growth and development of human life, and that when
verbal language fails, as it always must somewhere,
the language of action must be used, because talk
is a function of vitality, and wherever means of communication fail between men and between men and
God, there is also a failure of something that is
essential to human life.   We have seen that the healthy
soul necessarily uses the language of action when it
would give expression to thoughts and emotions which
it cannot yet analyse, because they ascend from the subconscious region where our instincts have their common
source, so that by association the consciousness of any

one instinct brings with it inexpressible hints and suggestions of them all. What rises in the consciousness is unutterable, for we cannot say " it is this and it is not that," for it is in reality the outflow of a living organism toward all that can enrich its existence, and the receptiveness of that organism toward the source of all enrichment. Yet, while it remains true that aspirations and appetites imply common associations, and that aspirations of affection, of love, of friendship, of the search for truth, of admiration, and of the desire for beauty and the worship of the Source of all, cannot be analysed because they imply one another, it is also true that we can analyse the language of action which has been used to express this unanalysable outflow, and we have endeavoured to explain its natural potency to relieve the soul and thus render it receptive to an inflow from its divine environment. God works through the power of suggestion, which we have seen to mean a method of bringing conviction to the whole mind, conscious and subconscious.

To some of us this explanation of the power of a Christian ceremony will, I fear, seem irreligious. But if so, let us ask ourselves whether our Lord's reiterated explanation, " Your own faith has saved you," detracted from His teaching that it was by " the power of God," " the finger of God," " the will of God," that salvation of soul and body was wrought. It is quite clear from His whole teaching that He regarded the power to heal and reform as of God, and as coming upon man in definite times and places from the transcendent Spirit of God. Yet He no less implies that the gift or power waited upon something that happened in the minds of men—upon the act of faith, which is the conviction of the whole mind, conscious and subconscious.

In an age when all other men looked to religious magic for relief from personal disabilities, it displayed marvellous insight to declare that faith—that is, an attitude of the soul—could reform conduct, heal the body, and cure mental insanities.   There is no more striking evidence of the way in which the mind of Jesus transcended the minds of His contemporaries, including His followers, than His insight into the potency of the inward attitude to heal and reform. When all the world believed that the power to heal body or soul resided in the magician or prophet, He saw—what science has now laboriously learned—that God works through a power of newness of life which arises within the needy soul.   To those who brought to Him the mentally helpless He said that their own conviction that the cure would be wrought was necessary in order to accomplish it in the patient.   He cast out no obsessions in Nazareth because of the unbelief of the populace.[1]   To the father of the boy subject to convulsions He said, "If thou canst believe."[2]   Any one who has tended the mentally feeble knows how much they are affected by the mental attitude of those who surround them.   To the poor woman who touched His garment expecting a magical cure He said, "Daughter, your faith has healed you."[3]   To the blind man He said, "What do you want me to do ?   Go, your faith has made you whole."[4]   To the converted courtesan He explained that the chain of evil habit was broken : "Your faith has saved you ; go in peace."[5]

The ecclesiastical mind is constantly turning back, thinking to find the Lord in the dim atmosphere of Church history.   The Christian too often thinks of Jesus Christ as in the past.   He is not there.   He has risen and gone before us into the future.   Again and again in Christian ages the reformer has found Him in the farthest vista of his own advancing path ; and we, entering an era of psychological discovery, find Him in front, awaiting us at the gate of a new day.

---

[1] Matt. xiii. 58.   [2] Mark ix. 23.   [3] Mark v. 34.
[4] Mark x. 52.   [5] Luke vii. 50.

VIII

SPIRITUAL EXPERIENCE

BY

A. CLUTTON-BROCK

AUTHOR OF "ESSAYS ON ART," "WILLIAM MORRIS : HIS WORK AND INFLUENCE,"
"SHELLEY : THE MAN AND THE POET," "THOUGHTS ON THE WAR," "THE ULTIMATE
BELIEF," "STUDIES IN CHRISTIANITY," "THE KINGDOM OF HEAVEN," ETC.

ANALYSIS

The two kinds of experience, one scientific, the other aesthetic.
The aesthetic always the sense of the personal.
So myth always expresses the personal.
Art implies that beauty is personal.
The belief in the personal in nature expresses our experience.

But we are afraid of this personal in nature.
The fairy angel we try to ignore.
We confuse her with actual women or with abstractions.
And she is ignored in our religion.
But not in pagan religion.
The Christian refusal.

But there is an orthodoxy which does not refuse.
It is the orthodoxy of Christ.
It brings the fairy angel close to us.

The certainty of spiritual experience.
Our desire to communicate it.
Worship an effort to share it, art to communicate it.
An example.

The need of self-surrender in spiritual experience.
The nature of the knowledge it gives us.
The need to act upon it.

VIII

SPIRITUAL EXPERIENCE

MEN, so long as they have been men, seem to have experienced each other, and all that is not human, in two different ways. The one kind of experience they express in knowledge and in theories built on knowledge, the other in art or myth. The one kind we call scientific, the other aesthetic, though the words are vague and do not clearly express the difference between the two kinds of experience. For the difference is this, that in the second or aesthetic kind of experience we are aware, or think we are aware, of something personal; that is to say, of something like ourselves, as we know ourselves inwardly, in all that is not ourselves. Nowadays, because of knowledge obtained by the other, the scientific kind of experience, it is commonly supposed that this sense of the personal in all that is not human is illusion, is itself but the theorising of primitive man, the error of his imperfect knowledge. In myths, we are told, primitive man expressed his theories of the behaviour of the sun and the moon and the seasons, or what not. He made stories of these theories, because he had not yet learned that a theory has its own form of expression. Afterwards he forgot why he had made the story, and came to believe it as a matter of fact. Hence religion. It is assumed that modern civilised man does not make myths but only theories. It is not understood that myths and theories are, and always have been, different things, the result of different kinds of experience, and that we still make myths no less than theories. Myths always have been, and still are, made to express the sense of the personal in all things. If ever they come to be believed as matters of fact, it is by dull men, who are always with us and who have never experienced what they express, or have denied their own experience.

Some years ago I was in the Maritime Alps in June, and I came to a spring in the shade of a sweet-chestnut tree on the southern slope of the mountain. Then I knew suddenly how southern peoples had come by their myth of the water-nymph. Standing myself in the blazing sunshine, I almost saw a water-nymph among the waters of that shade. Water-nymphs had always seemed to me frigid, unreal fancies ; but now the spring, in its shadowed beauty and contrast with the parched heat of the mountain side, became alive, became almost a person. It was not the legend of the water-nymph that brought her to my mind ; it was the life and beauty of the stream that almost brought her to my eyes. The stream seemed so clearly to be occupied with a lovely, friendly business of its own that I almost saw a lovely, friendly creature doing it. Then, for a moment, I knew what Paganism meant and why it was believed. I was a pagan myself, and saw what faith and beauty we have lost with it ; and I knew too why poets have always made and still make myths. The moment they experience nature intensely enough to make poetry about it, they also make myths about it. So Shelley made a myth about the Cloud, not frigidly or ingeniously or because other poets had made them, but because he could not otherwise express what he had experienced :

> I am the daughter of earth and water,
>   And the nursling of the sky ;
> I pass through the pores of the ocean and shores ;
>   I change, but I cannot die.
> For after the rain, when with never a stain
>   The pavilion of heaven is bare,
> And the winds and sunbeams with their convex gleams
>   Build up the blue dome of air,

> I silently laugh at my own cenotaph,
>   And out of the caverns of rain,
> Like a child from the womb, like a ghost from the tomb,
>   I arise and unbuild it again.

He did not believe all this as a matter of fact, nor was it allegory to him ; it happened to his mind and was the expression of his intense experience of clouds. And always, if we experience them intensely enough, they become personal to us and seem to be occupied with their own business. Coleridge has, consciously, expressed this feeling in a gloss to *The Ancient Mariner;* and he says that the experience came to the Mariner when he was wrought up to a certain intensity :

" In his loneliness and fixedness he yearneth towards the journeying moon, and the stars that still sojourn yet still move onward. And everywhere the blue sky belongs to them, and is their appointed rest and their native country and their own natural home which they enter unannounced, as lords that are certainly expected, and yet there is a silent joy at their arrival."

Yet modern writers often try to describe natural beauty without what they would call metaphor. The effort is vain ; the beauty so described is not beauty to us. Metaphor is but the beginning of myth ; it is the means by which poets communicate their sense of the personal in all beauty, even the beauty of nature, a sense which must be expressed in personal terms. Even a direct, simple sentence like " The silence that is in the starry sky " moves us because it is to us the silence of that which could speak.

So in poetry and all art there is an implied dogma that all beauty is personal. The artist affirms that in his art, even if he would deny it in his creed ; and our joy in his art is a joy in that sense of the personal everywhere which he communicates to us. It is not his own person that he tries to express to us, but the personal in that which is not himself. That likeness of which we are aware in all art, even music, and which we call

truth, is a likeness to the personal which the artist has
seen or felt and which he communicates to us, whether
in speech or lines or music. If he has not seen or felt
it, he cannot draw its likeness ; but when he can and
does, then we recognise it. The truth of art is not
a likeness to things as we see them, when we do not
feel the personal in them. The artist is not concerned
with impersonal or scientific facts at all ; he is concerned only with the personal that he becomes aware
of at a certain point of intensity. And often this personal ousts from a picture all impersonal fact so completely that the stupid are perplexed. They say it is not
like at all, because it is not like those impersonal facts
of which alone they are aware. But in music art escapes
from all facts that can be seen or stated in words or
paint. It is concerned with the personal altogether, not
with that in which the personal is manifested. It is
myth become a pure voice, sounds that are utterly
human, no matter how great their variety and com-
plexity. We are aware of the personal in the flight of
birds ; but the musician ceases in his music to be aware
of the birds. He gives us their motion and fellowship,
with all that is personal in it and nothing else. So we
often feel nature in music because the musician has given
us that personal in it which he has felt in nature. He
makes no reference to nature ; but we know the personal
which he expresses, that it is of nature ; we hear
the very voice of the water-nymph that he has almost
seen.

This implied dogma of the personal, a dogma not
stated but proved in the work of art, is necessary to the
mind of man. We cannot be content with the generic
impersonal world of things, functions, and processes
that science presents to us, because it is not the whole
of reality as we experience it. It is not that the one
kind of experience contradicts the other ; the personal
experience might itself be matter for science, and should
be. We are always passing swiftly and unconsciously

from one plane of experience to another ; as soon as we
see beauty and experience it intensely, we pass to the
sense of the personal, and there seems to be person outside us answering to person in ourselves.   But there
is nowadays a sharp conflict between art and science,
because science, trespassing beyond its proper business
of seeing things generically in classes and categories,
putting on the airs of philosophy in fact, often affirms
that to see them so is to see the only reality in them.
The artistic activity, it says, is mere trifling, however
pretty its products.   And artists themselves are apt to
believe this ; they have lost faith in the reality of that
experience which makes their art, and they have lost
faith in art as an expression of reality not to be otherwise expressed.   So they fall into frigid imitations of
the convinced art of the past, like those eighteenth-
century poets who talked about nymphs in whom they
had no belief ; or else they turn to realism, to an attempt
to describe things as they are seen scientifically, generically, with no sense of the personal in them.   The result
in one case is imitation art ; in the other not art at all,
but a kind of science without its validity or good faith.
Until artists can regain their faith in their own experience of the personal, art will remain frivolous and half-
hearted, or falsely scientific.

But why is it that we have so general a desire to deny
our sense of the personal in nature ?   Why do we wish
science thus to trespass beyond its proper function and
deny philosophically that there is a personal in nature ?
Why do we misunderstand myths and talk so much
nonsense about them ?   It is always fear that makes
men unscientific, and the modern world is afraid of its
own experiencing power.   There is something intoxi-
cating, bewildering, almost terrifying in this sense of the
personal in nature, something that drags us out of our
routine selves and makes us wretched and hungry when
we sink back into them.   " Thou hast touched me and

I am on fire for thy peace," says Augustine ; and we are afraid thus to be touched and fired by a reality not ourselves. It seems to us incompatible with the other reality of use and wont, and of things classified so that we may use and understand them. Poets themselves have cried out against the beauty which became personal to them and allured them like an enchantress that could never be possessed. Keats's *belle dame sans merci* is that beauty ; to be in thrall to her is to fall asleep and wake on the cold hillside and never forget the dream of her. If she is loved, it is for ever with mere desire ; and Euripides expresses the cruelty and peril of her in the *Bacchae*. Dionysus is *la belle dame sans merci* ; he is that personal in nature which leads men and women into the hills and makes them destroy what they love most; and then they wake and see what they have destroyed. In the *Bacchae* is expressed all the conflict in the nature of man between his two planes of experience. Euripides makes a tragedy of it ; but we try to escape from the tragedy by denying that one plane is anything but mere illusion ; and we do so, not because we are scientific, but because we are afraid.

We have locked up in the cupboard of the world, not a skeleton, but a fairy angel. We sit round the fire and talk of politics or religion or duty or the weather, and pretend not to hear when that winged creature flutters her wings and sings ; we stuff our ears against her as if she were a siren. That old story of the sirens is about her, and so is the story of the Lorelei and all such enchantresses. They express the fear of an earlier time, which it was not ashamed to confess. But we hope to rid ourselves of it by not confessing it, by denying the existence of the enchantress. The stories, we say, are not about her, but about the sun or the moon or the seasons. As for the *Bacchae*, we pretend not to know what it means. There is no fairy in the cupboard ; if there is anything, it is a skeleton, but most of us say there is nothing. We have only one kind of experience of reality, and that is the scientific. The other is all make-believe.

Yet, when the poets and musicians tell of the fairy angel we cannot help listening to them, for her beauty is in their speech and song :

> Lamp of Earth! where'er thou movest
>   Its dim shapes are clad with brightness,
> And the souls of whom thou lovest
>   Walk upon the winds with lightness,
> Till they fail, as I am failing,
> Dizzy, lost, yet unbewailing.

You see, Shelley himself says that she is dangerous, though he has let her out of the cupboard ; but he says it with her music. We try to enjoy the music, while we say that he is talking beautiful nonsense, but nonsense cannot be beautiful. And then, when the musicians make their tunes about the fairy angel, tunes half triumphant, half despairing because they can last only a moment, we pretend that those tunes are about some woman. Biographers tell us that this or that symphony of Beethoven was written when he was in love with a Boche princess ; but he was always in love with the fairy angel. There are even those who say that *la belle dame sans merci* was Fanny Brawne, and the *Bacchae* a political pamphlet. Perhaps Keats did try to persuade himself that Fanny Brawne was *la belle dame*. Shelley was always trying to persuade himself of such things. Mary, Emilia Viviani, Jane Williams, all in turn were Lamps of Earth to him. As it has been said, "The married life of geniuses is often unfortunate ; and the same is true of their wives ; " they cannot be married to the fairy angel. And that is why most of us deny her existence. The fairy angel is there, but if we allowed ourselves to believe in her she would put us out of conceit with our other plane of experience ; and we cannot always be aware of her. She comes and goes and leaves us on the cold hillside ; so we say that she neither comes nor goes, but is a myth

about something else. Or else we give her abstract
names like beauty, talk about it with a pretence of
scientific jargon, and say that beauty is truth, truth
beauty.   Keats said that—"him even."   All the
philosophers break their minds on beauty in their
anxiety to escape from the perilous desires and illusions of the poets.   The philosophers know, at least,
that beauty is not Jane or Mary or Emily ; and then
malicious men of science say that she is, that she is
a mere illusion of the sexual instinct.   That is the
language they use about the fairy angel in their anxiety
not to believe in her.   And then the theologians obtrude
themselves ; there is no fairy angel, they say, but only
God.   The mystics believe that the fairy angel is God,
but the theologians will not have it that God is anything
like a fairy angel.   They talk about Him drily and with
analysis, as the philosophers talk about beauty.   So both
try to keep the fact and its allurement at arm's length ;
they stuff their ears with wax against the siren's song.
And the devout try to drown it with Hymns Ancient
and Modern, the modern more fusty than the ancient ;
but the fairy angel continues to sing songs that are both
old and new—everlasting songs.   And in spite of our
efforts to ignore her, to explain the origin of her myths,
she is still there ; her origin is in herself, and she
remains as alluring and as dangerous as ever she was.
    Our religion ignores her, and that is why the poets
will have none of it.   A religion, to satisfy them, would
have the fairy angel singing at the heart of it.   Canon
Scott Holland once wrote a piece about the Isle of
Innisfree—how the tune of it would come into his mind
in the most incongruous places, at committee meetings
or in church, and how he would have a sudden desire
to say, " I will arise and go now to the Isle of Innisfree,"
and lead all the committee-men and sidesmen in a
dance after him.   The Isle of Innisfree is the home of
the fairy angel, and the song about it has in it her
music, which we recognise as soon as we hear it ; but

it is not often heard in church. It is not the voice of God
as we conceive Him; but if God does not and cannot
sing like that, then He is not inspired like Schubert or
Keats—which is absurd. If He exists at all, the uttermost beauty, the most extreme enchantment, must be
His; He cannot have left it to a dangerous fairy or to
obviously sinful artists.

The pagans did believe that this enchantment was
of God, or of many gods; they were so much aware of
the personal in nature that they saw gods everywhere, not
moral gods concerned to make men good, but wilful and
alluring, having only the goodness of the artist, the gift
of beauty, and also the vanity of the artist; being very
apt to destroy men like Pentheus, who were too dull to
see their charms. But we have denied all these gods,
and we say that there is one God, in whom we see
nothing of Dionysus or Apollo or Pan. In fact, most
of us see nothing in Him or of Him. But the pagans
had this advantage over us, that they did almost see
their gods. In that personal quality of nature that
we have schooled ourselves to deny, their gods were
glimmering and whispering:

> The wind in the reeds and the rushes,
>   The bees on the bells of thyme,
> The birds on the myrtle bushes,
>   The cicale above in the lime,
> And the lizards below in the grass.

These were the music of Pan, half heard, and it taught
man to make the music that is sweetest to himself, a music
not human, but the speech of nature become personal,
as nymphs are not human but the beauty of nature
become personal. In both there is a beauty that never
satisfies the desire it provokes. We think we are more
religious than the pagans, but most of us are less,
because out of fear we deny this personal quality in
nature and impoverish our own concept of God. All
the passion for the fairy angel we try to divert into the
passion of human love; that is the one romance for us

that is left.   So that the young may not be tempted by
the fairy angel, we encourage them to believe that they
have found her in Emily or Jane.   We sigh heavily to
ourselves in middle age—" I, too, thought that once ;
and how beautiful it was to believe that a fairy angel
existed ; how sad to know that she does not."   But we
lie to ourselves ; for we know, though we will not confess it, that she does exist, though she is not Jane or
Emily.   Better any infatuation about them than the
peril of believing in her.

Certainly the poets who have believed in her have
been sad, if not bad or mad.   Keats could never forget
those

> Magic casements opening on the foam
> Of perilous seas, in fairy lands forlorn.

For him they are cut off from reality, or he is made
forlorn by being cut off from their reality.   The word
is like a knell to toll him back again to his sole self and
to the loneliness of the other plane of experience.   But
it is the aim of religion to free us from that loneliness,
to make us aware of a universe in which there are
not merely things and processes and functions, but
everywhere person answering to ourselves ; and our
religion fails to do that more and more because the
fairy angel is left out of it, left to the poets, who therefore are not religious.   And because the fairy angel
is not in our religion it loses more and more the
power of expression, and more and more she begins
to call men away from it.   How can we achieve a
reconcilement ?

Some poets say there is none possible :

> Wilt thou yet take all, Galilean ?   But these thou shalt not take,
> The laurel, the palms, and the paean, the breasts of the nymphs in
>   the brake ;
> Breasts more soft than a dove's, that tremble with tenderer breath ;
> And all the wings of the loves ; and all the joy before death ;
> All the feet of the hours that sound as a single lyre,
> Dropped and deep in the flowers with strings that flicker like fire.
> More than these wilt thou give, things fairer than all these things ?

It is supposed that the Galilean teaches us how to escape from the peril of them by mere refusal. The early Church said that all the pagan gods were fiends; Apollo became Apollyon; but we have never quite forced ourselves to believe that, and Satan himself has for us some of the splendour of a pagan god. In fact, though we pretend to believe in a Trinity, we have split up the full idea of God into two, because we despair and are afraid of the uttermost beauty and delight. There is our God, and Lucifer; and Lucifer is the alluring half of God that we fear and deny and call the fallen angel. He is the beauty that seems to tempt us away from duty—Tintoret painted Christ Himself as tempted by him; he is, we think, incompatible with our life; he is the lovely danger at the heart of the universe. Milton makes him say, Evil, be thou my good; but it is rather we that say, Good, be thou my evil; because this ultimate beauty seems to us incompatible with our life, and is a good we despair of. Augustine speaks of a beauty old as new that he learnt to love too late; and that beauty is to him God. The theologians and the philosophers have split up that beauty also, from their fear of experiencing it. The theologians make a God of it, too personal in a narrow, ugly way; the philosophers make an Absolute, empty and arid. And between them the beauty old as new, the fairy angel, is vanished; and we are left with nothing to believe in that we can love with the whole of us. There is still the music of the poets, still the Isle of Innisfree, outside our religion, and so seeming mischievous, capricious, malign. Beyond God, beyond the Absolute, and still more real than both, there is this actual beauty in the sunset, so tender but not to us; in the spring, so gay but not with us; the beauty of the earth, that loves into the void. We call the earth a mother, but not ours. Nature is omnipotent, but she will not gather us into her peace; she makes a transcendent paradise of the universe, but leaves us outside it in exile.

So we feel towards the personal beauty of nature, and we feel so more and more the longer we deny it to be personal. It pains us, and the modern poet fills his song with that pain. There is to him a God in this nature but an unacknowledged God, unlike the other God whom some men worship and he cannot. Science tells us, dully and confidently, that this personal is not. The religious believe it, and in that belief are blind to the divine which was seen by the heathen in his blindness, and are left with a dull divine of their own, cut off from nature and immediate experience like a dried plant. It cannot have been so when men built the great cathedrals, which have the diversity, the swarming and dangerous beauty, of Nature herself. They were built as shrines of the beauty, old as new, which was almost imprisoned in them. But now we build tin tabernacles and imitation Gothic churches, with the fairy angel laughing outside them ; and we spend marble and gilding on eating-houses, trying to make another paradise with the fairy angel still left outside. We have utterly separated spirit and sense ; but that fairy angel is both, with a double allurement so strong that we fear it. So we are Manichees at heart ; for the Manichaean heresy is but the conscious, deliberate statement of a fear, and the assertion that it is wisdom and truth. The fear is latent in all men, and the facts of life seem to justify it. Spirit and flesh are manageable if we separate them, but fused together they sweep us away. So we are always trying to separate them, and to conceive of the universe itself as not one but two ; the one all and the other nothing ; the one real, the other unreal ; the one pure and cold and the other warm and foul. And, whether we are devout or sceptical, we are afraid of the reality in which matter and spirit are fused, and which the pagan saw and worshipped. We dare not even ask ourselves that besetting question, Is there something malign in the very heart of the universe? Is the uttermost beauty, delight, excellence hostile to us, uncompatible with our well-being, derisive of our native mediocrity? Are we but moths to its flame, moths for whom the only wisdom is to fly away into the darkness and cold?

That question is put again and again in poetry; it sounds in all the pleading of music—the desire of the moth for the star; it sounds even in the prayers of the saints. But the sensible man of the world says, "What nonsense. There is no star, and I am not a moth," and all the while he knows in his heart that he lies. He is a moth and there is a star; and he is not content to have refused his desire for it. The best he can do is not to think about it, and attend to business; but in that successful inattention of his no one loves him. We love those who cannot forget the star and who express their love of it in music. We call their music divine, even though we may smile at those who make it; and we remember them through the ages while we forget the men of business.

But with this Manichaeism, with this split between the two gods and between men into mediocrities and wild poets, there still persists faintly a great orthodox tradition between two heresis. To that tradition Christ is not the pale Galilean, the denier and forbidder; He is not one who would make us safe from the flame, nor is He the wild rebel who rushes like a moth into it and then weeps for his scorched wings. Certainly, Christ never denounces the fairy angel; and there is something of her in His Kingdom of Heaven, something that we have left out of it. If she is beautiful, so is His Kingdom; and the music which the poets have learnt from her is also in His speech: "Consider the lilies of the field, how they toil not neither do they spin; yet I say unto you that Solomon in all his glory was not arrayed like one of these." There at least is the personal in nature felt and expressed ; and, He tells us, if we see it, we shall not mistake riches for beauty. And some of the great Christian visionaries have spoken of God as if He were the fairy angel : " With Thy calling and shouting my deafness was broken ; with Thy glittering and shining my blindness was put to flight. At the scent of Thee I drew in my breath, and I pant for Thee. I have tasted, and I hunger and thirst ; Thou hast touched me, and I am on fire for Thy peace."

In Christ's Kingdom of Heaven there is allurement ; a man who sees it will give up all for it ; and He said that men must desert all duties for it, must leave father and mother ; He was exasperated with those who would not leave their duties for it. It was to Him an enchantment, but not malign ; for at the heart of it He saw, not *la belle dame sans merci*, but our Father which is in Heaven. Yet, because to us our Father which is in Heaven means the God whom in our timidity we have emptied of all enchantment, we do not see Christ among the poets and music-makers, His peers, but among the preachers and edifiers. We place Him among His own commentators as if He commented on life. He did not ; He made music about it, He spoke of it like a poet, but with an audacity beyond theirs. They have seen the fairy angel and desired her, but despaired ; He said, Live for her and forget everything else ; for she is God. Her beauty is not incompatible with life ; to see it is to know eternal life. The universe is not malign, tempting you with siren songs. Its music does not come and go, but sounds for ever if you will hear it. Nor is it only far away among the mountains and stars. There is the same wild beauty in the voices of children, for of such is the Kingdom of Heaven ; and in the light of a cottage window, and in any mother with her child. Chaucer says :

In reverence of Heaven's Queen
We ought to worship all women that been.

Christ puts it the other way.   In all women that be we ought to worship Heaven's Queen.

Implied in the Christian faith, but not yet clearly expressed, is the doctrine that we must discipline ourselves to find beauty if it is not to lead us and lose us in the wilderness.   In Swinburne's lines about the Pale Galilean, which I have quoted, we can almost see the beauty of the earth coming to life before our eyes and in our ears.   It is not merely women or flowers, or man's music separate from the sounds of nature ; there is the glimmer and whisper and scent of spiritual beings, refusing the last friendship with us, giving passion and unappeasable desire to the delight of the senses.   And the poets say that only through that delight can we know what spirit is ; while the preachers say that we must ignore that delight if we would know what spirit is ; and those who call Christ the pale Galilean think that He was one of the preachers.   They think that He superseded Paganism ; He said that He superseded the Pharisees.   He never said a word against the laurel, the palms, and the paean, the breasts of the nymphs in the brake ; and He was with the poets in this at least, that He told men to give up their routine for something wonderful, beautiful, and incompatible with routine. " Blessed are they which hunger and thirst after right- eousness ; for they shall be satisfied."   It is only in the last words that He differs from the poets : they lament that they are for ever unsatisfied ; He tells us that, if we hunger and thirst enough, we shall be satisfied.   And what does He mean by this righteous- ness, this Kingdom of Heaven, this seeing God, of which He is always speaking ?   One thing we know for certain : He means the utter yielding to a desire which at first seems unappeasable.   He tells us to have the courage of that desire ; and He denounces most those who have not the courage of it.   He did not denounce

Paganism, but that which is common to all exhausted religions, the stupid rules and ceremonies and sacrifices, the boredom which thinks it acquires merit by being bored, the stuffiness that shuts out from the tin tabernacle all the lovely danger at the heart of the universe, the stained-glass effigies of Himself that obscure what might be magic casements opening on the foam of perilous seas. He certainly looked out on the foam of perilous seas, and said that in the end they were less perilous than our safety. But He does impose a discipline on the hunger and thirst for beauty. We are to seek it and seek it until we find it in things that we have despised. It is not in its nature proud and distant, but humble and near, and we come closer to it, not by impatience but by patience. We can understand *la belle dame* only if we see her beauty also in the women and the children around us ; and then she will not be without pity for us, nor will she leave us to wake on the cold hillside. But we must see this beauty close at hand, we must see that children are of the Kingdom of Heaven, if we are to fill our religion with the wild beauty which it lacks, with the music of the Isle of Innisfree. St. Francis tried to bring that music into our religion ; but we think him quaint, odd, even a little mad. There was a time when the dance began to steal into our worship ; but it has been expelled, and now we only bow and kneel as if we were at Court.

A Church paper lately said that I took a merely human view of Christ ; but Christ Himself, and it was the essence of His doctrine, did not take a merely human view of any man. Now the despairing poets, no less than the men of business and the preachers, do take a merely human view of men. They say that we are cut off from this personal that is at the heart of all beauty by our own mediocrity ; but they cry for it even in their despair ; while the men of the world, and even the preachers, say that, if we tell ourselves firmly it does not exist, it will cease to exist for us. They would cut us off from all actual spiritual experience; or, at best, they tell us that spiritual experience is what it is not, that it consists in seeing the goodness of God in a sunset, and a text in the starry sky. But the poets at least know better than that; they do give us the beauty of the sunset and not a moral drawn from it. Christ tells us something different from both. He tells us that if we dare everything, sacrifice everything, we shall see His Kingdom of Heaven and be of it. He does not say that stout, comfortable men in black coats can tell us all about it. To be aware of it is a dangerous business; but, when you are utterly aware of it, then you will see, not *la belle dame sans merci*, but God Himself at the heart of it. Whether He speaks the truth or not is not for me to say, nor for any of us, least of all for the stout, comfortable men; but we may assume without superstition that He Himself saw what He took to be God, and the Father of us all, at the heart of it. The power of Christ over genera-tion after generation is not so much in the doctrine supposed to be His, which is constantly perverted and provokes revolt against its innumerable perversions, as in the intensity of His spiritual experience which all men still can recognise in the beauty of His speech. What He really says is always this—that He sees God in His Kingdom of Heaven and that we can see Him too. And He convinces us that He has seen God; no one ever had such a power of convincing. Thousands of those who refuse to call themselves Christians are unknowingly charged with His faith that there is a Kingdom of Heaven, so that His power of seeing it is not His alone but an inheritance for all mankind. We may begin with Paul: "I am utterly persuaded that neither death nor life, nor angels, nor principalities nor powers, nor things present nor things to come, nor height nor depth, no, nor any other creature, shall be able to separate us from the love of God, which is in Christ

Jesus our Lord." And we may end with these words of
William Morris :

> Ye know not how void is your hope and your living ;
> Depart with your helping lest ye undo me.
> Ye know not that at nightfall she draweth near to me,
> There is soft speech between us and words of forgiving
> Till at dead of the midnight her kisses thrill through me ;
> Pass by me and harken and waken me not.

In these passages, and many like them might be
quoted from all the centuries, there is the orthodoxy of
those who have found not merely *la belle dame sans
merci* in all beauty, who are not frightened by their
spiritual experience but assured by it. Indeed, the
mark of all full spiritual experience, whether it be of
beauty or of righteousness or of truth, is always
certainty.

> Here is the house of fulfilment of craving,
> Here is the cup with the roses around it,
> The world's wound well healed and the balm that hath bound it
> Cry out for one heedeth and leadeth you home.

Christ speaks of seeing God ; that is the most extreme expression of certainty ; Paul also of the Love of
God which is in Christ Jesus. The language of Morris
is different ; but the images of sex which he uses are
an under- rather than an over-statement of the warmth,
closeness, certainty of a passion which for him, as for
all the religious, is mutual. And it is this certainty
that gives to their words the convincing power of
beauty. But there is not one of them who says
exactly what he is certain of. The theologians have
worked upon the words of Christ and tried to turn
them into literal dogmas ; but in themselves they are
poetry, the expression of triumphant certainty rather
than of that about which He is certain. " The words
that I speak unto you I speak not of myself." That
which He has seen speaks in Him ; it is the very
spiritual experience that speaks in Him, and for all

men, and to all men ; and it is not merely Himself
who says them.   By this we may know the expression of
full spiritual experience, its certainty, and the sense of
a universal voice speaking in it.   And we too, when
we hear it, are certain and do not ask what we are
certain of.   For that universal voice is ours also ; it
lives in us long after the man who uttered it has
gone from us.   "Yet a little while and the world
seeth me no more ; but ye see me ; because I live,
ye shall live also."   That is true of all those who have
expressed spiritual experience for us, no matter in what
form.   They are gone ; but we see them still and
share in their life and their certainty.   When we hear
Mozart's *Ave Verum*, it is ours no less than his ;
we pass beyond time and change and out of the prison
of self into the freedom of that common certainty ;
we are no longer troubled with the desire of the
moth for the star, nor are we ourselves incompatible
with that which we experience.

But there is no division so deep as that between those
who recognise and value this experience and those who
do not.

When you have once experienced the Choral
Symphony, then, if some one tells you that he prefers
the Intermezzo from *Cavalleria Rusticana*, you are not
troubled—except for him.   You know that he has not
experienced the symphony ; if he had, he would not say
what he does say.   The gap between you is of the same
kind as the gap between one who has seen with the eyes
and one who has not.   Or rather it is even greater ; it
is the gap between the blind and the seeing, between
those who see and those who deny that there is anything to be seen.   It is a gap that cannot be overcome
by argument.   Yet those who see can never be content
to leave the blind in their blindness ; for spiritual experience is of such a nature that it is not consummated
until it is shared.   It is part of the affirmation produced by it, that all men can share it if they will ;

and it is not complete for any man, and does not produce the happiness of utter certainty, until all men do
share it, until the words—*Quod semper*, *quod ubique*, *quod
ab omnibus*—come true at last. That would be the
Millennium of which poets have dreamed—this certainty
coming suddenly to all men, like music in the night.
So it was Shelley saw the Millennium in *Prometheus
Unbound.*

"The trumpet shall sound"

> A sentinel was sleeping at the gate
> When there was heard a sound, so loud it shook
> The towers amid the moonlight . . .
> A long, long sound as it would never end ;
> And all the inhabitants leaped suddenly
> Out of their rest, and gathered in the streets,
> Looking in wonder up to heaven, while yet
> The music pealed along.

At the height of spiritual experience we always look
in wonder up to heaven while the music peals ; and it
seems to us that all must hear it. It is not for our
private ear ; if it were, it would not be the music of
heaven which speaks to the whole listening earth ; and
why are not all men listening ? Those who will not
listen seem to deny themselves the fellowship of that
music ; they refuse the Millennium and frustrate it
with their refusal ; they prefer their own bray to the
song of celestial nightingales. Perhaps that was what
Creighton meant when he said, "You may let the
ape and tiger die ; but you still have to deal with the
donkey." The human donkey, a libel on a charming
animal, is sceptical where he should be certain, sceptical
from mere insensibility and because he cannot hear
music for the noise of his own bray. He will listen to
nothing but another brayer, and that only on condition
that the brayer shall listen to him in turn. But we
must not think that the donkey is extinct in ourselves
and supreme in others ; he is intermittent in all of us.
A woman sitting next to you at a concert, who fans herself, munches chocolates, and looks at her nose in a bag-

mirror, may hear the music at some other time when you are deaf to it ; then you will be the donkey to her. So we are estranged from each other and filled with thoughts of murder ; but they will not help us to communicate our spiritual experience.

The chief purpose of worship is to draw us into the fellowship of spiritual experience ; and it is a useful rule of decorum that people should not fan themselves in church or eat chocolates or look at their noses in a bag-mirror. They know that in church such behaviour would prevent the fellowship of spiritual experience. But unfortunately there is another, more servile motive for decorum in church. We must behave ourselves there lest God should be offended ; and so church-goers put up with much in their services that cannot produce any spiritual experience, because they think they acquire merit by being bored. It is as if they were listening to a dull play at Court. One does not criticise the drama as it is performed at Windsor ; one acquires merit by being there. We must get rid of this notion of acquiring merit by going to church if we are to keep the services alive. We must apply this test to them : Do they produce in us a common spiritual experience ? Not always, for the failure may be in ourselves, but at least sometimes. Otherwise we are on the way to the prayer wheels of Tibet, or to the miner who wrote up his prayers over his bed and every night jerked his thumb towards them and said, " My sentiments."

But worship does keep us aware of the need for the fellowship of spiritual experience, and there can be no complete worship without art. For art exists because of men's desire to communicate their spiritual experience to each other, and so to consummate it. That desire accomplished is what we mean by expression. Expression comes of the desire to make spiritual experience complete by making it common. " This has happened to me, but not fully until it has also happened to you." The artist has the eagerness of the child who tells you all about it ; if he has not, he is only a proud, dull virtuoso. But, while the child speaks to one listener, the artist speaks to all mankind ; and he does not merely tell us about his spiritual experience ; he makes it happen to us. That is where he differs from the bore who tells us about his spiritual experience as something we must envy but cannot share. And that is where the artist is like Heaven, where there is more joy over one sinner that repenteth than over ninety-and-nine just men. For the sinner who repents is drawn into the fellowship of spiritual experience and makes it more complete for Heaven itself.

So, when we affirm the supreme value of a work of art, we affirm the supreme value of the artist's experience, which he has made ours. All art is the presentment in some form or other of that which, in reality, has produced spiritual experience ; and it is possible for art to exist because the same things will produce the same spiritual experience in all men, if only they can be rid of the obstructions to it in themselves. The artist by his power does rid us of these obstructions better than we can rid ourselves of them. We might meet a woman like Cordelia and see nothing in her ; she might be only a saucy miss to us ; but Shakespeare makes us experience her as he did. It does not matter that he may never have met just that woman ; she is for him a concentration of his spiritual experience of many women, without which he could not have drawn her. And she, with that beauty of character displayed in action and speech which is like the beauty of music, makes us cry " I believe " like a tune and like an actual human being whom we ourselves experience spiritually.

There is no difference in effect between the spiritual experience of art and the spiritual experience of reality ; only art communicates to us a spiritual experience of reality which most of us cannot get from it as surely and intensely as the great artist. The value of art consists

in this that, by its technique, plot, structure, composition—whatever the art may be—it does lead us into
spiritual experience with a certainty lacking to the
events of real life ; and the proper aim of all technique
and all method is so to lead us into spiritual experience,
not because the artist wishes to do us good, but because
the desire to communicate his experience is a part of
the experience itself.   And in the certainty with which
we are led into spiritual experience, and the sense of
certainty induced from the very start, lies the cumula-
tive power of art.   We know that we are being led, in
King Lear or the Choral Symphony, from the first
words, from the first notes.   They are full of surprises
for us, but not of disappointments ; what they promise,
that they perform, though in ways we never expect,
since they are not borrowed ways.

I know no better example of the nature of spiritual
experience, and of the unexpected manner in which art
may communicate it, than the end of the *Marriage of
Figaro*.   It is based on Beaumarchais' play, and the
libretto seems to leave most of the point of that play
out.   For the play, being satire, gives us negative
spiritual experience.   It shows us a society without
the values that are implied in Beaumarchais' *reductio
ad absurdum* of it.   But that is not Mozart's game ;
he cannot breathe in the negative world of satire
for long ; his music must be positive.   So the libretto,
seeking opportunities for Mozart's genius, leaves most
of the satire out ; it is mere intrigue without the point
of Beaumarchais' deadly bland demonstration.   Mozart
was not deadly or bland, and fools have thought that
in this music he was content to trifle.   But with the
waywardness of the artist he has his divine inevitable
surprise for those who can hear it.   It is an absurd
world and an absurd libretto that he accepts, as a child
will accept any story ; and he carries us along with
him as if he were just a charming child to whom
we listen, smiling in our superior wisdom.   And then

suddenly at the end he lifts us into the scene of general for-giveness ; and we, if we can hear the beauty of his music, know that this is reality, more real than all the logical tortures of Ibsen.   Of course, all these people are absurd and some of them worse ; the music has made fun of them and of all mankind.   But when at last they kneel down and forgive each other, the music transforms them and all mankind by a miracle that we must believe in. They are ourselves no less than themselves, and, because we forgive them with the inspired tenderness of Mozart, we forgive ourselves also.   There is a sudden relenting of the whole universe ; it is the parable of the prodigal son made universal in that music ; and at the moment of common confession and forgiveness all faces are turned upwards to feel the rain of the divine love. There is a sudden inrush of reality, undreamed of before ; but now we know that all the trifling has led up to it.   It is not merely these people, but all man-kind seen in a new way, made divine out of their very absurdity and part of a divine universe, and it is their recognition of their absurdity that makes them divine and turns our happy laughter to happy tears. Their confession of weakness lifts them to this heaven, more real than any heaven could be without a past of folly and error ; and then we know that nothing in the world is so beautiful as weakness made strong through confession of itself, as sin turned into holiness because it knows itself to be sin, as the ridiculous stepping into the sublime through self-ridicule.   And that this is reality, this is truth, Mozart convinces us, by making it happen with the surprise and the convincing power of life itself.

But for all spiritual experience, whether of art or of life, we need a self-surrender, a willing removal of obstructions in our own minds, a sacrifice of the obvious, of what is called common sense.   We must forget what the ego habitually says to us, so that we may hear

something else speak; we need to deny ourselves
and follow.   For spiritual experience is always surprising; it is not what our other kind of experience
leads us to expect.   Just as the man of science must
give up his theories before facts, so we must rid ourselves of all the inhibitions of habit that seems to us
wisdom, when spiritual experience offers itself to us.
Just because it is spiritual, it is always utterly new, and
tells us that we have been fools.   That we must confess
if we are to receive it, and confess with joy.   There is
an irony in all sudden revelation of truth, a *reductio ad
absurdum* of the whole of worldly wisdom, a revolutionary overthrow of all our traditions and precedents,
that we must consent to if it is to be a revelation to
us.   That is why beauty is terrible as an army with
banners—it is terrible to the old self—and why any
lovely action humiliates us when we see its loveliness.
It is not what we should have done, and yet it is utterly
right.   But how do we know that it is utterly right?
Not by calculating its results, but because we experience
it; and we cannot experience it unless we are prepared
to be proved wrong by it.   We must have the habit of
scepticism about all the possessions of our own minds
if we are to let truth happen to us; we must utterly
rid ourselves of the desire to be proved right.

But the donkey in us hinders us from doing this, and
at the last moment we are cut off from spiritual experience by that self-assertion which is fear of the unknown
splendour.   We are not the souls in Shelley's poem
who walk upon the winds with lightness; we reserve
judgement and beg leave to differ.   "That is not my
idea of a horse," people say when they look at Tintoret's
"Crucifixion," forgetting that it is his idea of a horse.   If
they meet a St. Francis they say, "That is not my idea
of seemly conduct."   Of Mozart they complain that
he is too tuny; of Christ Himself that He has a
devil.   And the reason always is, either that they do
not believe at all in a Kingdom of Heaven, or that they

x

think they know already just what it is. So they do
not recognise the true Kingdom of Heaven, the reality
compared with which they themselves are unreal. But
if we are to see it we must be ready to recognise it in
any form or shape and in the most unlikely people.
Think how unlikely Christ was to a learned Pharisee.
We must never say : Can any good thing come out of
Germany, or the Royal Academy, or the middle classes,
or any body or any thing that we happen to dislike ?
It is not our achievements or wisdom that matter,
but the Kingdom of Heaven ; and we matter only so
far as we are aware of it. To know that is to be humble,
but not with the 'umbleness of Uriah Heep. The great
men possessed by spiritual experience are not humble to
those who deny it ; they thunder, knowing that it is not
their own thunder. They let the power of God play
through them, and they are angry with those who deny
it, because it is not theirs, but God's. They could not
be so sure but for their humility.

There is a joy in this humility like the joy in
a lover's submission, and a pride like a soldier's
pride in discipline. But there is no rivalry with
any other regiment, no other army that we wish to
overcome. We are filled with *esprit de corps*, but the
corps is the universe itself ; and to be of the universe
and proud of it, to surrender your identity to it, and
then to have it given back a thousand times enriched,
that is a happiness compared with which all other is
counterfeit. To know yourself nothing, and then to
find yourself charged with all the power of that to
which you have yielded, that is the highest power man
can attain to. It comes, not with the will to power,
but with the sudden, irresistible confession of weakness
forced from us not against our will, but with it. For
this confession is made not merely for the self, but
for all mankind. It confesses that we are all absurd
infuriating creatures, and laughs in the very confession,
and it can hear Heaven laughing with it as well as at it.

And then it knows that, absurd and infuriating as we are, we rise above the angels in our confession and forgiveness of each other. They could not reach that subtle joy of tears and laughter ; those who have never borne the burden of their own follies cannot know what it is to let it slip from their shoulders. At the height of spiritual experience we are like the bandit who was imprisoned for years in a loathsome dungeon, until one day it occurred to him to open the door and walk out.

And at the height of it we have a certainty, if only in a glimpse, of the design of God. We know that sorrow has led to its own joy, folly to its own wisdom, sin even to its own holiness. Voltaire jibed at Leibnitz's doctrine that this is the best of all possible worlds ; but at the height of spiritual experience we know what he meant, or ought to have meant. Reality is the only reality ; our substitutes for it are figments of our minds, and not one of them could possibly be so good as what is. But this we know only when we see what is in spiritual experience, when we see it, not as a series of events, one pleasant and another painful, but rather as a piece of music in which all the notes have their place, both consecutive and simultaneous. One leads up to another and could not be what it is if it were not so leading up. And the self at one moment leads up to the self at another ; and the whole universe at one moment leads up to the whole universe at another ; and there is a oneness in both only seen at the height of spiritual experience. Then we rid ourselves even of the sense of waste, which at other times always intimidates and baffles us.

So there is nothing but spiritual experience that can give us belief, the full belief on which men act ; and all that scepticism which is deep enough to hinder or pervert action comes of the lack of spiritual experience, or the refusal to acknowledge its supreme authority and value. No man is utterly without it ; and our nightmare theories of the meaninglessness of all things come, not from the complete lack of it, but from thinking of ourselves as we are with all the spiritual experience of the past, but with all that experience proved to be false ; as if we had become what we are, soulless with the passion of immortal souls, through facts that are not. It is the bewilderment that has fallen away from spiritual experience and denied it, which turns the brain sick and makes men rush into blasphemy and savagery for relief. But all this is merely pathological, like those states of mind in which our identity seems to be divided and we are unreal to ourselves, since there is no self to be real to. Thinking about such a state is no cure for it ; you must think about something else, and then it passes. So the only cure for nightmares of scepticism is spiritual experience. Seeing is believing ; and only spiritual seeing can make us believe in spirit and its supremacy. A lover overwrought may, by thinking too much about love, persuade himself that he does not love, or even that there is no such thing as love. But when he sees the woman he loves, he knows that his thinking was all at the mercy of his nerves.

Yet the belief that comes with spiritual experience can be maintained only if it is acted upon. If we " see God," we must do what we have seen, otherwise spiritual experience itself turns to bitterness. And that, I think, is the real reason why men have feared the fairy angel so much and seen in her *la belle dame sans merci*. Either they have not connected the experience of beauty with their own actions, or they have made a false or base connection. They have seen a wild, distant, unattainable beauty in nature that allured them, but to no end ; they have heard a voice that led them nowhere. On that beauty, seen so, they could not satisfy their desires. But the doctrine of Christ, and of all the great visionaries, is that we can attain to the same beauty in ourselves, in our feelings, thoughts, and actions; we can be at one, not with nature in the scientist's sense, but with that personal in it which we see in spiritual experience. We can become like the lilies of the field as Christ saw them; and, when we do, they will not be to us flowers in the hair of the fairy angel, but, like ourselves, creatures and children of God.

IX

SPIRIT AND MATTER

BY

A. CLUTTON-BROCK

ANALYSIS

IX

SPIRIT AND MATTER

The Universal and the Particular

Spirit is a name given to something the very existence of which is often denied ; and those who believe in its existence often give an incredible account of it. It is my object to give an account of it not incredible and based on the common experience of mankind.

We are aware of matter with our senses ; and if we are aware of spirit at all, it is not with our senses. The first question is, then, Are we aware of anything not with our senses ? Of ourselves, perhaps ; but those who believe that matter is the sole reality must believe also that self-consciousness is an illusion. For them there is no self but merely matter in certain formal arrangements, functioning, as they say ; and self-consciousness is but an effect of that functioning. They insist that we have no knowledge of anything except with our senses, and that this knowledge is all knowledge by matter of matter.

Yet all the senses in combination applied to some one particular object could not produce any conclusion about that object, could not even tell us that it was an object. Smell by itself does not tell me that what I smell is also that which I touch and see ; nor do simultaneous smell, sight, and touch tell me that. A creature with only sense-perceptions could not go beyond them ;

there would be nothing in it to conclude that it was smelling, touching, and seeing the same object. It would in fact *consist* only of sense-perceptions and would have no notion of external reality at all ; and it may be that there are creatures which do consist only of sense-perceptions and have no notion of external reality. But man is not one of them ; he is aware of an object over and above his sense-perceptions of it ; and he calls that which is aware the self.

But still the question remains whether this self can be aware of anything but matter. Assuming, as we must, that the self is not merely a combination of sense-perceptions, is it still only matter, by some means which we cannot yet understand, aware of the existence of other matter ? Now the man who believes this believes also something more, namely, that it is the truth about matter. For him, therefore, besides matter there exists the truth about matter, which itself clearly is not matter and is not perceived with the senses. He may say that the truth about matter is a product of that matter which is his own mind, and exists only in his mind. But, if the truth is that and merely that, it is not the truth to him, and he cannot believe it. Truth means to us, not a product of our minds, but that which exists independently of them, that which would exist if we were not. The very word truth implies its independent existence ; the value for truth, to which we all appeal when we use the word, implies its independent existence. If we could believe that we made truth ourselves, we should no longer value it, and it would not be truth to us. When we speak of a bitter truth, an unwelcome truth, we imply that it exists independently of us and compels our recognition of its existence. If it did not, why should we not make for ourselves truths only comforting to ourselves ? The answer is that we could not believe them. Belief implies that what we believe in exists independently of our minds So the truth about external reality exists independently of our minds ; it is

not matter, though it be about matter, nor is it perceived with our senses.

Since metaphysics are concerned with the nature of
ultimate reality, it is impossible to prove any metaphysical statement. The aim of metaphysics is not to
prove any such statement, but to discover what other
beliefs are implied in any metaphysical belief. If a
man holds a certain metaphysical belief, you cannot
prove to him that it is false. But you may be able to
prove to him that other beliefs of his are inconsistent
with it, so that he will have to renounce either those
other beliefs or the metaphysical belief. So, to one
who says that he believes only in the existence of
matter, one may put it that that belief is inconsistent
with his other belief that he has attained to the truth
about matter, is indeed inconsistent with belief of any
kind, and so even with itself. For if only matter
exists, the truth about matter does not exist for us ;
it is merely an effect produced by matter upon matter ;
belief is an effect produced by matter upon matter.
But he who believes that cannot believe anything else,
or even that.

Turn now from truth to something which can be
much more easily confused with matter ; something
which most people suppose they perceive with their
senses, namely beauty. To us the truth about objects
is not the objects themselves ; but we may suppose that
the beauty of an object is the object itself, and that we
perceive it with our sense of sight or hearing. The
beauty of a tune is the tune ; and we hear that beauty.
Yet it is possible to hear the notes without hearing the
tune and so the beauty. The beauty of the tune does
not consist merely of the pleasant sound of the individual notes. Play the same notes in another order
and there is no tune and no beauty of the tune.
The tune is something we cannot perceive without the
sense of hearing ; but that which perceives it, and the
beauty of it, is not the sense of hearing. And, though

the notes are themselves merely sounds and material, the tune is not material ; it is something beyond matter and informing it. It is that relation of material things which we call beauty, and which, though it consists of material things, is itself not matter nor perceived with the senses.

And the perception of truth and beauty is a perception of — what ? not particular objects perceived with the senses, but universal relations not perceived with the senses, although we can be aware of them only through the medium of the senses. And spirit is the name given to that in us which is aware of these universals ; and they themselves, since they are not matter, though always perceived in or through matter, are said to be spiritual. The word spirit is an acknowledgement of their existence, and of the existence of something in ourselves, not sense, which perceives and values them. And there is another universal, another relation, in our own actions, which is spiritual and perceived by spirit, not by sense—that relation which is called righteousness. We are aware of it only in men and in their conduct ; yet it also is to us a universal relation like truth and beauty. It does not consist merely in particular actions or speech as we perceive these in others, nor in particular thoughts of our own as we are aware of them. It consists in the relation of action, speech, or thought to circumstance. Righteousness, in fact, is a certain arrangement of actions or speech or thoughts, like the arrangement of notes which makes a tune ; and we are aware of the righteousness as a universal relation, over and above the action, speech, or thought, though we cannot be aware of it apart from these. So we say that righteousness also is spiritual, and that spirit is aware of it. There is this difference between it and beauty or truth, that it is a universal we are aware of only in human beings, and perhaps sometimes in animals. We are not aware of it in mere phenomena or in inanimate objects.

But of this difference I will speak later. So there seem to us to be two kinds of reality, a reality of matter, of particulars, perceived by the senses ; and a reality of spirit, of universals, perceived through the senses but by spirit. But the mind of man refuses to believe in two kinds of reality ; the very phrase is a contradiction of itself ; for reality means that in terms of which all else can be explained, and there cannot be two kinds of reality each unable to explain the other. If there are, neither is to us quite real ; and we look for a further reality behind them, in terms of which both can be explained away. In despair of that further reality, some have said that there is no matter but only spirit ; and others that there is no spirit but only matter ; and, ever since men began to think at all, a pretty quarrel has raged between them, particularly over man himself. He is all spirit or all flesh ; but to himself, when he does not think too hard about himself, he remains both. To convince him that he is all one or the other makes him uncomfortable ; makes him feel that the universe, including himself, is fraudulent.

It is clearly fraudulent if he is all matter ; if life, consciousness, anything else you please, is, as they say, only a function of matter. For then the self, the very heart of reality to all of us, does not exist. On the other hand, if there is no matter but only spirit, why is this spirit so urgently aware of matter, so much in pleasure or pain over it. Why can I do nothing, perceive nothing, value nothing, without it ? I am living in a universe of phantoms, and the very agonies of Christ on the Cross were unreal. In fact the docetic heresy is true, not only of Him, but of all men and things. Let us then cut our throats so that we may rush out of this phantasmagoria the nearest way. Those who affirm the existence of spirit alone are insensibly led to think of it as a kind of invisible matter. It is to them spirit pretending to be matter and imitating it to the life, imitating it so that it deceives even the pure spirit which is ourselves. Spirit, to begin with, means to us that which is not matter, it does not mean spirit pretending to be matter ; and our own perception of spirit is to us the perception of something beyond matter, though manifested in or through it. We cannot be content if we are told that we do not perceive matter at all but only spirit pretending to be it. We might as well believe at once that spirit is all matter, if matter is all spirit. In either case an incessant trick is played on us by reality ; and reality itself is not to be trusted.

As for those who affirm the existence of matter alone, they are led insensibly to think of it as a kind of visible spirit. They cry that this matter is more than we ever dreamed of, is in fact the best possible substitute for that spirit which does not exist. We, for instance, are all matter ; and what fine creatures we are. It is a mistake to think of us as mere flesh. We are electrons or ions or what not, all incessantly whirling about ; and this whirling is itself far more glorious than any spirit could be, if there were such a thing. Let us sing our hymns no longer to a God who doesn't exist, but to the eternal whirl of which we also are a part. It must be good in itself if it can whirl into us ; and if it whirls out again, what does that matter ? We fade into the infinite azure of the past ; but the whirling goes on for ever, and the result of it is—just everything. Why therefore should we sulk ? Let us join the dance mentally as we do materially. The very mental refusal to do so is itself all part of the whirl. It is electrons at their highest state of eternally voluptuous excitement—a beautiful thought.

No ! we shall not be satisfied if we are told that reality is all spirit or all matter. Either way, half the content of reality is left out so as to make the rest easier to think about. But we may see the way towards a solution, through an analogy from art. In art there

seems to be the same difficulty about the universal
and the particular. In art, we are told, there are
always two things to be aimed at—unity of purpose or
design, and richness of content; and, so long as we merely
think about these, it seems that one is to be obtained
only at the expense of the other. But if an artist tries
to get one at the expense of the other, he is sure to fail
in his art. Design without content is not design at
all ; and content without design is not content. It is
only the presence of each that makes the other what it
is ; and the great artist attains to both, not by aiming
at one at the expense of the other, but by aiming at
both with equal intensity. The greater the work of
art the more there is of both in it. It is the passion
for both that actually produces a fusion of them, in
which they become one. And we think of them as
two, only for purposes of thought. Success in art is
the sameness of them ; it is only because we are so used
to failure that they seem to us different.

So, we may conjecture, it is with reality. It seems
to us to consist of matter and spirit, and we seem to
ourselves to be matter and spirit, because we so seldom
attain to any fulness of perception of it. For the most
part we are aware only of particulars, which we call
matter ; and the whole of us is not aware of them.
The senses are aware of different aspects of them, and
the self combines those sense-impressions into a perception of independent material reality. Then sometimes
we attain also to a perception of the universal in these
particulars ; but often, when we are aware of it, we
forget the particulars ; we think away from them to
the relation in which we have perceived them ; we pass
out of the immediate warm perception of the whole
reality, universal and particular, matter and spirit, to
a purely intellectual concern with the universal, which
perhaps seems to us then to be the whole reality, or
at least the higher, more significant, reality. But the
moment we separate it from the particular, we are

losing our perception of it ; it becomes to us far off
and faint and abstract, like a picture in which the artist
has aimed at unity of purpose without richness of content. When we are aware of both with equal intensity
they become one to us. Beauty is the beautiful thing ;
Truth is objects or phenomena behaving in a certain
way. There is in all truth and all beauty a character,
an identity, a precision, which they get only from the
particulars that are related in them. So this fulness
of perception is always a matter of degree for us, and
always we fall short of completeness. That is why we
make our division of spirit and matter, a division not
in reality itself, but only in our fragmentary perception
of it.

The Real and the Useful

Our difficulty is increased by the fact that we have
a past of ages in which we have conceived of things in
a relation of use to ourselves. Sense-perception indeed
does incite us instantly to sense-value. It is actually
a means of knowing what gives us pleasure or pain,
what helps us to live or hinders us from living. To
most animals perhaps the vision of an object has no
meaning beyond that of use, it suggests merely security
or danger, pleasure or pain ; and that is not concerned
with the object as an independent reality. But man
has gradually acquired a sense of the independent reality
of objects and has been able to contemplate them
apart from their use for him. We have language itself
because we have this power of disinterested contemplation. It has been said that animals have language,
since they can make sounds expressing their desire for
things. But that is not language, for it expresses only
the desire for a thing, never the thing itself. A cat
can mew for cat's-meat, as Samuel Butler has said, when
he hears the cat's-meat man ; but he cannot say cat's-
meat ; he can only say, I want cat's-meat, or rather
only, I want. He can make the sound of desire ; he

cannot make sounds purified of his desire, as he cannot
think of things apart from his desire ; and his desire,
sounding in all his noises, prevents that delicate differentiation of sound which is possible to man because he
can think and speak of a thing apart from his own
desire for it. That is how man has the power of
making nouns. The animal, unable to think of things
apart from his own use of them, never attains to nouns
at all and has no true language. So there is latent in
the first human speech, the artist, the philosopher, the
saint ; and it is by means of this very speech, and the
power of detachment which it implies, that man has
progressed, even in matters of use, so far beyond other
creatures.

And yet man is always being pulled back into thinking in terms of the relation of use. He can never
escape from it utterly, as he can never escape from the
struggle for life. It is a condition of his being. Like
other animals, he cannot help seeing objects in a relation of use to himself ; but while he sees them so he
cannot be aware of their full reality. For they do not
exist so that they may be of use to us ; the use is our
way of looking at them ; it is what the senses suggest
to us. But this always gives us merely the particular ;
and so long as we see things only or mainly in a relation of use to ourselves, we are not fully aware of the
universal in them which is a part of their reality.

But in so far as we can and do escape from the relation of use—and there is a constant effort of the spirit
to escape from it—we pass beyond mere sense-perception and sense-values to a perception and value of the
universal. Our escape is positive, not negative ; for we
cannot rise from the relation of use to no relation at all,
from one kind of perception and value into no perception and value. Beyond the relation of use we instantly
become aware of another relation, which, as soon as we
are aware of it, we value above the relation of use.
And in this new relation the object of perception

becomes more, not less, real to us, because it is related
not merely to us through our use for it, but to the sum
total of things. Its identity is not lost but heightened
in that new relation, as the identity of notes is heightened
when they are to us part of a tune. Because it is part
of a whole it is also far more itself than it was when it
was merely an item to be made use of. Thus to a
greedy boy a plum is merely something good to eat, it
is a member of the genus plum which, he knows, is
good to eat, and is distinguished from other members
of the genus only by looking more or less good to eat
than they do. That is the one point of distinction he
notices in it, because he sees it only in relation to his
own appetite. But an artist sees a plum in another
relation, the relation of beauty ; and because he sees it
in that relation it is not to him a member of the genus
plum which is good to eat, but is itself with all its
particular character and beauty. It is one note in the
music of beauty that he perceives, and it could not be
any other note. So he tries to paint its particular
character and beauty at one particular moment and
in certain particular circumstances. Yet the beauty
of which it is a part is also universal ; it is something
that he and not merely his eye perceives ; and his eye
perceives more of the plum because he himself perceives
the beauty of the plum. The very senses tell us little
in mere sense-perception. It is only when they are
enforced by spiritual perception that they tell us much.
It is only when we see things in some relation to each
other and not to ourselves that we see them fully.

Now the first spiritual perception, in order of time,
is the perception of beauty. It is not higher than any
other spiritual perception, but it must precede the
others if we are to understand the connection between
spirit and sense, and so between spirit and matter.
The sense of beauty, as we call it—thus insisting upon
the close relation between the universal beauty and its
particulars—is necessary to us if we are to grasp the

relation between other universals and their particulars.
In beauty we cannot separate the universal from the
particular, spirit from sense, or spirit from matter.
But those who pass on to the other universals, to
philosophy or morals, without an intense experience
and value of beauty, are always apt to think of the
universal with which they concern themselves as utterly
distinct from, or even as opposed to, the particular.
For them there is an opposition between spirit and
sense, and so between spirit and matter. They pass
from the actual experience of the universal in the
particular to mere thinking about the universal or to
mere acting upon it, upon what they call principle ;
and so they fall into error about the relation between
matter and spirit, about the very nature of reality.
Hence that Manichaean heresy which constantly infests
both thought and morals. It is, in all its different
forms and degrees of intensity, whether it be intellect-
ualism or asceticism, the result of the lack of actual
spiritual experience in its simplest and most immediate
form, the experience of beauty. But we are much
more aware of it in its effect upon morals than in its
effect upon thought.

It affects thought in a curious and unexpected way.
For man, knowing that he has the power of being
aware of objects out of the relation of use to himself,
and having a great desire to be so aware of them, is
apt to suppose that he can be so aware of them by
means of the pure intellect, that he can at any
moment switch off the animal in himself and switch on
the philosopher. He can no more do that than he can
switch off the animal and switch on the artist or the
saint. It has often been believed by philosophers in
the past that man is more capable of pure contemplation than of any other spiritual activity in its purity.
Their glorification of the reason is based on this belief ;
and the result of that glorification has been an immense
discouragement, since the pure reason by itself has done

for us far less than was expected of it. It has not discovered for us any certain truths about the nature of
reality, nor has it preserved us from obvious errors in
conduct. Mankind is impatient of philosophers and of
what seems their barren intellectual game, just because
of their glorification of that reason which has done so
little. Their error has been to trust in the reason and
in thinking about spiritual experience, without having
first enriched themselves with actual spiritual experience
in its simplest and most direct form, that is to say, with
the experience of beauty. They have been, for the
most part, mills grinding without any corn between
them ; they have trusted in the machinery without providing it with material ; and all the while it is not
machinery at all but a living part of themselves, subject
to error like all the rest of them. Now the error of
the reason, acting without enrichment, is to see the
universal as altogether separate from the particular, and
so to doubt the existence either of the particular or
of the universal ; and the reason falls into this error
because it believes itself to be pure and yet is, like all the
rest of the self, continually falling back into the relation
of use. We believe what we wish to believe, as we see
what we wish to see and do what we wish to do ; and
the errors of the reason are not merely individual
but generic, like all our other errors. The doctrine of
evolution, so much misapplied, might warn us that in
all things we have the habits of our own animal past,
and that we escape from them no more when we think
than when we feel or act. In fact, we need now to
apply that doctrine not only *in* our philosophy but *to*
it. So at last we shall make a conduit-pipe between
science and philosophy by means of psychology, a
psychology based on our awareness of our own animal
past. Kant gave us a Kritik of pure reason ; what we
need now is a Kritik of impure reason, based on the
knowledge that our reason, like all the rest of us, is
infested with habits acquired in the relation of use.

That Kritik will not make us despair of reason, any more than the same kind of Kritik so long applied to morals has made us despair of them. Just as our righteousness is always the effort to be righteousness, so our reason must be always the effort to be reason, to attain to a power of pure contemplation it never has attained to. It is not a machinery that works perfectly when we can separate it from the rest of ourselves ; it is a part of ourselves that we must always be purifying, and we cannot purify it except through actual spiritual experience, which, as I have said, begins with the sense of beauty. In that we are first aware of the universal ; and we see it indissolubly linked with the particular.

So, if we are to believe in spirit and to understand its nature, we must continue in our intellectual and moral activities still to see the universal thus indissolubly linked with the particular ; we must never fall into conceiving of them as separate or opposed. The world of particulars, as perceived by the senses, is not illusion, nor is the world of universals as conceived by the mind ; but each by itself is imperfect and misleading. The one is the notes without the tune, the other the tune without the sounds ; the one is chaos, nonsense, the other a mere pattern. Our business is not merely with the reason but with all the faculties, with the whole self, to be aware of both content and design, for we cannot be fully aware of one without being aware of the other.

Unfortunately it is possible for us to contemplate with the intelligence a world which still we conceive of as entirely in the relation of use to ourselves, and with the intelligence to take our conceptions of use entirely seriously. Where this happens the result is a barren and empty universal of the mere intelligence, and one that in its barrenness and emptiness appals us. We are apt to believe, for instance, that our notion of causation is itself a product of the pure intelligence, and a modern one. We argue about it as if it were itself necessarily, mathematically true ; but with all our arguing we are unable to state it even in a form satisfactory to ourselves. For it is not really a product of the pure or the modern intelligence, but a tool rather of the mind and one fashioned first by the primitive mind when it saw the whole universe in a relation of use to itself. A savage acquires the notion of causation when he discovers that, if he puts his finger in the fire, he will always suffer pain. And the savage is always making use of this law of causation, as we call it, in his struggle for life. It is to him, and still to us, a means of carrying on that struggle. We have through ages learnt to use the fact which we call causation for our own purposes, and still we see it and conceive it in relation to those purposes. Still it is to us a means, if not of using things, of discovering facts. It is the law of the universe, as we make use of the universe. We have acquired knowledge of causes and effects ; this knowledge has meant to us making use ; and we have flown to the further conclusion that where we can make use we know. But all we do know about causation is this, that in practice we can count upon certain things happening where certain other things have happened before. Mill said that the cause of anything is the total assemblage of the conditions that precede its appearance. But this definition has always been felt to be untrue, because it makes "the law of causation " useless to us. We never do know the total assemblage of the conditions, and yet we can observe causation and make use of it. So a different definition has been found, namely, that cause is a conception we find useful in our dealings with nature, that among the conditions of an event we find some from which, as a matter of fact, we are able to foretell the event. Those we call its cause or causes. In that definition it is frankly confessed that causation is a conception we make use of ; but it is still one so vague that it is useful to us rather because it gives us a kind of faith than because it helps us practically to discover or to make use of anything. It gives us faith that we shall

discover and shall make use, faith in a universal uniformity. And from this faith comes a sense of power ;
it convinces us that we are able to constrain that which
is not ourselves to our own purpose. The saying
"knowledge is power" is an expression of it. And
since we, through the action of causation, seem to be
able to exercise a compulsion on things, we come to
believe that causation itself is a compulsion exercised
upon all things, ourselves included, from outside. It
is the universal seen as compulsion, and seen so because
we see it in the relation of use. So we get the notion
of a compulsory universe, in which everything compels
everything else to do what it does not want to do,
and is itself compelled by this law of causation ; and
further, of a universe in which everything is made
for some use : once a use to men, then a use to God,
and now a use to an abstraction called Nature. Nature
wishes us and all things to survive or to attain to
some kind of perfection through the struggle for
survival ; and so we and all things are related to each
other only in terms of that struggle, whether we like
it or not. This relation is imposed on all things and
we conceive of all things, ourselves included, as passive
under it, as things seem passive under us when we make
use of them. All things are tied and bound to each
other by the chain of this relation ; all things are trying
to make use of each other, and cannot do anything but
try to make use of each other. Things appear to be
passive to us when we make use of them, and so we
think of all things, ourselves included, as passive under
the universal compulsion.

But a cabbage is not purely passive to us when we
grow it for the table. We use it, but we do not compel
it to grow. We can apply certain conditions of our own
choice to it ; but it answers to them in its own way and
according to its own nature. It has at least the power
of turning the nourishment we give it into itself ; and
the law of causation means to us that we can count upon

its turning that nourishment into itself and not into something else. Nourishment becomes something different in the cabbage from what it becomes in me, because the cabbage is a cabbage and I am I. Whatever happens to every living creature becomes in that creature something different from what it would become if it happened to any other creature. There is in all that lives an active contribution to every effect produced on itself, which means that the effect is not merely effect. It means that all that lives is a fount of original causation, or rather the words " cause and effect," if we mean anything by them at all, will not describe what happens to and in living creatures. The whole conception of causation is a conception of things not living but dead ; and it has grown up in our minds because things, when we make use of them, are to us not living but dead. We see them only in a relation of use to ourselves ; that is to say, as existing for us and utterly dependent on us. But no living thing exists for us or is utterly dependent on us ; we may exercise compulsion on it, but we cannot exercise compulsion on its nature. Yet our notion of causation is a notion of everything exercising compulsion on the nature of everything else. From it is left out the nature, the life, the identity of all things, that which in ourselves we call freedom. And since this obvious fact is left out of our notion of causation, we are unable to state the law of causation in a manner satisfactory to ourselves. We call it a law, but it remains merely a faith that things will continue to behave with a uniformity which enables us to make use of them.

It is a significant fact that mathematics, the science which is most free from the relation of use, the science in which man does not deal with things of use to him but with pure concepts or abstractions, is not concerned with causes and effects but with properties. The properties of a circle are not caused by any external or preceding conditions ; they are not caused by any other properties of the circle itself. They are the circle itself ;

they are that which makes it a circle. We may discover them one after another ; and we may discover
one because we have discovered another ; but they exist
simultaneously and do not cause one another any more
than we cause them by discovering them. The circle is
what it is by the law of its own being and not by the
pressure of circumstances. We know this about the
circle because we are able to contemplate it purely and
not as an object of use to ourselves ; and mathematics
is the type of all sciences because, dealing as it does with
pure concepts, it is freed from the relation of use. From
mathematics man first learned what pure science is. He
had to find a world purely of his own thought, before
he could understand how it was necessary to contemplate the real world if he was to see it as it is. Mathematics are to man a prophecy of reality, because in them
he can escape entirely out of the relation of use. But,
the moment we come to deal with actual things, there
is the pull of the relation of use upon our reason itself,
a pull as incessant as that of the attraction of gravity
upon our bodies. It is not merely a pull upon particular
processes of reasoning ; it enters into our very conceptions of reality, those conceptions that seem to us to
belong not to our minds but to reality itself.

Thus there is a perpetual incongruity in our conceptions of reality. We assume them to be single
and concordant, whereas there is a duality and conflict
in them, because we are always seeing things in two
different relations, namely, the relation of use to ourselves which will tell us nothing about reality, and that
other relation of which we become aware when we rise
out of the relation of use, the relation, as it were, of
notes in a tune. Of this relation we are most intensely
aware in ourselves. There are times when we become
to ourselves, not things making use and being made use
of, but notes in a universal tune, of which we are a part,
not by any compulsion, but because it is our own nature
to be a part of it. Only in becoming a part of it do we

find our nature, our identity ; then we act in a certain way, not because circumstances compel us, but because we are what we are, and because all other things are what they are. Then, too, we are aware of utter freedom, the freedom of the circle, which is what it is, and no external circumstances can make it otherwise. But we differ from the circle in this, that, being actual living creatures, and necessarily in some kind of relation with all other actual things, our task is not only to be what we are, but also to act what we are. In our relation with external reality doing is a part of being, as it is not with the circle. So we have to achieve that relation in which we are fully ourselves, and that is true of all actual things ; they are not, like mathematical concepts, merely in a relation of being, they are in a relation of action, which may be one of use or one of reality, one in which they attain to the freedom of being completely themselves. For us, at least, there are times, however rare, when the whole self seems to act in accordance with its own being, when our actions are our properties, when we know that we are not machines nor yet mere concepts, but notes in a tune finding their identity because they are in the tune.

A great piece of music has the mathematical quality ; but it has also passion aroused by a relation with external reality. Yet the external reality has not caused the passion so much as given it a subject matter through which it can express itself. So we in our supreme moments seem to get from external reality a subject matter through which we express ourselves. A circle has no subject matter ; it does not express itself but merely is itself. We at our highest are ourselves and express ourselves in action.

But we are ourselves and express ourselves only when we rise into a full perception of external reality and into a full relation with it, by escaping from the relation of use. We cannot pass out of the relation of use into no relation at all, into a higher and lonely

SPIRIT AND MATTER 331

egotism. Egotism is always the result of the tyranny
of the relation of use over the mind. The egotist
does not merely act, but also thinks and feels, in terms
of that relation. The higher egotist sees even his
dreams, his ideals, his moral effort, in terms of it ;
and so, even in them, he never escapes from himself.
He has them because others who were not egotists
have had them ; he is imitative, parasitic upon the
spiritual achievements of others ; but these achievements he sees always in terms of use to himself, and
so misunderstands and misuses them. Thus, in extreme
cases, a lunatic imagines himself to be God. He has
got the idea of God from others, but it means to him
only his own eminence, his own tyranny over all things.
He is unable to make terms with a God who is not
himself, because he sees God only in the relation of use ;
therefore he must himself be God if he is to believe
in a God at all. He attains to an imaginary tyranny
over all things because he cannot escape from the
tyranny of the relation of use over his own mind ; he
is so much at the mercy of circumstance, seeing it
only in the relation of use, that life would be intolerable
to him if he did not persuade himself that he was the
lord and master of circumstance. And in all egotism,
especially the egotism of religion, there is this desire
to be lord and master of circumstance. Men believe
in God that they may be masters of circumstance,
and imagine a God who will give them mastery ;
they make him a tyrant over themselves, that he may
delegate some of his tyranny to them.

But if we can rise out of the relation of use into
another relation, the relation of value, we are no longer
at the mercy of things, nor do we wish to be their
master. Rather we are more intensely ourselves, and
they to us are more intensely themselves, in this new
relation not of slavery or dominance but of value. Our
reality is heightened by our perception of an external
reality, of which we see the true nature because we

do not see it in a relation of use to ourselves. The perception and the value are simultaneous, are indeed one.

When this reality is altogether hidden from us by the relation of use, the universe is to us a nonsense universe. We are aware only of particulars in it, perceived by the senses and to be made use of. And, since many of these are useless or harmful to us, much of the universe has no meaning to us or an evil meaning. It is all something we would make use of if we could; but the chain of necessity that binds it, and through which we are able to make use of it, also limits its use to us, and even gives to it that tyranny over us which we desire to exercise over it. We are then related to all things as we should be to each other, if we had no aim except to make use of each other. We know that in human relations we must escape from use to value, if we are to know each other or to enjoy each other at all. A man who sees other men only in the relation of use is a criminal and has to be treated as such. So the universe treats us, if we see it only in a relation of use to ourselves; and it is as meaningless to us as civilised society is to the criminal. It punishes us, as society punishes the criminal, with the sense of its tyranny; it is to us a prison.

It is also what music would be to a man who looked to it for useful information. He would listen to the sounds, expecting them to tell him something of advantage to himself, and they would be mere noises to him in no relation with each other; for their relation with each other is not one of use to him, but of beauty. When that is not perceived they are nonsense, a chaos of noise. All art is both spirit and matter, and we cannot distinguish the one from the other in it. The spirit is the arrangement of the matter; in that arrangement the word is utterly become flesh. The matter is what it is because of the spirit; and unless we perceive the spirit in it the universal informing the particular, it is nonsense to us. So it is with the universe.

Now the natural sciences by themselves reveal to us a certain material coherence in external reality ; but, so long as it is merely material, it is to us like a geometrical pattern in which there is neither beauty nor meaning, nor even consistent use to ourselves. If we look for use to ourselves in it we find that it is part useful and part harmful. So we think of it as half friendly, half hostile, and we cannot see why it should be one, if also the other. So still it is nonsense ; and we, while we live in terms of use, are nonsense to ourselves, mere matter also forced by some external compulsion into the pattern ; and we think that this pattern, meaningless, unbeautiful, half useful, half harmful, is reality, and we ourselves are but as the rest of it.

In fact, the natural sciences by themselves give a coherence to reality which is self-contradictory ; for it is meaningless to us, yet coherence implies meaning. It is as if we found a grammatical structure in sounds without sense, or a machine which worked incessantly yet which had been made for no purpose. It is this coherence without meaning that appals the modern mind, so long as it seems the whole of reality. But the contradiction is in the mind itself, not in reality, in the mind that believes there can be a mechanical coherence, one to be perceived by the pure intellect alone, without also a spiritual coherence and meaning to be perceived by all the spiritual powers of the mind. The material coherence is but the beginning, the first hint or prophecy, of the spiritual coherence. But the mind gets no further towards seeing it if, from age-long habit, it looks for the meaning of the material coherence in use to itself. It has, in the mere discovery of fact, escaped from that atavism ; it no longer sees things merely as it wishes to see them, so that it may make itself comfortable among them. It makes theories which it tests incessantly by the facts. But still in its values the old atavism prevails, and it asks, What use is this coherence to me?

So long as it asks that question, the coherence, established and proved as it is, has no meaning for it. The value for truth by itself will not avail to discover the truth. It will show us the coherence but not its meaning. For the full perception of reality we need the full sense of the universal, as beauty and righteousness, as well as truth. And it is only by means of these three perceptions, all working together and throwing light on each other, that we can even advance towards a full perception.

The value for truth by itself will enable us to escape from the relation of use in the discovery of material facts; but, with the value for truth alone, we shall still remain in the relation of use in our valuing of those facts. We may try to rise out of it heroically; but truth alone will not show us any other relation to rise into. It will give us mere stoicism, in which we shall set our teeth and say that, though mere matter in a universe of matter, we will behave as spirit would behave if there were any spirit; though meaningless parts of a meaningless process, we will act as if we and it had meaning. Though faith, hope, and charity are virtues created by the illusions of man, yet we will make them our virtues. I can never believe that this stoicism is as hopeless and faithless as it pretends to itself to be.

For the fact that the pattern is meaningless to us does seem to imply always that it must have a meaning. Mere chaos could not suggest even that it ought to have a meaning; and if we were part of a chaos we should not be looking for one. We are not satisfied with a merely material meaning, with an explanation of all things in terms of the struggle for life, because that is not a meaning to us at all. It is not the meaning of our own spiritual perceptions, even of our

value for truth. But this unhappy stage which we
reach when we see a material coherence in things and
no other—what is it but a phase in our evolution, that
is to say, in our struggle towards fulness of perception.
The doctrine of evolution can warn us of this—that
our perception of reality is always a matter of degree.
We are not sharply separated from the beasts merely
because we are reasoning animals ; our very reason is
still subject to animal habits. Nor can we escape
suddenly from the perception of a merely material world
to the perception of a reality that is not material at all.
For that is a phantom of the mind. The beginnings of
the perception of reality in the lowest animals are to be
found in sensations, by means of which they are aware
not even of objects but merely that they themselves
feel ; or rather they are not even aware of themselves
as feeling, but only of their feelings. Self-consciousness
comes gradually and only with fuller perception of
that which is not self. Man is aware of self, of his
own identity, more and more as he becomes aware of
not-self. But even we have only fragmentary glimpses
of reality and, in them, are but fragments of ourselves.
So we cannot attain to complete self-consciousness by
ignoring external reality ; but only by being more and
more fully aware of it, of the universal in the particular,
of matter and spirit as one. Then we become to
ourselves one, like the tune in the notes, like the sense
in the words ; and the universe becomes one to us
also.

The Meaning of Evolution

It is strange that the doctrine of evolution has so
often led men to unhappy notions of the nature of
reality, seeing in it at best but a merely artistic process
with millions of experiments and failures for one
eventual masterpiece. That is Nietzsche's idea, the
idea of a man with a passionate sense of beauty, who
tries to see reality only in the light of that sense.

Beauty by itself will not satisfy the values of man; no excellence by itself, seen merely as excellence, will do that; there is still something cruel in mere triumphant excellence. It is like the mere virtuosity of art, the mere skill of Mozart. If a man sees only that in Mozart's music, he does not know why Mozart made his music; and it is to him a game which may please him in his hours of ease but will not answer the questions of his sorrow. If there is nothing but virtuosity in nature, nothing but the effort to produce masterpieces, then nature is a brainless artist not knowing why masterpieces should be produced. And there is this contradiction of the brainless artist, who produces masterpieces without knowing why, in all the talk about Nature when she is thought of as a mere blind process and yet called *she*; when she is praised for a loveliness she did not mean to produce, and all the while there is no *she* producing it but merely things being produced. The struggle for life does produce not merely life but masterpieces; which, if there is nothing but a struggle for life, is absurd.

We shall see our way to sense only if we take our sense of the masterpiece to be a sense of reality itself, if that sense is not merely a freak or by-product of evolution, but both the end and the means in the process. In that process we never escape from the struggle for life; but the struggle itself, with all the relation of use it imposes on us, yet makes us aware of another relation; and our effort is to be aware of that relation more and more. As we make use of particulars, in our very use of them we become aware of universals. Indeed, we ourselves, making particulars to be of use to ourselves, do also make universals. The mere craftsman, making things of use for the sake of their use, in that rises from the craftsman to the artist; in his own work he may see an image of what he can attain to in his perception of reality.

A man makes a pot or builds a house for use. Clay,

stone, are to him as yet only material to be made use of. But if he makes the pot or builds the house of good material and good workmanship, and if above all he designs it fitly for its purpose, then the pot or the house has, without his intention, a beauty that comes of its fitness for its purpose. This beauty, which I will call functional, is like the beauty of natural things as we perceive it without any sense of spiritual meaning in it. It is like the beauty of a pine growing in a rock and fitting itself by the design of its growth to its position. But the craftsman, when he sees this beauty, sees it as beauty, not merely as use ; he values it, as beauty, beyond use. And this perception of functional beauty as beauty, this value for it as beauty, leads him in his next work to emphasise the functional beauty as beauty, and so to turn it into expressive or artistic beauty, with a quality of his own self in it. He gives a more delicate curve to the pot and then a curve more and more delicate, until, in an age passionate for beauty, he attains to the masterpieces of the Sung pottery. But always the expression could not begin unless the workman were aware of functional beauty as beauty, not as mere use. That functional beauty is, as it were, given away to him with a pound of tea. It comes to him in his struggle for life ; but if he sees it as something not merely useful to him in that struggle, if he values it for its own sake, then he is led on to expressive art ; then from an intelligent animal he becomes a God, or at least an angel.

And it is the same in morals. Those virtues most valued by Christ Himself, love, self-sacrifice, fellowship, are, to begin with, instincts most valuable in the struggle for life, valuable to the herd at least, if not to the individual. The type of all love is the love of a mother for her child ; and that is an animal instinct without which the race could not survive. But man has the divine faculty of recognising it to be a virtue in itself and not merely a useful instinct. It has a value for

z

him that is not its survival value ; and because it is virtue to him, as functional beauty is beauty to the craftsman, he aims at it for its own sake and becomes morally expressive as the craftsman becomes aesthetically expressive. He extends it, from the particular relation of the mother with her child, to all other human relations, not because it is use but because it is virtue. And so it is with fellowship and self-sacrifice, both to begin with herd instincts. They too are recognised and valued as virtue, not as mere use, and are practised, not so that the herd may survive—often they are practised in defiance of the herd—but because they are virtues. All these virtues are wild virtues ; and when Christianity sets up the statue of the mother and her child for worship, it affirms that the universe is not unkind or unmeaning to the values of man ; that the highest virtues are to begin with wild virtues, springing out of nature herself and not imposed by the arbitrary will of God. In the mother, spirit and sense are one, and the divine beauty we see in her is one to our spirit and sense. It has its use ; and it stirs the heart and brings tears to the eyes, as no mere thing of use would do.

We can fancy what stirrings of the spirit there were in our distant forefathers when they saw their wives with the babe at the breast ; how they wished to share in that love ; how fiercely they would fight for the mother and child ; and how they worshipped the divine principle of generation that gave so much holiness and beauty to the world. And we can fancy them too looking at the pots they had turned, wondering at their beauty and then heightening it. We know that is how they became artists and how the passion for righteousness grew in them. But still to us nature, when it is merely nature, is an unknowing artist ; and the beauty of the visible world leaves us sad and baffled. It seems to speak, but not to us ; to pour out its beauty, but not with any desire for fellowship.

And so that beauty is to us not expression but an accident of phenomena, as the shapes made by hoar frost on the window have a chance resemblance to fern leaves. And men say that the beauty of nature has no existence outside their own perception of it, for they see in nature no will and no virtue. She, unlike the artist, sings about nothing. There is no experience of her own expressed in her own beauty, no value for anything, even for her own beauty. How therefore can there be beauty except in our perception of it? If there is no artist how can there be art?

Yet the savage made for himself myths of an artist, because he saw what he took to be art; without knowing it he answered in those myths a philosophic question we still put to ourselves and cannot answer. Because modern man sees both beauty and virtue in the works of man, and only beauty in nature, he is not assured of the presence of spirit in nature, and so comes to be doubtful of it in himself. But he will never be satisfied to see only beauty in nature; for beauty by itself makes no answer to his own spirit, nor can his spirit make answer happily to it. Only if he could find virtue as well as beauty and truth in reality outside himself could he see in it the promise of a final and complete fellowship with himself. Spirit is not spirit unless all the universals are manifested in it. All of them, however imperfectly, are manifested in man, but not outside him. So he remains lonely and hungry in a universe that seems occupied with its own business but will not speak to him; and he is always trying to accommodate himself to it, to assert its value and rightness, as he sees it; always telling himself that the desire of his own heart is foolishness that leads him astray. Yet still he cannot content himself with the truth that science offers him when it denies him the hope of fellowship; and he still looks back to the old myths of an artist who has expressed himself in the beauty of nature, or the later more moving myth of a God who is lover as well as artist. If those were made only by the heart of man, what was it that gave man the heart to make them? They are his answer to the nature of things; what in the nature of things caused him to make that answer?

A modern philosophy based on the doctrine of evolution has offered us a bright and cheerful substitute for the desire of man's heart. It is the very best margarine; if you had never tasted butter you might think it was butter. It tells us that the whole of reality, ourselves included, is evolving, and to what? The goal itself is in the future and not merely the attainment of it. It may be that there *will* be spirit in us and outside us. That hunger we feel for it is the very process of evolution working in us. We are hungry for the future of the human race, perhaps of the universe; we smell a dinner that is not yet cooked. The glory of life consists in this, that we live in a universe of change; and there is nothing, not even the goal of all change, fixed and stable. We make our hopes of the goal, our conception of it, and so the goal itself, as we go. Everything *solvitur ambulando*. Our very values are subject to change with everything else. They too are for something altogether in the future. If we say God, we mean the future. He Himself may evolve with our conceptions of Him; He and our values are notions that further the process of evolution in us; they are means to an end; and what we really value and worship is our own progress, or at best the progress of the universe. All good is but the scent of our own future. The savage had the scent of ourselves before him; we have the scent of other men far in the future; and they will have the scent of yet others. So, it may be, their values will be utterly different from ours with the incessant process of change. The very notion of a present, eternal, and absolute perfection has vanished from this way of thinking. It is sanguine, but in a political way, like a minister making a speech about our prospects in the war. It is entirely opportunist, and so contrary to the deepest faith of man, which cannot value its own values if they are only means to an end. We value them because they themselves are for universals existing here and now. Happiness for us means belief in those universals, belief that they are both in us and outside us. Our happiness is the answer within us to them outside us ; it is the sense of a fellowship of the absolute to which we belong. If we explain our values away in terms of something else, even of the progress of mankind, they cease to be our values ; for it is by means of them alone that we know what progress is. The whole creation groans and travails, but only creation ; and it groans and travails not towards its own future but towards something not itself, existing now, which gives it the very hope of the future. It has a future because it is aware of this something not itself, existing now and for ever, not subject to time and change. Just as Alice could not be satisfied with jam yesterday and jam to-morrow, but never jam to-day, so we cannot be satisfied with God yesterday and God to-morrow, but never God to-day.

Yet, if we could get the doctrine of evolution right, it might satisfy the desire of our hearts, instead of offering us a vain substitute for that desire. We are troubled and thwarted because we cannot find the whole of our desire in nature ; so we think of nature as having no likeness to ourselves. We look to it to help us, and find no help in it that we can count on. But this looking for help is but seeing it in the relation of use and so failing to see the reality of it. If we look to Nature for help, we think of it, or Her, as something more powerful than ourselves ; the stars in their courses fought against Sisera. But of course they did nothing of the kind ; and Nature does not fight with us or against us. There is no Nature in this sense, no power omnipotent, unintelligible, indifferent to us and our desires and values. All the talk about Nature as red in tooth and claw, or as superior to us in her calm or her justice, is mere myth-making, and a myth made out of our fears. If men pray to an idol, they get no answer from it, and Nature is an idol we have made because we see things in the relation of use to ourselves. This idol, seeking help from it, we see as superior to us in power, inferior in that it lacks our values; it is therefore a God that we worship but cannot value, like the heathen gods of the past. But evolution, though it can tell us nothing about God, can tell us this about Nature, that it is not God but less God than we are ourselves, more blindly groaning and travailing. It is not a vast, heartless, omnipotent process, imposing itself upon us against our wills, but a number of things with less will than we have, less consciousness, less sense of direction. Evolution has introduced us to our own poor relations ; and we are so generically snobbish that we are dashed to find ourselves thus related to all living things, perhaps even to things not living. Since the matter of ourselves is of the same kind as other matter we think that we are only matter. After all, we say, we are not what we thought ourselves, a little lower than the angels ; the spirit in us does not separate us in kind from all other things ; therefore there is no spirit in us. Science has told us the truth about our genealogy ; we are not angels that have seen better days, but animals still in the making. So we are dashed as if we had been the aristocrats of a world that has suddenly become a democracy. But aristocrats can share in the joy of a democracy if only they will accept it ; and there is a joy, an immense hope, in the doctrine of evolution, if we will accept it and utterly relinquish our old generic snobbery.

For what is the process of evolution but the effort of life to master completely all lifeless matter ? That matter exists to be the medium of expression for life ;

and life itself becomes more intense, becomes more completely life, as it masters matter and more and more makes it the medium of expression. Life, as we see it, is spirit expressing itself and becoming itself through the mastery of matter. The difference between ourselves and the lowest forms of life is one of degree, one of intensity of life. Consciousness is a greater intensity of life than sensation, reason than instinct, because it is a greater mastery over matter. And the aim of evolution is always more and more mastery, more and more intensity of life. The perfected universe would be one in which there was no matter not mastered by intensity of life, none that was not the medium of expression, conscious, willed, and so personal. What troubles and thwarts us in the universe, as we know it, is the vast mass of matter not mastered, or only imperfectly mastered, by life; because it is unmastered matter, less conscious, less will-full, less personal than we are, it seems to us alien and often hostile. We wish to make use of it, and fail, and often it seems to make use of us for some obscure, unvalued purpose of its own. We should know by this time that it is masterless, not master, and so less powerful than we are ourselves. We seek for a fellowship with it, but for a fellowship of use to ourselves; and, failing to achieve that, we despair of that fellowship of the future, prophesied to us in all the visions of heaven, that fellowship in which all things will be matter mastered by life and so mastered by our values, in which there will be no division at all between matter and spirit but everywhere and in all things expression, form, love, a beauty that makes answer to beauty, a choir of voices in a universal tune.

But this doctrine is impossible to us still, if there is nothing for us but a universal becoming. The effort of life to master matter is a blind effort, unless there is also somewhere in the universe a life that is master, a spirit to which all other spirit makes answer, and in making answer becomes more and more itself. For that very self which spirit desires to be must have an existing model. Prophecy, if there be any truth at all in it, is a prophecy for us of a destiny which already exists in that which is not us. The prophet foresees because he sees what is. And the " prophetic soul of the wide world dreaming on things to come," that universal soul of which we are more or less dimly aware, exists and is universal because of a universal to which it makes answer. The life everywhere striving to master matter, and to become more fully life through the mastery, could not strive, could not have a goal of its striving, if there were no master life to inspire it. It is that master life that we mean when we use the word God ; and as the most intense life we know, the life in ourselves, is more personal than all other life, so God is more personal because more intense life than we are ourselves. As St. John affirmed that God is love, so must we affirm that God is life ; and the word *is* is as much part of the affirmation as the words *God* and *life*. We are not yet fully life as we are not fully love ; but God is fully life as He is fully love. That is meant by the words " God is a Spirit " ; and we know dimly and prophetically what life is, what spirit is, because it exists already and fully in God.

Those who do not believe that personality is real, do not believe that life is real. For them it is merely an accident of matter, and there are for them no degrees of life, and so no values. For, as life is not real to them, so it is not good ; and lacking a standard of values they lack also a standard of reality—they seek for one and cannot find it. Because spirit is not real to them, matter is not real either. What can be real to beings for whom their own life, their own selves, is illusion ? The very mental process by which they discover the illusion of their own life and personality cuts them off from all power of discovering reality, for it is itself part of the illusion. They are imprisoned within themselves, those

selves that do not exist.   At best there is, for them, a
perpetual becoming of nothing to no purpose, which
sometimes, with a pathetic inconsistency, they call
progress.

But if you affirm progress, you affirm values and
their reality, not only for yourself but for the universe ;
and if you affirm values you affirm spirit, incomplete
in yourself, but, outside you and somewhere, complete.
Your values are the answer, the effort, of your incompleteness to that completeness ; they are the life in you
striving to become fully life, to master the matter
through which it must express itself.   It will not be
subservient to that matter, for in subservience it is not
fully life.   Life is mastery of matter, not so that it may
continue to exist—for the very anxiety to continue
proves that it is not master—but so that it may express
itself utterly in a full relation with all other life.   For
expression, as art tells us, is also communication, it is
a relation between one spirit and other spirits.   The
very effort at expression is an effort at communication.
What has happened to me is not complete until I have
made it happen also to others.   My experience is not
utterly mine until it is shared, nor am I utterly myself
until I am one with other selves in a relation like that
of notes in a tune.   The advance to that relation is
progress.

The doctrine of evolution, rightly held, makes us
aware that the advance, or the desire for it, is universal.
In all things there is life groaning and travailing to
become more life, first in mere sensation, then in consciousness ; life hardly differentiated in plants, in
animals differentiated, in man personal.   And we suffer
from our loneliness in the universe because all things
that we see have less life than we ourselves ; that is the
penalty of our precedence, of our greater consciousness
of what life is.   We demand more life, a closer relation
with ourselves in all things than they can achieve ; but
we also suffer because of the incompleteness of our life ;

matter not fully mastered drags us back into the relation of use. The life in us seems insecure, and we see all things as means of securing it. But seeing them so we misunderstand them. For they are not in their reality means of securing life to us ; they are like ourselves, life trying to be more life, and, even more than ourselves, troubled with the sense of insecurity. It is that trouble which makes them seem hostile to us, as we to them. Their loneliness is really greater than ours. But there is no conspiracy of them against us, or of nature against us and our values. For there is no such thing as nature, but only life everywhere trying to master matter and be more life. We ourselves are part of nature in that our life and our mastery of matter is imperfect ; but all nature is more than nature, in so far as there is the divinity of life, of spirit, in it. We must accept the truth of our genealogy if we are to share in the immeasurable hope which it offers to us ; we must rid our minds of those orders of precedence which once seemed a part of our very religion. God did not make the sun to be our candle ; He did not make dogs to be our pets, or midges so that we might learn not to blaspheme when they bite us ; He made all things not for us but to Himself, so that they might more and more attain to that life which is Himself. So long as we see the universe in the relation of use to ourselves, it remains cold, indifferent, meaningless to us ; but when we see it in relation to God, sharing the life which is God, but sharing it even more imperfectly than ourselves, then the process of nature is no longer a meaningless, intimidating mechanism, but pathetic and forgiveable to us even as we are to ourselves. Restless are the hearts of all things until they rest in Thee.

X

CHRIST THE CONSTRUCTIVE REVOLUTIONARY

BY

B. HILLMAN STREETER, M.A., Hon. D.D. Edin.

FELLOW OF QUEEN'S COLLEGE, OXFORD
CANON RESIDENTIARY OF HEREFORD
EDITOR OF "FOUNDATIONS," "CONCERNING PRAYER,"
"IMMORTALITY," "GOD AND THE STRUGGLE FOR EXISTENCE,"
AUTHOR OF "RESTATEMENT AND REUNION"

ANALYSIS

Christ the portrait of the Spirit.
The conservatism of the Church.
Christ the critic of tradition.
Christ as constructive thinker.
Christ and the Church of His day.

CHRIST THE CONSTRUCTIVE REVOLU-TIONARY [1]

CHRIST THE PORTRAIT OF THE SPIRIT

THE idea of Christ as "the portrait of the invisible God" [2] is central to the New Testament. It is, indeed, the climax of man's philosophy of God. Round about the throne of God, transcendent, illimitable, mysterious, clouds and darkness must for ever hang. "No man hath seen God at any time"; no man can ever hope to comprehend the incomprehensible. But in the personality of the Ideal Man we have an expression of Ultimate Being which we can understand. Moreover, we attain here to the highest and richest kind of understanding of which man is capable; for, to understand anything, it is not enough to look at it from without, we must have at least glimmerings of a knowledge from within; and in proportion as we rise in the scale of life, we can the better, by intuitive sympathy, understand the Ideal Man from within.

But the individual is the child of his time, the product of his family, his school, his country, or his church; his insight is limited by the interests and values of his environment. Hence the capacity even to understand, much less to follow, the highest is one which varies with the moral, intellectual, and aesthetic achievement of

[1] Certain portions of this Essay are reprinted, with considerable modifications, from an article by the author in *The Constructive Quarterly*.
[2] Col. i. 15.

the community. Granted, then, that Christ is the Ideal Man, it follows that we cannot yet have completely understood Him ; granted that in the Ideal Man we see God, there must still be much to learn about the character of God. If we believe that we find in Christ a unique revelation of the Divine, it follows from that very fact that the Christian revelation is necessarily a progressive one, and that Christianity in proportion as it ceases to be progressive ceases to be Christian. Theology has commonly ignored this inference, but History supports it.

"He that hath seen Me hath seen the Father." If so, it must be no less true to say, "He that hath seen Me hath seen the Holy Ghost." The Divine which is immanent in man, which speaks to us in the watches of the night — "from whom all holy desires, all good counsels, and all just works do proceed"—is not other than the Divine which creates and sustains the universe ; it is not other than the Divine revealed in Jesus Christ. Orthodox theology, no doubt, would not only admit, but vehemently assert this ; but popular Christianity is Tritheism with reservations. The average Christian does not in the first place think of Christ as the "portrait of the Father," still less often does he think of Him as the portrait of the Spirit also. Yet if the fundamental question for religion is, What is God like ? and if we are right in affirming that He is like Christ, then we must face all the implications of the statement, and we must apply it to our conception, not only of the Transcendent Divine which traditional theology has styled "the Father," but of the Immanent Divine which has been named the Holy Ghost.

To work out the full implications of the idea of Christ as the portrait of the Spirit would require a volume, or rather several volumes. In this Essay I select a single problem, definite and strictly limited. I ask myself the question, What was the attitude of the historic Jesus to the ideals and institutions, and, in particular, the religious ideals and institutions, of His time ? That is primarily an historical, even an academic, question ; but I ask it in the conviction that if I can read the answer to it rightly I shall have found the answer to another question, no longer historical or academic, " What saith the Spirit unto the Churches —now ? "

Europe of recent years has seen, facing one another in the realms both of thought and practice, two tendencies violently opposed. On the one side has been the spirit of autocracy and authority, clinging tenaciously to the methods and ideals of the past ; on the other is the spirit of a purely negative and destructive revolutionism, moral and political. Wherever either tendency has secured even a temporary predominance, disaster national and international has ensued. The only hope of humanity would seem to lie in the possibility of a middle course being found. Change is necessary, change political, social, economic, moral, and religious ; change in Church as well as State ; change far-reaching and revolutionary. But a great danger arises from the fact that, goaded to passionate reaction by timid conservatism, by lack of sympathetic understanding, or by something worse than this, on the part of the powers that be, the forces which make for change may express themselves in wild, unreasoning destruction. Construction is what the world most wants, but it must be constructive revolution ; and what the Church too requires is constructive revolution. To forestall my main conclusion—if I investigate the attitude of Christ towards the ideals and institutions of His day, I find an outlook and approach strangely appropriate to the present situation. Christ was no iconoclast, no lover of destruction for its own sake. If half that is said of Bolshevism is true, He would not have been a Bolshevist ; but He was a revolutionary. If He said that He " came not to destroy but to fulfil," He quickly added, " It was said to them of old . . . but I say unto you—something very different." He saw clearly that, without drastic change, fulfilment was impossible. His interest was in the creative and constructive ; but He knew, and was prepared to pay, the price. If, then, I call Him a *constructive* revolutionary, I put the emphasis upon the adjective, but with no intent to weaken the meaning of the noun.

THE CONSERVATISM OF THE CHURCH

If the first three Gospels are read without traditional preconceptions, the truth of this characterisation will, as I propose shortly to argue, become evident. But the whole habit of thought in the Churches is so conservative that it seems necessary, before doing this, to pause. Throughout Europe organised Christianity is regarded by reformers as the champion of the obsolete, whether politically, socially, or intellectually. In France, Italy, and Austria the Roman Church has been the bulwark of reaction, whether in politics or in education. In Russia, Orthodoxy and Autocracy were the twin pillars of the old régime. In Prussia, Christianity was openly claimed by the Kaiser as his ally against democracy. And in England, not the most enthusiastic sons and daughters of the Church of which, in spite of all its failures, I am proud to call myself a member can claim that it is usually to be found in the van of progress.

All large and ancient institutions have a tendency to settle down into well-worn grooves. But for the persistent association of the name of Christ with the spirit of reaction—so paradoxical to the reader of the Gospels—this explanation taken alone will not suffice. Other and deeper causes must be sought. History suggests two. First, the emphasis on the value of tradition due to reaction against Gnosticism and other pagan influences in the first four centuries A.D., which were the formative period of Christian doctrine. Secondly, the position of authority and the rôle of conserver of the past which the Church was called upon to assume in the reconstruction of European civilisation after the Germanic invasions which in the fifth century crushed the western half of the Roman Empire.

In the New Testament the main emphasis is on the future ; everywhere there is life and growth. The Spirit is thought of as ever revealing something fresh, as continually guiding into all truth. But in the third century [1] the traditionalist outlook triumphs. Why ? It was a sound instinct of the organism (may we not say it was *for that time* the guidance of the Spirit ?) that had gradually convinced that heterogeneous, half-educated community that its only hope lay in clinging to the tradition of a creative past. We shall never understand the Early Church, we shall never see the reason either of its successes or its failures, unless we clearly grasp that it was a Missionary Church—but one which, after the first generation, was cut off from its " home base." The Jewish nation, with a tradition of centuries of sublime ethical monotheism, and that burnt into its inmost life by heroic sustainment of exile and persecution, ought to have been that " home base." Had the Jews accepted Christ they would have become to the Graeco-Roman Empire what the Christian nations of Europe and America have been to the heathen world in recent times. Generation after generation of missionaries, nurtured in the traditions of the higher religion, would have gone forth to guide the newly founded Church. But the Jew rejected Christ. Thus the position of the Gentile Churches in the Roman Empire was precisely similar to that in which Christian missions in India or China would have found themselves had they been completely cut off from the European and American Churches within thirty years of their first foundation and left entirely to native leaders. Converts of the first

---

[1] In "the faith once delivered to the saints" of Jude, and "the form of sound words" of the Epistles (probably not genuinely Pauline) to Timothy, we get, even within the New Testament, the beginnings of the new attitude.

generation, however able, zealous, and self-sacrificing
they may be, can never free themselves entirely from
the associations and ideas of the pagan environment.
Home, school, and national customs and literature necessarily leave marks of old religious outlook and usage
which conversion to a new faith, however sincere, cannot
at once obliterate.　Just as relics of heathen customs and
superstitions crop up in Christian communities in India,
Africa, or China, so the history of the growth of Christian doctrines and institutions during the first six centuries is largely the history of the gradual infiltration
of Greek, Roman, and Oriental ways of thought.　Nor
was the process, as some too hastily assume, one entirely
to be regretted.　From Roman statesman, Greek philosopher, and Oriental mystic the Church learnt much
that was worth learning as well as much that had better
have been unlearnt.　But from the third century A.D.
the Graeco-Roman civilisation was consciously decadent.
Science was dead, education declining, art and literature
all but stagnant.　Look about for growth and you will
find it—in the spirit of superstition and despair.　In
such an age it was the salvation of the Church that,
while adventurous in practical experiment, it was
conservative in things of the mind.　As it was, alike
in doctrine, ethics, and devotion, Christianity absorbed
too much from its environment. It was preserved
from a quite fatal dilution by always looking back.

Consider again the situation that arose when, in and
after the fifth century, fresh relays of barbarians kept
pouring over the Alps and the Rhine, and the civilisation of Western Europe was in ruins.　Whatever was
saved from the ruins was saved by the Church.　Slowly
and painfully a new civilisation took its place.　What
was built up new among the ruins was built up under
the protection and guidance of the Church.　That is
the central fact of European history.　But in that age
the Church could only rebuild by pointing men to the
past.　In undertaking this work of reconstruction the

Church was true to the spirit of Jesus. To save and to inspire, to restore and to create, is to carry on the work of Christ. But—and this is the essential point—at that date, and under the special circumstances of that period, construction necessarily entailed a moral and intellectual attitude towards the past which, in so far as it has lasted on beyond those special circumstances, is alien to the real genius of Christianity.

First and foremost, what the wild barbarian then needed was discipline, the habit of obedience to authority and law. Europe, like Israel, had need of the Law before it could appreciate the Gospel. The Church, therefore, was right in standing predominantly for Authority and Law—right, that is, at that period—but in so doing it lost sight of what St. Paul found to be the deepest thing in Christianity : " where the spirit of the Lord is there is liberty."

Again, so long as the Church was the main conserver of the broken fragments of a great civilisation, so long as the general level of education, science, art, and literature was far below that of the old Roman Empire, just so long it seemed the function of the builder to preserve, to imitate, to reproduce the past. So long as the Golden Age was really in the past, the cause of progress itself demanded an attitude of looking backwards. But Christ taught that the Kingdom of Heaven [1] was yet to come.

In the great period of the Middle Ages, the essentially pioneering and creative spirit of Christianity begins to find fuller expression—and that not alone in art and architecture. A St. Francis essays a revolution in Christian ethics ; and the line of thinkers from Anselm to Aquinas dare a " New Theology." Few but students realise what innovators these were. Indeed, they did not realise it themselves.

[1] I hold that, to our Lord, the idea of the Kingdom of Heaven included the corporate regeneration of society on earth as well as a life in the world to come. The evidence is, to my mind, conclusive against the view of some recent scholars that it included the latter only.

The Renaissance of the fourteenth and fifteenth centuries reinforced in a new way the backward look of Europe. The Church, to its credit, was to the fore in the revival of learning. But learning meant the study of the Humanities, that is, of the great writers of the classical period of Greece and Rome ; and the study of the Humanities again implies a Golden Age in a distant past. Down to very recent times, European education in general has been, and clerical education still is, mainly on Renaissance lines. It has tended to suggest, as the ideal of intellectual attainment, acceptance and imitation rather than invention and experiment.

But to-day, outside the Church, men are looking *forwards* for the Golden Age. The really live intellectual activity of the present age is not so much conservative as adventurous. Its motto is not learning but research, not acceptance but criticism, not imitation but invention. Experiment and fresh construction are the dominating ideas, not only in natural science and engineering, but in economics, in art, in philosophy, and in political and ethical ideals. Outside organised Christianity the motto of the idealist in every department of life is, " Behold I make all things new." What does this mean but that the Spirit of Christ is often to be seen in what is called " the World " more clearly than in any of those societies which claim to be His " Church."

The fact is one which may be explained by past history, which may be excused by human infirmity. It is not one to be acquiesced in.

CHRIST THE CRITIC OF TRADITION

Christ was essentially a critic of tradition, but especially of religious tradition—whether on its theological, moral, or ecclesiastical side. No small part of His recorded utterances is in criticism of contemporary conceptions of the character of God, of current notions of right conduct, or of that ecclesiastical tradition by which the word

of God was made of none effect. And it is important
to notice that of the Church He was a severer critic than
of "the World." He has much to say against the
Pharisees, very little against Herod or the Roman
government — though He certainly did not admire
them.[1] What He most deplored was the failure of
the religious — both in regard to teaching and to
practice. Taking the commandment, "Love God, love
thy neighbour," as the criterion of true religion, He
found that the theologies, the moralities, the ecclesiastical ordinances of His time tended to disguise and
overlay, or even to make impossible, the weightier
matters of the law.

But what Pharisaism did for the Law and the
Prophets, traditional theology has done to Christ.
Starting from the assumption that His revelation of
the Divine was final, it has looked for the finality not
in the spirit but in the letter. It has failed to see that
if Christ was the critic of tradition, then in all ages the
spirit of Christ must impel men to criticise contemporary tradition. His followers have turned Christ Himself into a tradition, and those who in His spirit have
criticised that tradition have been cast out. The living
prophets they have stoned while rearing the sepulchres
of the dead—thus witnessing to themselves that they
are the true sons of those that slew the prophets.

The supreme moral activities of the modern world
have been two—the humanitarian movement, *i.e.* the
effort to realise in practice the brotherhood of man ;
and the scientific passion of truth for truth's sake.
Consider the precept, "Love God and love thy neighbour," and, if I mistake not, it will appear that in
these two movements the best elements in the modern
world outside the Churches have come much nearer than
most of those within towards realising its implications,
and therefore in applying the spirit of Christ to the
actual conditions of the day.

[1] Luke xiii. 1-2, 32.

The greatest blot on the history of the Church in modern times is the fact that, with the glorious exception of the campaign to abolish slavery, the leaders in the social, political, and humanitarian reforms of the last century and a half in Europe have rarely been professing Christians ; while the authorised representatives of organised Christianity have, as often as not, been on the wrong side. This indictment, however, is a commonplace ; and, at any rate so far as words go, its justice is readily admitted by the leaders of all the Churches to-day.

It is conceded [1] that the Churches have been backward to adapt to new conditions the commandment, " Love thy neighbour." It is less commonly recognised that they have failed even more conspicuously in regard to the commandment, " Thou shalt love the Lord thy God." If God is the source of righteousness, beauty, and truth, only he can love God who is also a lover of these. The Churches have, it must be admitted, never tired in urging the love of righteousness—though they have often taught that to be righteous which manifestly is not. Some of them in fane and rite and hymn have trained men to love beauty, but in ways narrow and restricted, and, as time has passed, progressively more conventional. But where do they stand in regard to the love of truth ? Few men have the capacity to be discoverers in the realm of knowledge, and of those who have the capacity some may properly put first the claims of other duties. But all men can be taught to value truth, to see ignorance, error, and superstition, even though they share them, as a misfortune of the soul ; and on the most important things of all to decline to be put off with shams. Here certainly the Church has failed. I may have been unfortunate, but it is certainly the fact that I have never heard a single sermon devoted to emphasising the all-important fact

---

[1] Cf., for instance, the recent Report of the Archbishop's Committee on the Church and Labour.

that *the love of truth* is a fundamental element in the love of God.

The Churches have, it may be readily conceded, never wanted persons convinced that they hold the truth, and prepared if necessary to die for it The fatal mistake has been to take for granted that the individual, or his own section of the Church, already apprehends all truth, or at least all that can be known of truth. And this is not an intellectual but a *moral* failure. In the Middle Ages such a position was intelligible. At that time science and philosophy, equally with theology, were matters of tradition, to be accepted on authority. When in one sphere of know-ledge a question could be decided by a word of Aristotle or Galen, it was reasonable in another sphere to take as final a text of St. Augustine or St. Paul. Only the greatness of antiquity was realised, not its limitations. The indefinite possibility of acquiring new knowledge, and the fact that truth is not won by blind acceptance of tradition, but is the reward of diligent and courageous search, had not yet been demonstrated to the world. Nor did the spectacle then obtrude itself at every turn of men of good will differing on vital beliefs ; such men in general accepted without demur the rulings of a Church whose intellectual even more than its moral prestige was virtually unchallenged. But for us it is a mockery to call that a love of truth which is not also a love of the search for truth, which does not include the hope that more of truth may be discovered. In the intellectual as much as in the moral sphere, " I count not myself yet to have apprehended " is the fitting attitude of the truly religious mind. To take up any other to-day implies some element of moral weakness.

Sometimes the claim to have an exclusive monopoly of truth reflects a native arrogance in the individual claimant ; more often it expresses the corporate arro-gance of a Church. But arrogance, as the world has learnt of late in the sphere of world politics, is only the more harmful if it takes the form of a claim by a group rather than by an individual to be in an exclusive sense the chosen people. Religious controversialists do not realise how phrases like "Catholic truth" or "Protestant truth"—as if truth, like sardines, was something of which you can have different brands—strike the outsider as the supreme desecration of the word truth. But in most cases apparent arrogance is really doubt disguised. It results from a timidity which dares not face facts for fear these facts should be unpleasant—a timidity rooted at bottom in unfaith, in an apprehension, unconfessed even to the man himself, that science or criticism may after all have disproved some cherished tenet of religion, or even religion itself. It can be justified only on the theory, explicit or implicit, that human reason is a trap set by God for man—a theory degrading to our conception both of God and man. The dogmatist is own brother to the sceptic, and there is a deep pathos in the inner life of many of the most blatant defenders of tradition. The very vehemence of their affirmation is the measure of their secret doubts—"The lady protests too much methinks."

To love God is to hate delusion and to long to know that which really *is*. It is to know that reality is more than we, or our friends, can ever grasp completely, but never to rest content with what we have as yet attained. The love of truth is perhaps that aspect of the love of God which is the most completely disinterested. "The philosopher," says Samuel Butler, "must be one who has left all, even Christ Himself, for Christ's sake." And those who are prepared, if necessary, to give up Christ Himself for truth's sake will get back more of Christ than they gave up—if not in name or in form, at least in the appropriation and inspiration of His spirit. Those many thousands who have given up, not only the things of this world but the hopes of a world to come, for the sake of what seemed to them to be the truth, have that spirit. They show a love of God more real than those who dare not put their beliefs to the test of inquiry—and that even though the actual conclusions held by these worshippers of truth may in the long run turn out to be false and those held by the others to be true. "Whosoever would save his life shall lose it" applies especially to religion just because that is the very soul of life.

But while the world — or rather its best men — have been seeking truth, the Church has been interested in defending tradition, with the result that the intellectual leadership, which in the Middle Ages belonged to the Church, has passed to the scientist. And the scientist, once outside the boundaries of his own subject and in the sphere of philosophy and ethics, has not infrequently led men wrong, to their no small hurt. Yet for this hurt too the Church is more than half responsible, for it has been the attitude of the Church towards the search for truth that has, quite unnecessarily, made science the traditional enemy, and thereby prejudiced its devotees against an impartial consideration of the truth for which religion stands.

I am far from asserting that we ought lightly to surrender a formula or a legend which has been closely bound up with sacred beliefs. I am far from saying that a man is not often justified in clinging to moral principles or fundamental beliefs which he may not be able intellectually to defend. The intuitions of the race and the inherited beliefs of the past often rest on a diffused experience and a basis in reason which eludes the grasp of the science or philosophy of the day. It is not by the Church's tenacious hold on these, it is not by her fond clinging to hallowed associations, that the conscience of Europe has been shocked ; that attitude men respect, even when they do not share it. But it has been and is shocked by the failure of the Church to appreciate the supreme *moral* value of truth and of the search for truth ; and by the arrogance, both real and seeming, of the dogmatic temper, which it contrasts with the humility of the great scientists. The world knows, what the Church has forgotten, that of a genuine love of truth there is only one test—a readiness to admit on sufficient proof that an opinion previously held may be wrong.

Apologists often point out that when a conflict has arisen between traditional views and modern hypotheses, whether of science or criticism or history, it has not infrequently happened that the traditionalist has ultimately been found in point of fact to be the nearer to the truth. This may be so, but it is irrelevant. The Church's attitude to truth has been a *moral*, not an intellectual, failure. To be mistaken about a matter of fact, or to entertain for a time a false hypothesis, is to be guilty of an error which time and further inquiry will correct. Absolute devotion to truth and making mistakes about the truth are quite compatible. Science often makes mistakes. But not to be interested in discovering truth, to make a virtue of the fact under the name of " faith," worst of all, deliberately to suppress one's interest, under the name of " the sacrifice of the reason " or " the asceticism of the intellect," is (for those who have the requisite mental capacity and training) openly to renounce obedience to the commandment, " Thou shalt love the Lord thy God with all thy *mind*." Nothing is nobler than the impulse which moves man to offer up his best and dearest to his God ; nothing more pathetic than the delusion that he must first slay the thing he offers —whether it be his first-born in the flames of Moloch or his reason at the altar of Christ.

To a God really worthy of man's worship only that sacrifice of the reason can be pleasing which consists, not in its stultification, but in its devotion to the elucidation of truth. And this will often be a painful sacrifice. To pass out from the cosy fireside of a dogmatic faith into the cold blasts of criticism and science ; to put to the test of real inquiry beliefs without which life does not seem worth living ; to apply the knife where one suspects a tumour even if it touch the heart—this is the "asceticism of the intellect" that is required of our age ; this for us is the strait gate and narrow way which leadeth unto life. "You have learnt something," says Bernard Shaw, "that always feels at first as if you had lost something." But in the end there is gain—gain for the seeker, gain for the Church.

During the last half-century there has been real advance among the leaders of the Churches in the recognition of the moral and religious value of the scientific temper. But these gains have been largely forfeited through lack of courage in many of those who *do* realise the need for change, but hesitate to apply their knowledge in popular religious teaching. Plain speaking, they fear, might upset old people ; it might unsettle young people ; it might offend the rich ; it might disturb the poor. But granted an element of risk, granted that tact, discretion, and moderation are virtues, and even characteristically Christian virtues, still they are not the only virtues. From the way many people talk one might suppose that the injunction against offending the weaker brother was the one which is styled "the first and great commandment." When I read the Gospels and recollect that the Pharisees were "the religious public" of the day, I am often surprised to find how little careful Christ seems to have been about shocking what a lady, writing to *The Challenge* lately, called "the just susceptibilities of religious people." Indeed, I must frankly admit that the one objection to the belief that He was morally perfect which I have found it difficult to meet, is derived from the apparently exaggerated severity of His language to and about the Pharisees, who, with all their limitations, undoubtedly stood, as a body, for religious earnestness and self-sacrifice. Recent research has made it evident that—whatever the shortcomings of individuals—the Pharisees as a whole were conspicuous for religious zeal and earnestness. It may be that in the Gospel tradition our Lord's antipathy towards them has been exaggerated ; personally I think it has been, but it cannot have been altogether invented. It is at least evident that the " humbug " of which He accused them lay, not so much in the insincerity, as in the futility of their beliefs. Not otherwise Plato deemed the unconscious "lie in the soul," that inability to recognise the good and true which misleads the man himself, worse than the conscious verbal lie which is meant to mislead others. Truly a hard saying ; but Christ and Plato here seem to concur that, not sins committed, but false values and ideals are the worst peril of the soul.

A fruit tree will bear no fruit unless it be occasionally pruned, and progress is impossible without a painful disturbance of cherished and accepted customs, institutions, and beliefs. That is why the age-long passion of India for religion has produced results so disproportionate to its longing. Prophet after prophet there has seen high visions, but there has been lacking the Elijah and Josiah to make a clean sweep of evil custom and ancient superstition. The Reformation, with all its crimes and limitations, did that for Europe ; but in India the good seed has been choked by the thorns among which it has been sown. Half-truths are a stage on the road to truths, good laws a stage on the road to better ; but once that stage is past, half-truths become deadly errors, and the good is the worst enemy of the best. Christ had the courage to recognise, the courage to proclaim, this fact. "Destroy this temple, and in three days I will raise it up." " Ye have heard that it was said to them of old . . . but I say unto you. . . ." Think what the Temple meant to a Jew, think what the Law, and you will realise—or rather you may dimly guess, no one born out of Jerusalem could fully realise—the revolutionary, the iconoclastic

ring which sayings like these had for His contemporaries.
By the side of them the programmes of our modern
leaders seem tinkering timidities.

Christ as Constructive Thinker

The amount of concentrated constructive thinking
that lies behind the sayings of our Lord is commonly
overlooked.   Their brevity, their simplicity, their
lucidity, and the fact that most of them read like
obiter dicta, disguise the hard thinking they imply from
unreflective readers—but only from the unreflective.
Many folk are impressed by obscurity and elaboration,
but these are really either a substitute for thought or
an evidence that the matter treated has not been
thought right out.   Where the matter does not admit
of exact expression the real thinker knows it.   He
ceases to define and tries rather to suggest a meaning ;
so Plato in his myths, and all the poets.   Of course
where trivialities only are concerned, or where deep
things are dealt with in superficial ways, a cheap epigram
is easy.   But wherever the thought is admittedly profound, terseness and lucidity of expression are a test of
intensity and clearness of thinking.   No really valuable
idea can be " put into a nutshell " unless the matter it
deals with has been the subject of prolonged meditation.
He knew what he was talking about who said, " I wrote
a long book because I hadn't time to write a short
one."

Consider, again, the relation of Christ's teaching to
earlier Hebrew thought.   In Jewish religious tradition
we can distinguish, in the main, five different strains.
There is the Law—at its best in Deuteronomy, where
law becomes less a code than a call to personal service.
There are the Prophets, with their passion for social
righteousness, their indifference to ritual requirement,
their conviction of man's responsibility to God, and
their concentration on His moral attributes.   There is

the Wisdom literature, with its sober, practical idealism directed towards the problems of everyday life. There is the intense personal religion of the Psalms, with their note of absolute trust in the goodness of God and His power to heal and save. Latest of all—most of it, except for the book of Daniel, too late to be included in the canon— is Apocalyptic, in form fantastic, in spirit inferior to the direct ethical simplicity of the old prophecy, but enriched with the new vision of the resurrection of the dead and the life of the world to come. Each of these made its distinctive and characteristic contribution to religion.

From the study of these turn to the sayings of Christ, and note the appropriation of all that is best in each, combined with a rejection of whatever in any of them is of inferior value. He shows not only the courage to reject tradition when it is wrong, but the insight to reaffirm it when it is right. Yet His teaching is not a kind of florilegium of the Old Testament; it is no mere collection of undigested titbits ; it is a fresh creative synthesis. Like the wise scribe that He spoke of, He brings out of His treasury things new and old. But they are not just brought out, and left at that ; they are fused into a new and coherent philosophy of life, thought out from first principles, clearly grasped and thoroughly applied. They form a positive and constructive statement of religious and ethical outlook unique in the history of human thought.

It is worth while to point the contrast between this thorough and thought-out method of approaching traditional ideas and two elements in our contemporary acceptation of Christianity.

(1) Good intentions, or the uncriticised dictates of the individual conscience, are commonly held to dispense with the need of thought on moral issues. So long as a person is striving vigorously to live up to the accepted ideal which in his own particular coterie or set is labelled Christian, he is supposed to be dispensed from

asking the previous question whether or not this ideal
really is in accordance with the mind of Christ. Some
one once said to a friend, "So-and-so is a very good
man but very narrow." His friend replied, "If goodness means in the last resort God-likeness, *can* a person
be narrow and also good?" It is often supposed that,
provided you work hard and are sincere, it does not
matter whether the cause you work for is the best;
and that if you are prepared to sacrifice yourself for an
ideal, it does not matter much how distorted the ideal.
Bishops may be heard deploring the narrow-minded
fanaticism of some incumbent, but excusing or even
commending him on the ground that "he is such a
good worker." I wonder if it ever occurs to them to
ask whether such men existed in our Lord's time and
what He thought about them. The blind guides who
held up false ideals, the conscientious traditionalists
who took away the key of the Kingdom of Heaven,
were not excused by Him because they acted in accordance with their conscience or because they were animated
by the best intentions. And the results of the heroic
efforts of some "who compassed sea and land to make
one proselyte" are characterised by Him in language
which suggests that it is not always a sufficiently
extenuating circumstance to be "one of the hardest
workers in the diocese."

(2) At the present time there is nothing which is
more needed than a body of sane, clear-headed idealists
to think out and offer to the world a constructive lead
on the moral, social, and political problems of the day.
For example, everybody feels that the industrial revolution and the elaborate State organisation of the
modern world has presented the problem of the relation
of rich and poor, and of employer and employed, in
a wholly new form. The Churches, to their credit
be it said, have never forgotten the claims of the sick
and needy. They have worked, they have prayed,
they have paid; they have done everything but think

—but maybe that was the one thing needful. Methods of dealing with poverty or sickness which were most appropriate in Palestine or Greece two thousand years ago are not likely to be adequate to-day. But, with some conspicuous but relatively few exceptions, the Church has left it to organisations like the Fabian Society to do their thinking for them, and, if not to find solutions, at any rate to be foremost in the search for them.

Take, again, the various problems relating to sex —the position of women in general, the control of the birth-rate, prostitution, venereal disease. Not only the present but the future welfare of humanity depends on looking these questions squarely in the face ; on first finding and then applying the right solutions. Here, if anywhere, is a field where the Churches might have been expected to give a lead. If sexual relations are outside their province, there is not much left inside. Here, again, it is not " good intentions " but intelligence that is to seek. Immense and undoubtedly well-meaning effort has been put into a blind defence of ecclesiastical tradition, to preclude any reconsideration of the conditions of divorce or to prevent marriage with a deceased wife's sister. To the solution of the really burning problems the one outstanding contribution which what is known as specifically Christian public opinion has made, has been an organised conspiracy to ignore their existence. In religious circles thorough and constructive discussion of them has been boycotted in the name of decency ; and this attitude, more than anything else, has retarded the possibility of discovering the right solutions. " To the pure all things are pure." Plain speaking need not be coarse speaking—indeed, a really Christian outlook naturally expresses itself with simplicity and good taste. It is subterfuge and innuendo, not direct speaking, that implies and encourages the prurient mind. In recent years much has been done to break down this conspiracy of silence and to force public opinion to face these questions. But this has been mainly accomplished, in spite of the shocked opposition of the religious,[1] by free lances like Mrs. Josephine Butler, or, more recently, by acutely un-ecclesiastical writers like Mr. Bernard Shaw.

CHRIST AND THE CHURCH OF HIS DAY

Our Lord's attitude towards the religious body of which He was a member will become clearer if we remind ourselves that the Jewish people at that date was a community approximating more nearly to what we now call a Church than to what we call a State. As the result, partly of the Exile, but still more of the subsequent city-building of the successors of Alexander the Great, the Jews had ceased to have an independent national existence, but had become something like an inter-national brotherhood having branches in every important city in the Roman and Parthian Empires. They no longer even spoke one common language, and were held together by a bond which, though nominally racial, was actually religious, since in every generation any who ceased to believe or practise the religion became assimilated to the surrounding peoples, while numerous proselytes, attracted by the religion, became incorporated as members of the chosen people. Hence, though still based mainly upon race, the community had become in essence and idea less of a nation than a Church.

What, then, was our Lord's attitude towards this Church ?

A certain man had a fig tree planted in his vineyard ; and he came and sought fruit thereon, and found none. Then said he unto the dresser of his vineyard, Behold, these three years I come seeking fruit on this fig tree, and find none : cut it down ; why cumbereth it the ground ? And he answering said unto him, Lord, let it alone this year also, till I shall dig about it, and dung it. And if it bear fruit, well : and if not, then after that thou shalt cut it down.[2]

---

[1] Cf. *Life of Josephine Butler*, p. 55.   [2] Luke xiii. 6-9.

The axe is laid unto the root of the tree. Time—
but only a short time—will be given for amendment.
At present "it cumbereth the ground," but there is
still hope.

This was His judgement. But it was one to which
He had come, not willingly, but with infinite regret.

And when he was come near, he beheld the city, and wept
over it, saying, If thou hadst known, even thou, at least in
this thy day, the things which belong unto thy peace! but
now they are hid from thine eyes.[1]

O Jerusalem, Jerusalem, which killest the prophets, and
stonest them that are sent unto thee; how often would I have
gathered thy children together, as a hen doth gather her brood
under her wings, and ye would not![2]

And what other view can the Spirit of Christ suggest
to us to-day? We, too, can look back with pride and
affection on a great inheritance, on a past which is
eloquent to us, through religious monuments like our
great Cathedrals, or the Book of Common Prayer, or
in that tradition of civil and religious liberty and pure
family life to which Puritanism has contributed so
much. Yet only the purblind can fail to see that,
while we have been pondering on a mighty past, the
present has been slipping away from us, and the
Kingdom is passing away from the Churches, as of
old it passed from the Jews to "a nation bringing
forth the fruits thereof."

What, then, should be our attitude towards the
Historic Church? The axe is laid at the root of
the tree; the year is given to dig and to tend. There
are many of the younger generation who think that
the sentence of final condemnation has been already
spoken, that men of good will had best leave the
organised Churches to perish gently of senile decay,
while they themselves seek ampler opportunity to carry
on the Master's work outside. My own judgement is

[1] Luke xix. 41-42.   [2] Luke xiii. 34.

otherwise. I hope and believe that Jerusalem, even in this her hour, will recognise the things which belong to her peace, and that the Christian Church to-day, unlike the Jewish Church of old, may have the insight and the courage to face that Constructive Revolution—in theology, in forms of worship, in organisation, in practical activity—through which alone it can realise its destiny in the uplifting of mankind.

There has come upon the world a supreme crisis, a crisis clamorous with the need for reconstruction—reconstruction all along the line, political, social, moral, religious. The world is looking for guidance ; but the guide must be one who has the courage to discard what is obsolete and the insight to create what is new. It is looking for the guidance of the Constructive Revolutionary. I have tried to show that this is precisely the kind of guidance given by our Lord. The Church claims to be a body inspired by the Holy Spirit. What is this Holy Spirit? It is no other than the spirit manifested in the life of Christ. If Christ, I reiterate, is our portrait of the Father, He is no less our portrait of the Holy Ghost. We have seen how the characteristic expression of the Spirit as seen in His life is constructive thought and creative effort. The idea is not new, but it has never been worked out. *Creator Spiritus* is no modern title, but it answers to a most modern need. Man and his civilisations have always needed re-creation, but other ages have been barely conscious of their lack. We know our need. That is a new fact in human history. To-day every one is crying out for reconstruction : some in hope, others in despair ; all are crying out for the creative spirit. And this, if only we will see it, is the spirit manifested in the life of Christ.

Veni Creator Spiritus.

INDEX OF SUBJECTS

INDEX OF SUBJECTS

375

Immanence, 1
  in Stoic philosophy and Athanasius, 10
  of the Creative Spirit, 19
  and transcendence, 21
  Divine immanence in Nature, 111
Immortality—
  belief in, 205
Incarnation, the, 6, 10
India, 364
Infallibility, verbal, 202
Inspiration, 36, 44
  of the Church, 61
  in Old Testament, 122
  of persons, not books, 200
  criterion of, 201, 215
  in Christ, 221, 222
  in the ordinary man, 222, 223
  unexplained factor in, 218, 219
Instincts, the, 88-94
  the conflict of, 94-96
  conversion of, 96-102
Intelligence, 325. *See also* Reason

Jesus—
  the historic, 350
  the Baptism of, 127 *n.*
  See also Christ
Judaism, 176

Kingdom of Heaven, 293, 294, 295, 306, 355 *n.*
Koinonia, the, 137, 138
  the organ of spiritual insight, 145
  results of, 145-154

Language, 227-230
  necessary for progress, 232
  language of action, 236, 237
  language of action in religion, 240, 244
  sacramental language, 250
Law, 265
Liberalitas, 195
"Lie in the soul," 364
Loaf, the, 142
Logos, the—
  history of the doctrine of, 179
  See also Word

Magic, in time of Christ, 276
Manichaean teaching, 177, 292, 293, 323
Mass, the, 267, 274. *See also* Ceremonial
Mathematics, 328, 329, 330. *See also* Calculators
Matter, 313, 314
Mediocrity, 293

Merit—
  supposed to be acquired by going to church, 301
Metaphysics, 315
Middle Ages, the, 357, 361
Mind, the modern, 10, 338
Miracle, 29
  subordinate position of miracles, 130
Monotheism—
  Hebrew, 6, 202
  its supposed uniqueness, 203
Music, 284, 293, 299, 332
  analogy of conductor, 161, 171
  See also Schubert, Beethoven
Mystery—
  of the Kingdom, 64
  in St. Paul, 139, 140
  mystery religions, 245, 272
Mysticism, 213
  "Pauline mysticism," 149
  of Plotinus, 234
Myths, 282
  misunderstood, 285

Nationalism—
  in Jewish religion, 8
Nature, 342
  "the religion of," 6
  "laws of," 27
  in Anglican Church Catechism, 175
  in New Testament, 175
  and grace, 179
  beauty of, 289
New Theology—
  in Middle Ages, 355

"Otherness," 211, 214, 221
Oxyrhynchus Logia, 269

Paganism, 289
  Christ and, 295
Pantheism, 4
  the Higher Pantheism, 5
Particulars, 319, 323
Paulicians, 144 *n.*
Pentecost, 112, 119, 124
  a modern Pentecost, 155-157
Perception, 318, 319
Personal, the, 281, 284, 285, 309
Personality—
  in God, 166, 199
  reality of, 344
  enhancement of the, 162
Pharisees, the, 295, 357, 363
Philosophers, 323
Poetry, 236, 237
Power, III. *passim*
Prayer, 47, 48, 262

Preachers, 294, 295, 296
Presbyterian Communion service, 267 n.
Private property, 157
Prophets, the Hebrew, 206, 212
  monotheism of, 205
  experience of, 205, 206
  and mystics, 213
Proverbs, 233, 234, 248
Psycho-analysis, 263
Psychology—
  as reconciling science and religion, 115
  its analysis of conversion, 207
  "crowd" psychology, 234
Psychotherapy, 113, 162 n., 263
Puritanism, 370

Quakers, 261, 263

Real Presence, 268
Reality, 307, 318
  not two kinds of, 317
Reason, 324
  "the sacrifice of the," 362
  See also Intelligence
Reconciliation—
  miracle of, 139
Reformation, the, 364
Relics, 169, 170
Religion—
  language of action in, 244
Renaissance, 356
Revelation, 214
  "Revelation" and "revelation," 203
Revolution, 351
Rhythm, 269
Righteousness, 316

Sacraments, the, 244, 246, 247
Salvation Army, the, 128
Savages, 239
Scepticism, 307, 308. See Illusion
Sciences, the natural, 333
Scripture—
  idea of verbal infallibility of, 202
  Old Testament, sublimity of, 7
    Spirit in, 122
    the Psalms, 8
    the 23rd Psalm, 37
  New Testament—
    experience of power in, 112
    ethical significance of holiness in, 123
    grace in, 193-195
    nature in, 175, 176
    emphasis on the future, 353
    the Synoptic Gospels, 147
    the Acts, 129
    supposed mythical accretion in Acts, 131

Scripture, New Testament (contd.)—
  Ephesians, 140, 146, 175
  Philippians, 146
Selection, 217, 218
Self-consciousness, 313, 335
Senses, the, 313
Service, the Presbyterian Communion service, 267 n.
Seven, the, 134
Sex, 101, 102, 288, 298, 368
Slavery—
  the campaign to abolish it, 358
Solitude, 233
Spirit—
  God as indwelling Spirit, 6
  the Holy Spirit, meaning of, 25, 120, 155
  influence of the Holy Spirit, 51
  goal of, 54
  coming of, 119
  existence of spirit often denied, 313
  spirit and matter, 317
State, the, 247
Stoicism, 234
Subconscious mind, 40
  reflection, 207
Suggestion, 41, 77, 253, 254, 259
  abuse of, 255
Supernatural, the, 30, 31, 32
Symbols, 169, 170, 241
  not a pretence, 241

Telepathy, 45, 46, 161, 262
Theism, 5, 6
Theology, popular theology on disasters, 53
"Togetherness," 138
Transcendence of God, 13
Trinity, the, 26, 291
Tritheism, 11, 53
  in popular Christianity, 350
Truth, 314
  the criterion of, 215
  love of, 359
  "Catholic" and "Protestant" truth, 360

Universals, 316, 323
Universe—
  its meaning to us, 332
Use, 321

Value—
  contrasted with use, 321, 331
  spiritual values, 153
  aesthetic value, 271
  survival value, 338
Visions—
  of Isaiah, 210

INDEX OF PROPER NAMES

379

THE END

Printed by R. & R. Clark, Limited, *Edinburgh.*

Second Impression.   *8vo.*   **10s. 6d.** *net.*

Edited by Canon Streeter.

IMMORTALITY

AN ESSAY IN DISCOVERY

CO-ORDINATING

SCIENTIFIC, PSYCHICAL, AND BIBLICAL RESEARCH

CANON STREETER.
>THE RESURRECTION OF THE DEAD.
>THE LIFE OF THE WORLD TO COME.

A. CLUTTON-BROCK.
>PRESUPPOSITIONS AND PREJUDG-MENTS.
>A DREAM OF HEAVEN.

THE REV. C. W. EMMET, B.D.
>THE BIBLE AND HELL.

J. A. HADFIELD, M.A., M.B.
>THE MIND AND THE BRAIN.
>(A DISCUSSION OF IMMORTALITY FROM THE STANDPOINT OF SCIENCE.)

THE AUTHOR OF "PRO CHRISTO ET ECCLESIA" (L. DOUGALL).
>THE GOOD AND EVIL IN SPIRIT-UALISM.
>REINCARNATION, KARMA, AND THEOSOPHY.
>THE UNDISCOVERED COUNTRY.

DEAN INGE in *THE GUARDIAN.*—" The volume is important, interesting, and stimulating. . . . There is much for which we may cordially thank Canon Streeter and his colleagues."

CAMBRIDGE REVIEW.—" An intensely interesting volume, and very timely. . . . The book offers a sorely needed comfort to its readers—comfort of no unworthy sort—and spiritual stimulus; there is little more that an author could wish to achieve, and we believe many readers will be grateful to Canon Streeter and his colleagues."

LONDON: MACMILLAN AND CO., LTD.

Second Edition. *8vo.* **10s. 6d.** *net.*

Edited by
Canon Streeter and Miss Dougall.

CONCERNING PRAYER

ITS NATURE, ITS DIFFICULTIES AND ITS VALUE

CANON STREETER.
> GOD AND THE WORLD'S PAIN.
> WORSHIP.
>> I. THE NATURE OF WORSHIP.
>> II. THE PSYCHOLOGY OF PUBLIC WORSHIP.

THE AUTHOR OF "PRO CHRISTO ET ECCLESIA" (L. DOUGALL).
> REPENTANCE AND HOPE.
> PRAYER FOR THE DEAD.

THE REV. HAROLD ANSON, M.A.
> PRAYER AS UNDERSTANDING.
> PRAYER AND BODILY HEALTH.

EDWYN BEVAN, M.A.
> PETITION (SOME THEORETICAL DIFFICULTIES).

R. G. COLLINGWOOD, M.A.
> THE DEVIL.

THE REV. LEONARD HODGSON, M.A.
> INTERCESSION.

RUFUS M. JONES, M.A., D.Litt.
> PRAYER AND THE MYSTIC VISION.

THE REV. W. F. LOFTHOUSE, M.A.
> PRAYER AND THE OLD TESTAMENT.

THE REV. C. H. S. MATTHEWS, M.A.
> THE EUCHARIST—AN ANGLICAN VIEW.

THE REV. N. MICKLEM, M.A.
> THE EUCHARIST—A FREE CHURCH VIEW.

A. C. TURNER, M.A.
> FAITH, PRAYER, AND THE WORLD'S ORDER.

ATHENÆUM.—"Nor will any reader be able to lay the book aside without feeling that he is enriched by many new and striking thoughts."

LONDON: MACMILLAN AND CO., LTD.

Eighth Impression. *8vo.* **10s. 6d.** *net.*

Edited by Canon Streeter.

FOUNDATIONS

A STATEMENT OF CHRISTIAN BELIEF IN TERMS OF MODERN THOUGHT: BY SEVEN OXFORD MEN

THE REV. B. H. STREETER, M.A.
THE HISTORIC CHRIST.

THE REV. R. BROOK, M.A.
THE BIBLE.

W. H. MOBERLY, M.A.
THE ATONEMENT.
GOD AND THE ABSOLUTE.

THE REVS. A. E. J. RAWLINSON AND R. G. PARSONS.
THE INTERPRETATION OF THE CHRIST IN THE NEW TESTAMENT.

THE REV. A. E. J. RAWLINSON.
THE PRINCIPLE OF AUTHORITY.

THE REV. N. S. TALBOT.
THE MODERN SITUATION.

THE REV. W. TEMPLE.
THE DIVINITY OF CHRIST.
THE CHURCH.

TIMES.—" It is the endeavour to put into fairly popular language the . . . position of the young men who seem to claim that they can speak on behalf of their generation. They have gone further than their Victorian predecessors. They believe that they have gone deeper down to the ' Foundations.' It is an unmixed gain that we should have their statements presented to us in a form so free from the jargon of party and from the distressing discord of controversy."

HIBBERT JOURNAL.—" It may be that this book will constitute a turning-point in the history, not of a party, but of the Church of England and of the Church in England."

LONDON : MACMILLAN AND CO., LTD.

3

BY CANON STREETER.

RESTATEMENT AND REUNION. A Study in First Principles. Crown 8vo. 2s. 6d. net.

CHURCH QUARTERLY REVIEW.—"This is an admirable book— admirable alike in its sincerity, its faith, and its all-embracing charity. We may doubt whether Mr. Streeter's position is tenable in the Church of England, but even those of us who most disagree with him will wish that it might be so. . . . Of Mr. Streeter's second and third chapters it is difficult to speak with too much praise. We hardly know whether more to admire the wisdom and truth of what he says, or the sympathy and understanding with which he speaks of those with whom he disagrees."

BY THE AUTHOR OF "PRO CHRISTO ET ECCLESIA"
(LILY DOUGALL).

PRO CHRISTO ET ECCLESIA. Crown 8vo. 5s. 6d. net. Globe 8vo. 2s. net.

BOOKMAN.—". . . Such a gem is *Pro Christo et Ecclesia*. . . . It will permanently influence the mind of the reader, and will implant higher thoughts of the meaning of Christianity, and of the attitude of the religious towards it."

CHRISTUS FUTURUS. Crown 8vo. 4s. 6d. net.

TIMES.—"A laborious and fascinating discussion on many things—prayer, the ascetic life, inspiration, demonology, war, and the like. Its effect is not only to stimulate thought but to excite obedience and to spread sincerity."

ABSENTE REO. Crown 8vo. 6s. 6d. net.

RECORD.—"This is a book to be read and pondered over. . . . Every page has a thought-arresting sentence, and its spirit is as excellent as its style is lucid."

VOLUNTAS DEI. Crown 8vo. 6s. 6d. net.

SPECTATOR.—"It is our author's pleasure to set us thinking and to leave us thinking."

THE PRACTICE OF CHRISTIANITY. Crown 8vo. 5s. 6d. net.

ATHENÆUM.—"It is a well-considered examination of Christ's teaching, not as it appears in ecclesiastical confessions, but as it bears upon social problems ; and it is at once a criticism and a challenge."

THE CHRISTIAN DOCTRINE OF HEALTH. A Handbook on the Relation of Bodily Health to Spiritual and Moral Health. Crown 8vo. 2s. net.

LONDON: MACMILLAN AND CO., LTD.